The Old Burying Ground

FIRST PRESBYTERIAN CHURCH YARD

Caldwell (Horse Neck)
Essex County, New Jersey

INSCRIPTIONS
AND MORE
ABOUT THE FOUNDING FAMILIES
OF
CALDWELL, NEW JERSEY

Compiled by
Carol Personette Comfort

HERITAGE BOOKS
2021

HERITAGE BOOKS

AN IMPRINT OF HERITAGE BOOKS, INC.

Books, CDs, and more—Worldwide

For our listing of thousands of titles see our website
at
www.HeritageBooks.com

Published 2021 by
HERITAGE BOOKS, INC.
Publishing Division
5810 Ruatan Street
Berwyn Heights, Md. 20740

Heritage Books by the author:

Cedar Grove Cemetery, Cedar Grove, Essex County, New Jersey

*Early Cemetery Inscriptions and Early Pastors: Fairfield Reformed Church
(Gansegat Reformed Dutch Church) Fairfield, Essex County, New Jersey*

*Old Burying Ground, Cemetery of the First Presbyterian Church:
Orange, Essex County, New Jersey*

*St. Mark's Episcopal Cemetery, Orange, Essex County, New Jersey, (Near the Southwest
Corner of Main Street and Scotland Road, Adjacent to the First Presbyterian Church
of Orange). History of the Cemetery; Expanded List of Interments; and
Early History of St. Mark's Church, Revised Edition*

*The Old Burying Ground, First Presbyterian Church Yard,
Caldwell (Horse Neck), Essex County, New Jersey*

International Standard Book Number
Paperbound: 978-0-7884-1331-5

CONTENTS

History

The First Presbyterian Church at Caldwell, earlier called the First Presbyterian Church at Horse-Neck, and **its cemetery** are listed in the New Jersey Register of Historic Places (ID#1069). It stands at 326 Bloomfield Avenue, Caldwell, New Jersey.

> *THE CHRISTIAN PATH*
> *THE CHRISTIAN PILGRIMS,*
> *WHO THIS PATHWAY TROD,*
> *ARE NOW IN HEAVEN*
> *AND WALK WITH GOD*

"The path was an old Indian trail used by the settlers to attend weekly religious services at the old meeting house of the Mountain Society, the forerunner of the First Presbyterian Church at Orange. They came by foot some walking from as far away as Caldwell then known as Horse Neck before they built their own meeting house to become known as the First Presbyterian Church at Caldwell. The Christian Path marker still can be seen on the grounds of the St. Cloud Presbyterian Church." (John Crosby Brown. West Orange History.com)

1779, July 19: Deed of Parsonage Lands: donors: Caleb
Hetfield, William Crane and Noah Crane.
"...the said congregation to be known by the name of the First
Presbyterian Church in Horse-Neck...and also for the use of a
place of burial for the said Congregation and Inhabitants
...containing ninety acres and forty-seven hundredths of an
acre."(An Historical Survey of the First Presbyterian Church, Caldwell,
NJ. Rev. C.T. Berry. Newark. 1871)

"During this year, at mere nominal cost (10 shillings), the
society purchased 52 acres of land in the 'Little Piece'. The
land was used as a source of revenue." (i.e., wheat growing
and pasturage) (History of Essex and Hudson Counties. W. H. Shaw)
In June 1873 they sold the plot for $1,853.00 to use in the
building of the new church.

1784, December 4: "meeting called to effect a church
organization in Horse-Neck.: Mr. (Rev. Jedediah) Chapman,
moderator. 40 attendees signed the Confession of Faith of the
church of Christ at Horse-Neck. Nine of these families were
members of the Mountain Society at Orange. Elected both
Elders and Deacons were Samuel Crane and Silas Baldwin.
Elected elders were George Personett, Joseph Harrison,
Aaron Tompkins and William Gould."

1787 February 19: "At a meeting of the parish called
Horseneck, properly notified for that purpose the 19th of
February last, Trustees were chosen, and the parish regularly
incorporated, agreeable to a law of this state; and hereafter is
to be known by the name and style of the First Presbyterian

Church at Caldwell." (New Jersey Journal & Political Intelligencer of Elizabethtown. June 13, 1787)

There are written reports of over 530 burials in the Church Yard from 1788 to 1881. The number of those missing must be thoughtfully surmised. (See the Chronological List of Burials)

Old Burying Ground: Tablet on fence

The First Presbyterian Church at Caldwell
OLD BURYING GROUND
In use ca. 1788-1881
Land given in 1779 for a church and for "... a place
of burial for said Congregation and Inhabitants."
Contains graves of early Caldwell area
families, including veterans of
The American Revolution
The War of 1812   The Civil War

Reverend Stephen Grover, the church's first pastor and for
whom President Grover Cleveland was named, lies here.

Church and cemetery are listed in the State Register of
Historic Places.

1788, March 16: The earliest stone reported standing in 1904, 1925 and 1955:

In Memory of
Susanna, Wife of
Timothy Gould

*She Died March
16th,1788 Aged
27 Years 1 Month
and 8 Days*

1796 April 6: The new Meeting House was dedicated and the congregation assembled there for the first time.

1808: It was voted: "That the Care of the meeting house and **Burying Yard** be sold at Vendue to the lowest bidder and the articles to be as follows: That the purchaser brush the Seats, Sweep the floor and Sand it 6 times the ensuing year...and to have the pasture of **the burying yard** but not to put anything in larger than Calves or Sheep."

1847: "**The burying ground** had first been enclosed by a fence in 1804. By 1847 this fence had fallen into disrepair, and George Canfield, the village wheelwright and undertaker, was paid for mending the fence."

1854: After a new cemetery was being considered, the congregation voted:
"That we appoint a Committee to lay a tax of One dollar on all such persons as have moved out of the Congregation and have friends now laying in **the Old Yard**, providing that there is room so to inter them by their Friends and that no new grounds shall be opened but to such as reside in the Congregation at the time of their decease and have themselves or Families either attended or belonged to the Church."

"Up to this time, the facilities of **the Old Burying Ground**
had been available to all residents of the parish, without
charge, irrespective of their church affiliation, but now, the
space becoming so congested, this step was found necessary
to preserve burial places for their own congregation."

1867, April: It was"Resolved. That Jonathan Provost be
associated with the President of the Board with authority to
give written permits to inter in **the old burying ground**, and
that such permits be only given in cases where members of
the same family are buried there, and when there is
unoccupied ground adj oining that may be used for the
purpose."

1872, November 29th: The first Meeting House was
destroyed by fire.

1873, Febuary: "The Committee was about equally divided
as to the location of the (new) church: part in favor of
occupying a portion of **the Grave Yard** & a number
decidedly opposed: - nothing was decided." Four days later
on on April 11, 1873 it was "Resolved, that neither Church
or Lecture room be located on **the old Burying Ground**, but
parallel with the old Church foundation on the Western side:
three members voting for the above Resolution the   Balance
of Trustees and Committee not voting, preferring to locate
the Lecture Room **upon the Yard**, if the consent of the
friends of those lying there could be obtained for their
removal: (but the resolution was considered carried)."

<u>Cornerstone - 1874</u>

FIRST
PRESBYTERIAN CHURCH
ORGANIZED   A.D. 1784
DEDICATED   A.D. 1796
REBUILT   A.D. 1874

1875 November: The first service was held in the new church

1881, May 5: Latest stone in the **Old Burying Ground** reported in 1925 and 1955:

Abram Personett
died May 5, 1881
in the 92nd year
of his age

1881, June: "Resolved, that further interments in the <u>**old**</u> <u>**burying ground**</u> be prohibited;" and in the following January it was decided to level the mounds. No interments were made after that date.

Then a committee on the Public grounds belonging to the Society in the neighborhood of the church, with directions that the grounds be properly cared for, nuisances abated and that they have authority to enclose **the grounds** as well as practicable and to exercise a general care and supervision over the same.

Monument: 1934

*"THERE ARE TIMES WHEN IT IS RIGHTEOUS
TO FIGHT AS WELL AS TO PRAY"*

- - - -

*REV. JAMES CALDWELL, IN WHOSE HONOR
THIS COMMUNITY WAS NAMED,
EARLY ESPOUSED THE COUNTRY'S CAUSE
IN THE WAR FOR AMERICAN INDEPENDENCE.
CHAPLAIN--DEPUTY QUARTERMASTER--
GENERAL IN WASHINGTON'S ARMY.
STERLING PATRIOT - FEARLESS PREACHER
MARTYR ON FREEDOM'S ALTAR*

-----

*ERECTED BY THE NEW JERSEY SOCIETY
SONS OF THE AMERICAN REVOLUTION
NOVEMBER 24, 1934
1734-1781*

1955: "There is at the present time (1955) no register in existence of the burials in the **old grave yard**. Whether one was ever kept, we do not know." (Lockward, p.179)

"In the early 1980's the **Old Burying Ground** was almost razed to create a parking lot. Resistance from descendants of those buried there included Rachel A. Farrington, Ruth Crane Shepard and Personette Gould Baldwin, then one of the Church's oldest and longest members. The debate convinced the Church to spare **the Old Burying Ground** and today it now receives cremated remains. Damage done by time, weather, neglect and vandals has eliminated many of the stones, but **the Old Burying Ground** remains a poignant reminder of the history of Caldwell and its people." (Caldwell Merchants Association; caldwellmerchants.com)

Today, 2018, the Caldwell Heritage Room of the First Presyterian Church at Caldwell offers a self-guided tour of **the Old Burying Ground.**

NOTE: Much of the above information is gleaned from: A Puritan Heritage. The First Presbyterian Church in Horse-Neck (Caldwell, N.J.) Lynn G. Lockward. 1955

INSCRIPTIONS
AND MORE

"The persons mentioned in the following gravestone records are grouped into families so far as the information on the stones themselves will permit, and arranged alphabetically according to heads of families when practicable." (njhs)

NOTE: As with any compiled genealogical record, researchers should regard this information as helpful and check data with independent research.

SOURCE KEY:

CAPITAL letters - indicate a record has been found

(.....) - no proof found

njhs - NJ Historical Society. 1904

gmnj - Genealogical Magazine of N. J. 1925

lgl - A Puritan Heritage. L.G. Lockward. 1955

photo - see findagrave.com

military service: "1775:...all male persons, above sixteen and under fifty years old...shall be enrolled in the Militia Corp. Essex County shall furnish 6 companies of 64 men each, officers included."

ADAMS

Adams, **EZEKIEL**   b. (abt. September 1814)
(gmnj)   d. September 25, 1866
(NJ Will #16255G,1866)

Ezekiel Adams
died September 25, 1866
Aged 52.0.5

wife, Martha M.   b. (abt. 1815)
(NJ Deaths & Burials)   d. (January 30, 1895)

daughter, **RHODA M.**   b. (abt. 1846)
(gmnj)(NJ Deaths Burials)   d. February 10, 1864

Rhoda M.
Daughter of Ezekiel
and Martha M. Adams
died February 10, 1864
Aged 18 years, 10 months
and 8 days

Notes:
--1850 Census, p.228, South Ward, Newark, NJ: Ezekiel
Adams, age 35 mason; Martha M. age 34; Rhoda M. age 3;
all b. NJ
--1860 Census, p.300, 3Wd, Newark: Ezekiel Adams age 47,
mason; Martha age 45; Rhoda age 13; and boarders
--1870 Census: 3Wd, Newark: Martha Adams, widow, b. NJ,
keeping house

--1895 January 30. Martha Adams: d. Caldwell, Age 80, widow, father b. England

- - - - -

ALBERT
ALBERTS

Albert, Charles B.	b. (abt. 1825)
(NJ Deaths 1670-1988)	d. (February 5, 1899)
	Age 74
wife, **RACHEL** (Brown)	b. (abt. 1830)
(gmnj)	d. February 10,1864

Rachel Brown
Wife of Charles Albert
died February 10, 1864
Aged 34 years

Notes:
--Charles, prob. son of Hezekiah Alberts (1791-Dec. 1871) and Charlotte Budd, d.1855 (bur. Hackensack Cem, Bergen Co. NJ)
--Charles m. December 27, 1848, Rachel Brown, dau. of Ephraim Brown and Maria Bogert (NJ Marriages 1670-1980)
--1850 Census, p.179, Lodi, Bergen Co., NJ: Charles Albert, age 25, farmer; Rachel, age 23; Hezekiah, son, age 10 mos. all b. NJ
--1860 Census, p.509, 8Wd. Newark: Charles Albert, age 30; (blank) Albert, age 30; Hezekiah, age 11; Maria, age 6; all b. NJ

--1860 Census, p.100 Caldwell: Charles Albert, age 29, laborer; Rachel age 28; Hezekiah age 10; Maria, age 8; all b. New Jersey (near Ephraim Brown, age 66, b. NJ, huckster and his wife, Maria, age 59, b. NJ)

--1880 Census, p.417.2 Caldwell: Marcus Stager, age 28, farmer; Maria, age 26; Hester E., age 4; Eliza Belle, age 2; Margaretta, age 9 mos. b. August; Charles Albert, age 55, father-in-law, widower, laborer; all b. New Jersey

--February 5, 1899: Chas. B. Albert, N. Caldwell, Age 74, farmer, b. N. Caldwell (NJ Deaths 1670-1988)

Children of Charles Albert and Rachel Brown:
Hezekiah Albert, b. February 1848; m. (?)Lily Blair; m. #2, 1911, Newark, Anna Smith
Maria Albert, b. March 1855; m. abt. 1875, Marcus E. Stager
(bur. Prospect Hill Cemetery, Caldwell, N.J.)

- - - - -

ALLEN

Allen, Alpheus   b. (June 12, 1813)
"son of Daniel and Jane"   d. (November 19, 1876)
Paterson Daily Intelligencer   (bur. Cedar Lawn Cemetery Paterson, NJ.) *aged 63.5.7.*

first wife, **MARY O.** (Burnet)b. (August 18, 1815)
(gmnj) (photo)   d. April 11, 1852

Mary
wife of Alpheus Allen

died April 11, 1852
Aged 37.6.0

dau., Frances Jane   b. (abt. 1837)
(NJ Deaths & Burials)   d. December 26, 1853
                      Paterson NJ. *Aged 17*
                      (?bur. Cedar Lawn Cemetery)

Notes:

--Alpheus, son of David Allen and Jane Personett.

--Alpheus, great grandson of George Personett, Esq., q.v.

--Alpheus m. October 24, 1835,Presbyterian Church, Hanover, Morris Co., NJ: Mary O. Burnet, daughter of Job B. Burnet and Mary (Hedges?); Mary, bapt. June 9, 1816 at Hanover. (NJ Births and Christening: 1660-1980)

--Alpheus m. #2, aft. 1852, Sophia ....., b. abt. May 1833; d. aft. 1900

--1840 Census, p.9, Caldwell Twp (Cedar Grove): Alpheus Allen (adj. to grandfather, John Personett, Esq.)

--1850 Census, p.81, Caldwell Twp: Alpheus Allen, age 38, shoemaker; Mary, age 35; Frances, age 13, daughter; Edwin, age 11; William W., age 9; Mary L., age 7; David O., age 5; all b. New Jersey; near Elijah Anderson, q.v.

--1859 Paterson City Directory: Alpheus Allen, tobacco cutter, 63 Hamburgh Avenue

--1860 Census, p.504, North Ward, Paterson, Passaic Co., NJ: Alpheus Allen, age 48, tobacconist; Sophia age 27; Wallace age 19, clerk; Louisa age 17; Oscar age 14; Jennie age 3; all b. New Jersey; adj. to Stephen Allen, tobacconist

--1865 Census: Paterson: Alpheus Allen; Sophia; Oscar; Jane

--1870 Census, p.277A, Colesburg, Hardin Co., KY:
Alpheus Allen, age 58, b. NJ, miller; Sophia, age 27, b. NJ;
Jennie, age 12, b. NJ
--1876 November 20: "*In this city, on Sunday, Nov. 19th, 1876, Alpheus Allen, aged 63 years, 5 months and 7 days...funeral Nov. 22nd...Interment at Cedar Lawn.*"
(Paterson Daily Guardian, Nov. 20, 1876)
--1880 Census, p.38C, Paterson: Sophia Allen, widow, age 47 b. NJ; Jennie, dau., age 22 b. NJ, dressmaker
--1900 Census, p.129A, 2Wd, Paterson: Sophia Allen, b. May 1833, age 67; Jennie b. Oct. 1859

Children of Alpheus Allen and Mary O. Burnet:
Frances Jane Allen, b. abt. 1837; d. Dec. 26, 1853
Edwin Allen, b. abt 1839;
Wallace William Allen, b. abt 1840; m.Elizabeth (Packer?)
Mary Louisa Allen, b. April 18, 1842; d. May 1909,
       Paterson; m. July 27,1864, Ralph Turner
David Oscar, b. abt. 1845; d. February 23, 1866; 'Oscar'
       Allen: Served: Civil War. Pvt. Co. C, 25th Regt. NJ
       Volunteers

Child of Alpheus Allen and Sophia .....:
'Jennie' (Jane) Allen, b. abt. October 1858; d. aft. 1900

- - - - -

ANDERSON

Anderson, Elijah   b. (July 5, 1798)
                           d. (February 14, 1883)

(bur. Bethel Cem., Sleepy
Creek, West Virginia)

wife, **JOANNA**   b. September 28, 1798
(gmnj)   d. March 10, 1866

Joanna
wife of Elijah Anderson
born September 28, 1798
died March 10, 1866

Notes:

--1850 Census, p.81, Caldwell Twp: Elijah Anderson, age
52, farmer; Joanna age 51; Harriet N. age 27; David D. age
23, blacksmith; Cyrus A., age 21, cigar maker; Sarah Jane,
age 19; Frances M., age 17, female;all b. NJ; (near Alpheus
Allen, q.v.)

--1860 Census, p.106, Caldwell Twp: Elijah Anderson,age
61, no occupation; Joanna age 61; adj. to Jno. C. Anderson,
age 35, shoe manufacturer; Jane C., age 23; Josephine C. age
7; William T., age 4; all b. NJ

--1870 Census, p.168, Noblesville, Hamilton Co., Indiana:
Jason S. Kitchell, age 42, physician homeopathic, b. NJ;
Harriet, age 40 b. NJ; Isabelle age 17 b. NY; Fanny age 13 b.
Iowa; Minnie, age 5, b. Ohio; Elijah Anderson, age 72 b. NJ,
no occupation

--1880 Census, p.3B, Sleepy Creek, Morgan Co., West
Virginia: John C. Anderson, age 55 b. NJ, farmer; Caroline,
wife, age 54 b. NJ; William L. son, age 24 b. NJ; Agatha,
dau. age 19 b. NJ; Jno. C. son, age 15 b. NJ; C. Harry, son,
age 12 b. NJ; Elijah Anderson, father, widower, age 81 b. NJ

--1893: Elijah "was a farmer in New Jersey ..." (Biographical Record of Madison and Hamilton Counties, Indiana. Chicago. 1893)

Children of Elijah Anderson and Joanna .....:
Harriet N., b. abt. 1823; m. April 14, 1852, Noblesville, Indiana, Dr. Jason Sylvester Kitchell
John C., b. abt. 1825;
    m. December 1, 1852, Jane Caroline Tuttle
David D., b. abt. 1827; m. Elizabeth (Hicks?)
Cyrus A., b. abt. 1829; m. Sarah E. .....(?)
Sarah Jane, b. abt. 1831
Frances M., b. abt. 1833

- - - - -

ARBUTHNOT

Arbuthnot, William   b. (abt 1781)
                         d. (December 30, 1852)

wife, Mary (Howell)   b. (February 19, 1782)
                         d. (April 7, 1854)

son, **PETER MORRISON**   b. (August 5, 1825)
(gmnj) (njhs) (lgl) (photo)   d. September 10, 1827

Sacred
to the memory of
Peter Morrison
son of Wm.
and Mary Arbuthnot
who departed this life

Septr. 10th, 1827
aged 2 years. 1 month.
5 days

Notes:
--William Arbuthnot, b. Ireland, son of Samuel Arbuthnot;
m. 1808, Kingston, Somerset Co., NJ, Mary Howell, dau. of
Stephen Howell and Mary Stout.
--1850 Census, p.79A, Caldwell Twp: William Arbuthnot,
age 69, b. Ireland, farmer; Mary, age 68 b. NJ; Mary Jacobus,
age 31; William Jacobus, age 10; Eliza Jacobus age 8;
Monroe Jacobus, age 6; children b. NJ

Children of William Arbuthnot and Mary Howell:
Elizabeth Arbuthnot, b. abt 1812; d. 1830;
        m. July 4, 1828, Simon E. VanNess
Christopher Howell Arbuthnot, b. Apr. 18, 1814; m. Julia .....
Mary Ann Howell Arbuthnot, b. February 17, 1816; d. March
30, 1905; (bur. St. Mark's Cemetery, Orange, N.J.) m. #1, Monroe
        Jacobus, Sr.; m.#2, Nicolas Miller
Samuel Arbuthnot, b. abt. 1820; m. Sarah E. .....
Stephen Arbuthnot, b. abt. 1824; m. Jane Adelle Masker
Peter Morrison Arbuthnot, b. Aug. 5, 1825; d. Sept. 10, 1827

- - - - -

BACKUS

Backus, **CALVIN G.**
(gmnj) (njhs) (photo)
(NJ Will #15862G,1864)

b. (February 12, 1812)
d. August 8, 1864

Calvin G. Backus
Died
Aug. 8, 1864
in his 53d year

first wife, **ELIZABETH** (Post)
(gmnj) (njhs)   b. (abt. 1812)
                                 d. March 26, 1847

Elizabeth
wife of
Calvin G. Backus
died March 26th, 1847
in the 35th year of her age

second wife,   b. (January 15, 1817)
Charlotte Williams Personett d. (October 3, 1905)
(widow of John T. Lockward,q,v,) (bur.Prospect Hill Cemetery)

son, **JAMES**   b. (February 3, 1844)
(gmnj) (njhs)   d. August 18, 1845

James
son of
Calvin G. & Elizabeth
Backus
died Augst. 18th. 1845
aged 1 year, 2 months,
& 15 days

Notes:

--Calvin, son of Daniel Backus; m. #1, July 18. 1835, Elizabeth Post; m. #2, September 30, 1849, Charlotte Williams Personett, widow of John Townley Lockward, q.v.; dau. of Abram D. Personett, q.v.

--1850 Census, p.78A, Caldwell Twp: Calvin G. Backus, age 38, tobacco mfr; Charlotte, age 36; Henry, age 10; James H., age 3; Lewis G. Lockward, age 11; Harriet Lockward, age 8; all b. New Jersey

--1860 Census, p.99b, Caldwell Twp: Calvin G. Backus, age 48, tobacco mfr; Charlotte, age 46; Mary C., age 31; Henry F., age 21; Harriet Lockward, age 10; James F. age 13; Edmund, age 10; Fanny, age 7; Clara, age 5; John Kushmall, age 20, laborer, b. Germany

--1870 Census, p.112A, Caldwell: Abraham Personett, age 80; Charlotte L. Backus, age 53; Mary K. Backus, age 33; James A. Backus, age 23; Edmund P. Backus, age 19; Fannie Backus, age 16; Clara L. Backus, age 13; Lewis Grover Lockward, age 31, tobacconist

--1880 Census, p.401B, Caldwell: Charlotte Backus, widow, age 63; Edmond P., son, age 29, lumber dealer; Clara L., dau., age 22; all b. NJ

--1900 Census, p.257A, Verona: Henry Ahlborn, b. Dec. 1850, Germany, bronze powder mfr; Clara L. b. Feb. 1857; Henrietta b. Nov. 1887; Louisa, b. July 1889; Marion b. July 1891; Dorothy, b. Feb. 1896; Charlotte Backus, b. Jan. 1817, mother-in-law, widow

Children of Calvin G. Backus and Elizabeth Post:
Mary Catherine, b. abt. 1837; m. Mahlon Speer
Henry Francis, b. February 1839; m. #1, Ada Marshall
        Dustan; m. #2, Justina Melrose Harrison
Harriet Lockward, b. abt. 1841

James H., b. February 3, 1844; d. August 18, 1845
James Augustus, b. 1847; m. Jane Thomas Gould
(Grandfather of actor, Jim Backus)

Children of Calvin G. Backus and Charlotte W. Personett:
Edmund Personett, b. abt. 1850; d. July 15, 1932,
Brentwood, Los Angeles Co., California
m. Cora Elizabeth Leavenworth, d. 1914
(b. Prospect Hill Cemetery, Caldwell)
Frances C., b. January 2, 1854; d. February 16, 1928
m. Nov. 17, 1874, Thomas Clinton Provost
(bur. Prospect Hill Cemetery, Caldwell)
Clara Leanna, b. February 22, 1857;
m. February 22, 1887, Henry Ahlborn
(bur. Prospect Hill Cemetery, Caldwell)

- - - - -

BACORN
BECAREN

Bacorn, **DENNIS**   b. (abt. April 5, 1743)
(gmnj)(njhs) (lgl)   d. May 16, 1791
(NJ Will #741807423G. Int.1792)

Dennis Bacorn
who was drowned at the Little Falls
May 16th, 1791
aged 48 years. 1 month & 11 days

wife, (Trinche Casted?)   b.
                                 d.

Notes:

--Dennis, son of Job 'Becaren' and Jannitie Crancheyt

--November 21, 1730: Marriage of his parents: "Job Becaren j.m., b. in Basthon (Boston), and Jannitie Crancheyt, j.d., b. in Phillips Burgh, both live here." (First Record Book, Old Dutch Church of Sleepy Hollow, Tarrytown, New York)

--April 30, 1743: Baptism - "Thunnas, child of Job Becaren, Jannitje (Cranckheyt) his wife; witnesses: Harrick Crancheyt, Maragrietie his wife" (First Record Book, Old Dutch Church of Sleepy Hollow, Tarrytown, New York)

--1789 December 2: "Were married Denis Beckhorn & Trinche Casted" Presbyterian Church, Caldwell (lgl)

--?1789 Census, p.4, Newark Twp: Dennis Beckhorn; p. 5

--1792 September 24: Will: "Bacorn, Dennis, of Essex Co., Intestate. Adm'r - Frederick Bacorn. Fellowbondsman - William, Gould; both of said Co." (NJ Wills: Lib. 34, p.57)

--?See: John, son of Hercules Becorn and Anne Brown bapt. 1800, Second River Ref. Church

- - - - -

BALDWIN

Baldwin, Alfred Deforest	b. (March 4, 1820, NY)
	d. (May 16, 1887)
	(bur. Rosedale Cemetery, Orange)

wife, Frances Jane	b. (May 25, 1821)
(nee Saulpaugh)	d. (June 22, 1902)
	(bur. Rosedale Cemetery, Orange)

daughter, **FLORENCE**   b. April 18, 1848
(gmnj)   d. September 15, 1848

Florence
daughter of
Alfred D.
and Frances Jane Baldwin
born April 18th
and
died Septr. 15th. 1848

Notes:
--1850 Census p.197 Orange Twp: Alfred D. Baldwin, age
30 b. NY merchant; Frances J., age 29 b. NY; Elmira V., age
11 b. NY; Alfred D., age 6 b. NY
--1860 Census p.334 1Wd Orange: Alfred D. Baldwin, age
36 b. NY merchant; Frances J. age 35 b. NY; Alfred D. age
16 b. NJ clerk; Eliza A. age 7 b. NJ; Frances M. age 3 b. NJ;
Eliza A. Fanman age 16 b. NY
--1870 Census p.203 East Orange: Alfred Baldwin, age 50 b.
NY; Frances age 49 NY; Frances M. age 18 b. NJ; Philip A.
age 13 b. NJ; Elizabeth G. age 8 b. NJ; Mary Butler age 23 b.
Ireland domestic
--1880 Census p.486.2 East Orange: Alfred D. Baldwin, age
60 b. NY parents b. NJ 'out of business'; Frances J. age 59 b.
NY parents b. NJ; Frances N. age 28 b. NJ music teacher;
Elizabeth G. age 18 b. NJ; 1 servant; 2 boarders
--1900 Census, East Orange: Frances Baldwin, age 79 b. NY;
Alfred D., age 57 b. NY Oct. 1843; Frances N.,dau. age 49 b.
NJ. Oct. 1851, musician; Philip A., age 44 b. NJ Oct. 1856,
bookkeeper; Elizabeth G., age 39 b. NJ Dec. 1861, librarian

--1910 Census, East Orange: F. L. Baldwin age 57, single, b. NJ; P. A. Baldwin, brother, single; ELizabeth, 47, sis, single

Children of Alfred D. Baldwin and Frances Jane Saulpaugh:
Alfred D., b. Oct. 1843; d. 1911; (bur. Rosedale Cem.)
Florence, b. 1848; d. 1848; (bur. First Presb, Churchyard, Caldwell)
Elmira V., b. abt 1849
Frances N., b. Oct. 1851; d. 1914 (bur. Rosedale Cemetery)
Elizabeth A., b. abt. 1853; d. bef. 1862
Philip A., b. Oct. 1856; d, 1918 (bur. Rosedale Cemetery)
Elizabeth G., b. Dec. 1861; d. June 21, 1927 (?bur. Rosedale)

- - - - -

Baldwin, Amos	b. (March 20, 1792)
	d. (January 27, 1858)
	(bur. Prospect Hill Cemetery)
wife, Rachel (Crane)	b. (October 16, 1794)
	d. (March 17, 1855)
	(bur. Prospect Hill Cemetery)
son, **SILAS**	b. (October 2, 1830)
(njhs)(lgl)	d. May 27, 1850

Silas, son of
Amos & Rachel Baldwin
died May 27th 1850
aged 19 years. 7 months
& 15 days

Notes:

--Amos, son of Ephraim Baldwin,q.v., and Phebe Perry
--Amos m. September 9, 1818, Rachel Crane, dau. of Oliver
Crane and Susanna Baldwin
--1850 Census p.81 Caldwell Twp.: Amos Baldwin, age 58,
farmer; Rachel, age 56; Ephraim, age 28, shoemaker; Harvey
H., age 23, sawyer; Sarah, age 22; Susan, age 17; Lydia, age
13; Marcus, age 10; all b. NJ (listed between Alpheus Allen
and Elijah Anderson)

Children of Amos Baldwin and Rachel Crane:
Oliver Crane, b. 1819 d. 1881; m. 1850, Mary C. Osborn
Ephraim, b. September 25, 1822, d. 1902 (Prospect Hill Cem)
Harvey H., b. April 11, 1825; d. Feb. 16, 1857. Age 33
Sarah, b. August 2, 1827; m. abt. 1848, Mahlon Griffith
Silas, b. October 1830; d. May 27, 1850, Age 20
Susan M., b. March 18, 1833;
        m. 1876, Cornelius Brooks
Phebe Jane, b. 1835
Lydia, b. November 16, 1836
Marcus Crane, b. August 27, 1840; d. Nov. 12, 1854, age 15

- - - - -

Baldwin, Caleb Hilbert   b. (November 6, 1810)
                              d. (April 5, 1898)
                              (bur. Riverside Cemetery,
                              Amaposa, Jones Co., Iowa)

first wife, **MALVINA M.** (Potter)
(gmnj)(njhs) (lgl) (photo)   b. (abt. 1809
                                  d. May 8, 1848

Malvina M.
Wife of
Caleb H. Baldwin
and daughter of
Isaac & Abigail
Potter
died
May 28th.1848
in her 39th year

Notes:
--Caleb Hilbert Baldwin, son of Noah Baldwin, q.v.;
--Caleb m. #1 Malvina Maria Potter; m. #2 Dec. 1860,
Abigail S. Swain; m. #3 April 1881, Mrs. Hannah Broom
--1850 Census: Caleb H. Baldwin - not found
--1850 Census p. 80 Caldwell Twp: Samuel O. Harrison age
33 farmer; Naomi A. age 3; Elizabeth B. age 8 mos.; Milton
N. Baldwin age 12; Samuel S. Dobbin age 31 painter;
Hannah M. age 30; Mary L. age 6;all b. NJ; 2 other persons
b. Ireland
--1850 Census, p.88&89, Caldwell Twp: Naomi Baldwin,
age 64; Mary Dodd, age 76; Hannah Baldwin, age 59; Joseph
V. Baldwin, age 41, farmer; Noah O. Baldwin, age 35,
farmer; Esther Baldwin, age 33; Louisa Baldwin, age 25; all
b. NJ; Mary D. Baldwin, age 2, b. NY; George Tepley, age
25, b. England, laborer
--1860 Census, p.109, Caldwell Twp: Caleb H. Baldwin, age
49 b. NJ, merchant; Abby, age 59, b. NJ; Noah M., age 20, b.
NJ, clerk
--1870 Census, p.113, Caldwell: Caleb H. Baldwin, age 59,
b. NJ, butcher; Abby, age 66 b. NJ; M. Frank, age 27, b. NJ,
butcher

--1880 Census, p.443.3, Anamosa, Jones Co., Iowa: Trumen Tuttle age 79 b. PA, parents PA, artist; Elizabeth Tuttle, age 60, wife, b. NJ, parents b. NJ; "C. W." Baldwin, age 69, boarder, shoemaker, b. NJ, parents b. NJ
--1885 Iowa State Census, Family #69, Anamosa, Jones Co., Iowa: Caleb H. Baldwin, age '74' married b. NJ, boot & shoe merchant; Hannah, age 68, b. NY

Children of Caleb Hilbert Baldwin and Malvina M. Potter:
Noah Milton,b. abt. 1839; m. Phebe Catherine Baldwin
Anna Elizabeth,
Marcus Franklin, b. 1842; d.1889(Served Civil War)
Mary Dodd, b. 1848; d. 1803; m. James Nixon Mager

- - - - -

Baldwin, **Mr. DANIEL**   b. (abt. April 1770)
(gmnj)   d. October, 1795

Mr. Daniel Baldwin
d. Oct. , 1795
aged 25.6.3
who left a wife and two sons,
James and Bartholomew
to lament his loss

wife .....   b.
                               d. (aft. 1795)

Notes:
--"Daniel, son of Mr. Ezekiel Baldwin" (gmnj)

--?Daniel, son of Ezekiel Baldwin (1719-1885) and Sarah Baldwin

Children of Daniel Baldwin and .....:
James, b. bef. 1795
Bartholomew, b. bef. 1795

- - - - -

Baldwin, Elias (gmnj)	b. (abt. 1764) d. (1852)
wife, Permelia	b. d. (bef. 1850)
son **ELIAS ALLEN** (gmnj) (njhs) (photo)	b. September 8, 1803 d. November 3, 1806
son, **DAVIS BAYLES** (gmnj) (njhs) (lgl) (photo)	b. January 12, 1804 d. September 1, 1804

In Memory of
Davis Bayles Baldwin
who was born Jan. 12.1804
and died Sept. 21. 1804
and
Elias Allen Baldwin
who was born Sept. 8. 1803
and died Nov. 3.1806

Children of Elias & Permelia Baldwin

Notes:
--Elias, son of Ezekiel Baldwin (1736-1822)
-- Elias m. bef. 1780, Permelia nee (Bayles?) (Mitchell?)
(Smith?)
--1850 Census, p.69, Caldwell Twp: Elias Baldwin, age 85,
farmer; Smith Baldwin, age 55; Amanda Shipp, age 51, all b.
NJ
--1793 Will of John Mitchell of Morris Co. NJ names
"grandchildren": Mitchell Baldwin; Daniel Baldwin;
Margaret Baldwin; and other grandchildren named Mitchell:
John, Jeremiah, Hyla. (Lib. 33. p.322)Witness: Isaac Mitchell

Children of Elias Baldwin and Permelia .....:
?Mitchell, b. abt. 1780; d. 1873 (bur Lakeview Cemetery, Cayuga,
        Cayuga Co., NY); m. Betsy Brown
?Daniel, b. 1783; d 1843 (bur. Lakeview Cemetery, Cayuga)
?Margaret, b. bef. 1793
Smith, b. abt. 1795; unm. in 1850
Elias Allen, b. 1803; d. 1806
Davis Bayles, b. 1804; d. 1804

- - - - -

Baldwin, **ELIZABETH**   b. (abt. 1776)
(gmnj) (njhs) (lgl) (photo)   d. November 3, 1844

Elizabeth Baldwin
died Novr. 3d. 1844
in the 68th year
of her age

Notes:

--(?) possible sister of Noah Baldwin, q.v.

- - - - -

Baldwin, Ephraim   b. (abt. 1765)
(NJ Will 8134G.Int. 1795)   d. (abt. 1795)

wife, **PHEBE** (Perry)   b. (abt. 1769)
(gmnj) (njhs) (lgl) (photo)   d. March 20, 1828

Phebe
wife of
Hiram Baldwin
and also of Ephraim Baldwin, decd.
died March 20th 1828
in her 59th year (?)

Notes:
--Ephraim, b. abt. 1765, son of Silas Baldwin, Sr., Founding
Elder and Deacon of the Church.
--Phebe Perry, dau. of Arthur Perry and Jane Ball; m. #1:
Ephraim Baldwin; m. #2: Hiram Baldwin, q.v.
--1795 August 11: Will: "Baldwin, Ephraim of Essex Co.
Intestate: Adm'rs Phebe Baldwin and Samuel Perry;
Inventory by Enos Martin and Stephen Fordham."
(Lib. 33, p.498 File 8134-8137G)

Children of Ephraim Baldwin and Phebe Perry:
Amos, q.v., b. March 20, 1792; d. 1858

- - - - -

Baldwin, **GABRIEL LEWIS** b.
(gmnj) (njhs) (lgl)   d. June 1, 1838

Gabriel Lewis Baldwin
died June 12th 1838
aged 1 year
(gmnj "aged 14 yrs.")
(njhs "1 year") (lgl "1 year")

Notes:

- - - - -

Baldwin, Hiram   b. (January 19, 1776)
                                    d. (aft. 1828?)

wife, **PHEBE** (Perry)   b. (abt. 1769
(gmnj) (njhs) (lgl)   d. March 20, 1828 (?)

Phebe
wife of
Hiram Baldwin
and also of
Ephraim Baldwin, decd.
died March 20th 1828
in her 59th year

Notes:
--see Ephraim Baldwin
--Hiram, b. January 19, 1776; bapt. Presbyterian Church at
Caldwell; son of William Baldwin and Sarah Martin

- - - - -

Baldwin, **IRA**   b. (August 27, 1813)
(gmnj) (lgl) (photo) (GAR Marker) d. March 12, 1863

In the hospital at Newark
Aged 49.6.3

wife, Emeline (Dobbins)   b. (abt. 1818)
                           d. (aft. 1890)

daughter, **ABBY E.**   b. (abt. January 1842)
(gmnj) (njhs) (lgl) (photo)   d. March 6, 1843

daughter, **ELIZABETH**   b. (abt. July 9, 1843)
(gmnj) (njhs) (lgl) (photo)   d. March 10, 1849

Abby E.
died March 6, 1843
aged 13 mos. 7 days
and
Elizabeth
died March 10th, 1849
aged 5 yrs. 7 mos. & 29 ds.

Children of Ira and Emeline Baldwin
(Lockward says: "2 grandchildren of Ira & Emmeline")

son, **HARVEY**   b. (abt. April 29, 1843)
(gmnj) (njhs) (lgl) (photo)   d. January 8, 1863
Served: Civil War, Co. D, 26th Reg't, NJ Vols.
Lincoln U.S. Army Gen. Hospital; typhoid fever

In the Hospital at Washington, D.C.
Aged 19.8.10

Notes:
Served: Civil War, Co. D, 26th Reg't, NJ Vols.; d. U.S.
General Hospital, Newark, NJ (?); chronic diarrhea
--Ira, son of Stephen Baldwin and Betsy Kitchell
--Emeline, dau. of John? Dobbins, q.v.
--1850 Census, p.84, Caldwell Twp: Ira Baldwin, age 37,
shoemaker; Emeline, age 32; Harvey, age 5; all b. NJ; (adj.
to John G.? Dobbins age 65, farmer and wife, Sally, age 58)
--1860 Census, p.95, Caldwell: Ira Baldwin, age 47,
shoemaker; Emeline, age 43; Jno. age 10; Harvey, age 15; all
b. NJ
--1870 Census, p.130 Caldwell: Emeline C. Baldwin,age 52;
P. A. Matthews, age 24, no occup.; all b. NJ
--1887-90 Orange City Directory: Emeline Baldwin, res.
Bloomfield Avenue near Gould Avenue, Caldwell
--1890 Veteran Schedules, Caldwell Twp: Emeline C.
Baldwin, widow of Ira Baldwin, 26th NJ Inf., res. Caldwell
--Civil War Pension Index: Emeline C., mother of Harvey
Baldwin, 26th NJ Inf.

Children of Ira Baldwin and Emeline Dobbins:
Abby Esther, b. 1842; d. 1843
Elizabeth, b. 1843; d. 1849
Harvey, b. abt. 1845; d. 1863;
John, b. abt. 1850

- - - - -

Baldwin, Marcus Young   b. (June 20, 1823)

(gmnj)   d. (May 18. 1904)
                                          (bur. Prospect Hill Cemetery)

wife, **ELECTA CATHARINE** (Dobbins)
(gmnj)   b. July 1, 1848
                                          d. September 17, 1864

*Electa Catharine
daughter of Joseph and Abby
Dobbin
born July 1, 1848
died September 17, 1864*

Notes:
--Marcus, son of Noah Baldwin,q.v., and Naomi Baldwin
--Marcus m. 1850, Electa Catherine Dobbins; dau. of Joseph
Dobbins, q.v.
--1850 Census, p.68, Caldwell Twp.: Marcus Y. Baldwin,
age 27, wagon maker, b. NJ; at res. of Alfred C. Gould
--1850 Census, p.85, Caldwell Twp: Joseph 'Dobbin' age 53,
farmer; Abby, age 48; Catharine E.(Electa), age 22; Eliza
Ann, age 26; all b. NJ
--1860 Census, p.105, Caldwell: Marcus Y. Baldwin, age 37,
farmer; Electa C., age 32; Joseph W., age 4; Emma C. age 6;
Abbie Dobbins, age 56; all b. NJ; 1 laborer
--1870 Census, p.110, Caldwell: Marcus Y. Baldwin, age 46,
farmer; Emma C. age 16; Joseph W., age 14; Abby Dobbins,
age 66; all b. NJ; 1 boarder
--1880 Census, p.406.4, Caldwell: Marcus Y. Baldwin, age
55, b. NJ, widower, teamster; Arthur O'Neil, age 60,
widower, laborer, b. NJ

--1900 Census, p.12B, Florham Park, Morris Co., NJ: Marcus Y. Baldwin, b. June 1823, widower, boarder, b. NJ; at res. of George Budd

Children of Marcus Young Baldwin and Electa C. Dobbins: Ann Eliza, "b. Oct. 24, 1852, Caldwell; of Marcus Baldwin and Electa C." (NJ Births & Christenings) Emma Catherine, b. 1855; d. 1940; m. Phineas A. Matthews Joseph Wilbur, b. abt. 1856; d. 1873

- - - - -

Baldwin, **NOAH**   b. (May 12, 1785)
(gmnj) (njhs) (photo)   d. March 13, 1832
(NJ Will 12280G.Inv.1832)

In
memory of
Noah Baldwin
who died March 13, 1832
in the 48th year
of his age

wife, Naomi Baldwin   b. (March 26, 1786)
                             d. (September 22, 1871)

daughter, **HANNAH MARIA** b. (March 24, 1819)
(gmnj) (njhs) (lgl)   d. November 5, 1819

Hannah Maria
daughter of Noah
& Naomi Baldwin

died Novr. 5th. 1819
aged 7 months. 9 days

Notes:
--Noah Oscar Baldwin, Elder in the church for 33 years; also
served as Deacon and Trustee
--Noah Baldwin, son of Joseph Baldwin and Elizabeth
Young; m. 1808, Naomi Baldwin, dau. of Joseph Baldwin
--1850 Census, p.88&89, Caldwell Twp: Naomi Baldwin,
age 64; Mary Dodd, age 76; Hannah Baldwin, age 59; Joseph
V. Baldwin, age 41, farmer; Noah O. Baldwin, age 35,
farmer; Esther Baldwin, age 33; Louisa Baldwin, age 25; all
b. NJ; Mary D. Baldwin, age 2, b. NY; George Tepley, age
25, b. England, laborer
--1860 Census, p.104, Caldwell Twp: Noah O. Baldwin, age
45, farmer; Emily, age 35; Edward, age 3; Naomi age 74;
Hannah, age 69; Esther, age 43; Louisa, age 35; Mary, age
12; Barney Budd, age 60, laborer; all b. NJ
--1870 Census, p.106, Caldwell Twp: Noah O. Baldwin, age
54, farmer; Emily, age 44; Naomi, age 84; Hannah, age 78;
Esther, age 52; Ann L., age 43; Mary, age 22; Edward H.,
age 13; Barney Budd, age 70, farm labor; all b. NJ

Children of Noah Baldwin and Naomi Baldwin:
Joseph Varnum, b. 1809; d. 1892; m. Mary Ann Eliza
        Harrison (1829-1907. (both bur. Prospect Hill Cemetery)
Caleb Hilbert, q.v., b. 1810; d. 1898;
Sarah Elizabeth, b. 1813; d. 1850; m.Samuel Orton Harrison
        (bur. Prospect Hill Cemetery)
Noah Oscar, b. 1815; d.1899; m. Emily Gould
Esther Crane, b, 1817; d. 1881
Hannah Maria, b. 1819; d.1819

Hannah Maria, b. 1820; d. 1886; m. Samuel S. Dobbins
  (bur. Prospect Hill Cemetery)
Marcus Young,q.v., b. 1823; d. 1904; m. Electa C. Dobbins
Anna Louisa, b. 1825; d. 1900
Zenas Ashmun, b. 1828; d. 1903; m. Martha E. Coil
  (bur. Pataha Flat Cem., Pomery, Garfield Co., Washington)

- - - - -

Baldwin, Robert	b. (abt. 1776?)
(NJ Will 14169G.1852)	d. (April 1, 1852)
wife, **MARY**	b. (abt. October 1780)
(Mary Denman Gould)	d. (April 14, 1854)
daughter, **HETTY ELIZA**	b. (abt. 1810)
(njhs)	d. June 20, 1815

Hetty Eliza
daughter of
Robert and Mary Baldwin
died June 20, 1815
aged 5 years

Notes:
--Robert, b. abt. 1776; son of Zadoc Baldwin
--Robert m. February 6, 1800 Mary Denman Gould dau. of
Gen. William Gould, q.v.
--1850 Census p.87 North Ward Newark: Robert Baldwin
age 74 b NJ no occupation; Mary age 71 b. NJ; Lucius age
34 b. NJ works 'free stone quarry'; William age 30 b. NJ
farmer; Margaret Tierney age 20 b. Ireland

Children of Robert Baldwin and Mary Denman Gould:
Johnson Gould, b. 1801, d. 1870, m. Jane Broadwell
Hetty Eliza, b. abt. 1810; d. 1815
Lucius David, b. September 4, 1815; d. November 24 1882;
    President of the City Council of Newark
Hettie Elizabeth, b. abt. 1816; m. Jonas Smith Crane
Phebe H., b. abt. 1817; m. William H. Harris
William W., b. abt. 1820

Baldwin, Silas   b. (abt. 1751)
                           d. (1807)
                           (d. Bloomfield)

Founding Elder and Deacon

wife, Sarah (Harrison)   b.
                                d.

Notes:
Silas Baldwin is included here as a Founding Elder and
Deacon. "Silas Baldwin was descended from the early
settlers of Newark, and his family settled in Bloomfield. He
was known in later life as Deacon Silas.: (Lockward. p.78)
--"Presbyterian Deacon and noted for his piety. It is said he
wore a hole in the Ground near his house by his knees in
prayer." In 1795 he and his brothers were among the
organizers of the First Presbyterian Church at Bloomfield.
--Silas Baldwin, son of David Baldwin and Eunice Dodd; m.
Sarah Harrison, daughter of Moses Harrison and Abigail
Foster. After his death she m. Ephraim Morris.

Children of Silas Baldwin and Sarah Harrison:
David Silas, b. 1783; d. abt. 1855, age 72; m. Elizabeth Kent
   res. Pennsylvania, Ohio, Michigan
     (named in 1812 Will of Rachel Crane Baldwin, widow
     of his Uncle Simeon Baldwin)
Amos, b. 1785; d. 1807; consumption
Abigail, d. bef. 1812; m. Caleb Tompkins; (2 children Joseph
and Sarah/Sally of Abigail Tompkins, dec'd named in 1812 Will of
Rachel Crane Baldwin, widow of their Uncle Simeon Baldwin)

- - - - -

BANKS

Banks, David, Esq.	b. (1740)
	d. (1811)
	(bur. First Presb. Churchyard Memorial Garden, Newark)
wife, Susan (Crane)	b. (1746)
(widow of John Plum)	d. (1821)
	(bur. First Presb. Churchyard Memorial Garden, Newark)

Notes:
This family included relevant to Stephen Gould, Esq., q.v.,
and Holmes Pearson Nichols, q.v.
--David Banks: printer and publisher of law books: Banks &
Brothers; later Banks & Gould.
--Will (signed May 1811; proved Feb. 1815; File 10882G)
David Banks of Newark: wife, Susan; dau., Mary Meeker;
dau., Sally/Sarah Gould; dau. Susan Holmes; dau. Catherine;
son David;'grandchildren Dr. Charles Graham had by my

daughter Lucetta'; Executors: wife Susan, son David, and son-in-law Stephen Gould (Will on sheepskin-extremely fine-first part of the will engraved thereon. Will Transcriber's note)

Children of David Banks and Susan Crane Plum:
Mary, m. Stephen Meeker
> "Stephen Meeker, of Elizabethtown to Polly Banks of Newark. by Rev. Dr. MacWhorter on Saturday evening last." (Sentinel of Freedom. Feb. 1797)
> (?)William Gould m. 1817, Newark, Mary Meeker
> (?)Mary Meeker, wife of Stephen Meeker, died 30 Sept. 1827; (bur. First Presb. Churchyard, Elizabeth, NJ)

Sally/Sarah, b. 1779; m. Stephen Gould, Esq., q.v.
Susan, b. Oct. 1782; " August 26, 1806. Samuel Rathburn Holmes married Susan Banks, daughter of David Banks of Newark, by Rev. Dr. MacWhorter" (Sentinal of Freedom)
> m. #2, May 1818, Stephen Gould, Esq., q.v.

Catherine,
Lucetta, d. bef. 1811; m. Dr. Charles Graham
David, b. 1786; d. 1871; m. Harriett Lloyd (1798-1886) (bur. Green-Wood Cemetery, Brooklyn)

- - - - -

BARNETT

Barnett, **GEORGE W.**   b.
(gmnj) (photo)   d. (December 15 1865)

Geo. Barnett
Co. D

11th N.J. Inf.

Notes:
Served: Civil War; "Enlisted July 12,1862 for three years Co. D; 11th Reg't; NJ Volunteers; discharged at Convalescent Camp Alexandria, VA July 18, 1863, disability" Pension: July 2, 1863. New Jersey. Pvt. Co. D., 11 Inf. Government Headstone shipped to Caldwell, New Jersey --Battle of Fredericksburg. ..arriving December 14th (1862) the Regiment marched to Franklin's Crossing...soon ordered to cross the river to the front line. Two companies D & I...among the wounded was George Barnett of Co. D. " (History of the Eleventh New Jersey Volunteers from its Organization to Appomattox. Thos. D. Marbaker. Trenton. 1898) --(??)Sally Gould m. 1811, Newark, John "Barned"

- - - - -

BATES

Bates, John	b. (abt. July 1771)
	d. (1818)
wife, Mary/Polly (Lindsley)	b. (February 6, 1771)
	d. (January 14, 1823)
	Age 51
	(bur. First Presb. Church Yard Morristown, N.J. photo)
son, JOHN LINDSLEY	b. October 26, 1798
(gmnj) (njhs) (photo)	d. October 19, 1819

Sacred
to the memory of
John Lindsley Bates
son of
John and Mary Bates
born Octr. 26th, 1798
died Octr. 29th. 1817
aged 19 years and 3 days

Notes:
--John, son of David Bates and Phebe Tappan; m. at Hanover, NJ, January 1795, Mary Lindsley, dau. of Benjamin Lindsley and Sarah Kitchell

Children of John Bates and Mary Lindsley:
John Lindsley, b. October 16, 1798; d. October 19, 1817

- - - - -

Bates, Philemon   b. (1766)
                         d. (October 20, 1840)
                         (bur. Colosse Cem., Mexico, Oswego Co., NY)

wife, Susan (Beach)   b. (June 12, 1779)
                         d.

daughter, ELECTA DICKERSON
(gmnj) (njhs) (photo)   b. (abt. July 3, 1802)
                         d. February 21, 1809

daughter, NANCY CATHERINE

(gmnj) (njhs) (photo)   b. (abt. February 1808)
                                         d. April 14, 1808

For children of
Philemon & Susan Bates

Electa Dickerson
died Feby. 21. 1809
aged 6 years. 7 months & 18 days

Nancy Catharine
died Apr. 14.1808
aged 2 months

Notes:
--Philemon, son of ?William Bates and Mary/Polly Dodd
--Philemon, m. June 12, 1779, Susannah, dau. of Capt.
Enoch Beach and Hannah Young
--"Mr. Bates built a cider mill and distillery, and was a
hard-working and ambitious business citizen; but he became
involved in transactions outside his business, and failed."
(History of Essex and Hudson Counties. p. 834)
--He was at various times a partner of Nathaniel Douglass
and Thomas Cochran and Andrew Ray.
--Susan named in the 1814 will of her father Enoch Beach;
executors:Philemon Bates and Farrand Kitchell

- - - - -

BEACH

Beach, DANIEL   b. (abt. November 16, 1743) (gmnj) (njhs) (lgl) (photo)   d. December 31, 1824

Sacred
to the memory
of
Daniel Beach
who died
Decr. 31st. 1824
aged 81 years. 1 mo.
& 15 days

wife, JOANNAH (Pierson)   b. (abt. October 15, 1749)
(gmnj) (njhs) (lgl)   d. January 7, 1825

Joannah, relict of
Daniel Beach
died Jany. 7th. 1825
aged 75 years. 2 mos.
& 23 days

Notes:
Served: Revolutionary War
--Daniel Beach, Esq., son of Josiah Beach and Anna Day

Children of Daniel Beach and Joanna Pierson:
Maria, m. William F. Munroe
Nathaniel,
Thomas,
Jonathan, q.v., b. October 7, 1773

- - - - -

Beach, James H.   b. (abt. March 1825)
                         d. (aft. 1910)

first wife, HENRIETTA OLIVER
(gmnj)   b. (abt. 1827)
                         d. April 20, 1852

Henrietta Oliver
wife of James Beach
died April 20, 1852
In her 25th year

daughter, MARY CECILIA   b. (abt. September 6, 1851)
(gmnj)   d. March 7, 1852

Mary Cecelia
Daughter of James Beach
Died Mar. 7, 1852
Aged 0.6.1

Notes:
--James H., son of Timothy Beach; m. 1848 at Caldwell, Henrietta Oliver
--1850 Census: p.91 Caldwell Twp: James H. Beach age 25 carpenter; Henrietta age 20; infant son (Wm. A.) age 2 months; Thomas Courter age 19 carpenter; all b. New Jersey
--1860 Census: p.99 Caldwell: James H. Beach age 35 carpenter; Maria...age 25; William A. ... age 10; Joseph E. age 4; Henrietta A. age 2; Adaline Beach age 17; all b. NJ
--1870 Census: p.681.. 13Wd .. Newark: James H. "Beeck" age 45 carpenter; Anna M. age 35; William A. age 20

printer; Joseph E. age 14 works at japanner shop; Henrietta
R. A. age 12; Ida G. age 4; all b. NJ
--1880 Census: p.430D Caldwell: James H. Beach age 52 b.
NJ carpenter; Anna Maria age 42 b. NJ father b. NY mother
b. NJ; Ida June dau. age 14 b. NJ; 1 servant
--1900 Census: p.7B 9Wd Newark: Thomas Hodson b. Apr.
1854 m.23 yr. b. NJ father b. England mother b. Scotland
paper hanger; Henrietta b. Feb. 1858 NJ; George b. Feb.
1878 plumber; Jennie b. Sept. 1879 clerk at factory; Ida b.
Jul. 1881 clerk at factory; Harry b. Jan. 1886 office boy;
James H. Beach b. March 1825 widower father-in-law; all b.
New Jersey
--1910 Census: p.61A&B 3Wd Newark: Thomas Hodson age
56 paper hanger; Henrietta age 52; Jennie age 30
bookkeeper; Ida bookkeeper; James H. "Beeck" age 86
widower father-in-law; all b. NJ

Children of James Beach and Henrietta Oliver:
William Alonzo, b. March 14 1850
Mary Cecilia, b. 1851; d.1852

Children of James H. Beach and Anna Maria .....:
Joseph E., b. abt 1856
Henrietta A., b. abt 1858; m. Thomas Hodson
Charles H., b. abt. 1862, d. July 23, 1864
Ida June, b. April 17 1865

- - - - -

Beach, Jared   b. (June 2, 1804)
                                  d. (September 2, 1886)
                                  bur. Prospect Hill Cemetery

wife, Eliza (Canfield)

b. (May 12, 1813)
d. (March 20, 1889)
bur. Prospect Hill Cemetery

son, JUDSON IRVIN
(gmnj) (njhs))(photo)

b. (March 16, 1837)
d. June 6, 1844
(also at Prospect Hill Cem.)

*Judson Irvin
son of Jared & Eliza Beach
died June 6th 1844
aged 7 years. 2 mos.
& 21 days*

daughter, EMELINE
(gmnj) (njhs) (photo)

b. (abt. March 30. 1853)
d. September 24, 1853

*Daughter Emeline
Died Sept. 24, 1853
Aged 0.5.25*

Notes:
--Jared, son of Timothy Beach and Sarah DeCamp; m.
November 14, 1833, Eliza Canfield, dau. of Matthias
Canfield, q.v., and Elizabeth Crane
--1850 Census; p.84 Caldwell Twp: Jared Beach age 46
carpenter; Eliza 37; Matthias 12; Erastus 9; Cyrus C. 4; Eliza
Jane 3; Joseph E. age 6 months; John J. Mann, age 20,
carpenter; William H. Bond, age 21, carpenter; all b. NJ
--1860 Census; p.102 Caldwell: Jared Beach age 56
carpenter; Eliza age 48; Owen M. age 21 carpenter; Watson

age 19 carpenter; Cyrus age 17; Jane age 14; Joseph age 10; Ella age 5; all b. NJ

--1870 Census p.125 Caldwell: Jared age 64 carpenter; Eliza age '34'; Owen M. age 30 law student; E. Watson age 28 farmer; Cyrus age 25 carpenter; Joseph age 21 carpenter; Jane E. age 23; Ella F. age 13; all b. NJ

--1880 Census p.403.2 Caldwell: Jared Beach age 75 farmer; Eliza 64; Owen M. age 41 attorney at law; Erastus W. 38 farm labor; Cyrus C. age 36 farm labor; Jane E. age 32; Flora E. age 24; Joseph E. age 30 carpenter; Elvina age 23 son's wife; Eliza E. age 2 son's daughter; all b. NJ

Children of Jared Beach and Eliza Canfield:
Augustus Rawson, b. 1834; d. 1869; m. Hannah M. Willis
Judson Irvin, b. 1837; d. 1844
Owen Matthias, b. 1839; d. 1888
Erastus Watson, b. 1842; m. 1877, 'Elvina' Kirk
Cyrus Canfield, b. 1844
Jane Eliza, b. 1847
Joseph Edgar, b. 1849; m. #1 Mary Emma Wardell;
      m. #2 Mary Emma Baldwin
Emeline Phebe, b. 1853; d. 1853
Flora Ella, b. 1854

- - - - -

Beach, JONATHAN   b. (abt. October 7, 1773)
(gmnj) (njhs) (lgl) (photo)   d. April 12, 1842
(NJ Will 13184G.1842)

Jonathan Beach
died April 12th, 1842

68 years 6 months
& 5 days

wife, SARAH   b. (abt. 1785)
(gmnj) (njhs)   d. January 3, 1847

Sarah Beach
died Jany. 3d. 1847
in her 62nd year

daughter SARAH M.   b. (abt. August 28, 1822)
(gmnj) (njhs) (photo)   d. May 29 1842

Sarah M. Beach
died May 29th. 1842
aged 19 years.
9 months & 1 day

daughter, HARRIET P.   b. (abt. July 30, 1829)
(gmnj) (njhs) (lgl)   d. February 8, 1846

Harriet P.
daughter of Jonathan
and Sarah Beach
died Feb. 8th, 1846
aged 16 years. 6 mos.
& 9 days

Notes:
--Jonathan, son of Daniel Beach, q.v.

Children of Jonathan Beach and Sarah .....:

Sarah M., b. 1822; d. 1842
Harriet P., b. 1829; d. 1846

- - - - -

Beach, Zophar   b. (abt. 1735)
                                  d. (before 1808)

wife, ELIZABETH   b. (abt. 1744)
(gmnj) (njhs) (lgl) (photo)   d. March 13, 1808

In Memory of
Elizabeth Beach
widow of Zophar Beach
who departed this
life on the 13th of March
1808. In the 64th
year of her age.

Notes:
--Zophar, son of Josiah Beach and Anna Day; m. Elizabeth
"More?"

- - - - -

BEDFORD

Bedford, Moses B.   b. (February 22, 1810)
                              d. (August 9, 1859)
                              (bur. Fairmont Cemetery?,
                              Newark, NJ)

wife, Eliza (Backus)   b. (November 12, 1814)
                              d. (February 2, 1872)
                              (bur. Fairmont Cemetery?)

daughter, MARY ELIZABETH
(gmnj) (njhs) (lgl)   b. (January 13, 1836)
                              d. September 19, 1853

Mary Elizabeth
only daughter of
Moses & Eliza Bedford
died Septr. 19th. 1853
aged 17 years.
8 months & 6 days

daughter, SUWARROW S.   b. (March 20, 1842)
(gmnj) (njhs) (lgl)   d. July 6, 1843

Suwarrow S.
died July 6th.1843
aged 1 year. 3 months & 16 days
Children of Moses B. & Eliza Bedford

daughter, SUWARROW A.   b. (August 23, 1846)
(gmnj) (njhs) (lgl)   d. May 21, 1847

Suwarrow A.
died May 21st.1847
aged 8 months & 28 days
Children of Moses B. & Eliza Bedford

Notes:

--Moses, son of Timothy Bedford and Matilda Beach
--Eliza, sister(?) of Calvin G. Backus, q.v.
--1850 Census; p.80, Caldwell Twp: Moses B. Bedford age
40, b. NJ, shoemaker; Eliza, age 36 b. NY; Wellington B.,
age 16, tobacconist; Mary E., age 14; George R., age 12;
Silas E., age 10; Augustine M. age 6; Edward A., age 2; all
children b. NJ
--1860 Census; p. 244, Rahway, Union Co., NJ: Eliza
Bedford, age 46, b. NY; Wellington, age 26, 'cegar maker';
Randolph, age 23, 'cegar maker'; 'Edmonds' age 19, carriage
trimmer; Augustus, age 16, clerk; Edward, age 12; Alonzo,
age 10; Charles, age 6; Mary F., age 1; Moses, age 49,
shoemaker (Moses died August 1859)
--1870 Census; p. 455, 5Wd. Newark: Eliza Bedford, age 55,
b. NY; Augustus M., age 24, b. NJ, 'segar maker'; at res. of
John and Matilda Waterfield

Children of Moses B. Bedford and Eliza Backus:
Wellington B., b. 1833; m. Phebe .....
Mary Elizabeth, b. 1836; d. 1853
George Randolph, b. abt. 1838; m. Elizabeth .....
Silas Emmons, b. abt. 1840; d. August 1870;
        m., 1860, Myra Miranda Youmans
Suwarrow S., b. 1842;d. 1843
Augustus M., b. May 1845; m. Henrietta C. .....
Suwarrow A., b. 1846 d. 1847
Edward Calvin, b. abt. 1848; m. (?)Amelia .....
Alonzo Lawrence, b. 1850
Charles A., b. 1853; m. 1885, Margaret H. Bagan
William A. b. abt. 1857
Mary F., b. 1859

- - - - -

BOND

Bond, Abner

b. (October 23, 1766)
d. (April 3, 1840)
bur. Honeoya Falls Cemetery,
Monroe Co., New York

wife, Mary Elizabeth (Gould)

b. (March 30, 1773)
d. (February 6, 1868)
bur. Riverview Cemetery,
Oregon, Ogle Co., Illinois

daughter, ELIZABETH
(gmnj) (njhs) (lgl) (photo)

b. (December 19, 1790)
d. September 19, 1794)

In Memory of
Elizabeth. daughter of
Abner & Mary Bond
Who died Septr. 29th. 1794
aged 3 years. 9 months
& 16 days

daughter, CHARLOTTE
(gmnj) (njhs) (lgl) (photo)

b. (November 9, 1792)
d. August 2, 1793

In Memory of
Charlot. dau'r. of
Abner & Mary Elizabeth Bond
Who Died Augt. 2d. 1793

Aged 8 months
& 23 days
Sleep on beloved babe.

Notes:
--Abner, son of William Bond and Keturah Earl
--Abner m. June 27, 1790, Mary Elizabeth Gould, dau. of Joseph Gould and Sarah Ward
--1850 Census, p.264, Mendon, Monroe Co., NY: Charlotte Bond, age 50, b. NJ; Mary, age "28" (78), b. NJ
--1860 Census, p.0, Image 218, Rockford, Winnebago Co. Illinois: Emily Sanford, age 40, b. NY; Mary Bond, age 87, b. NJ; Ellen M. Townsend, age 26 b. MA; Julia Hovey, age 19, b. IL

Children of Abner Bond and Mary Elizabeth Gould:
Elizabeth, b. 1790; d. 1794 NY
Charlotte, b. 1792; d. 1793 NY
Mary Elizabeth, b. 1794
Zebedee, b. 1796; d. 1884, NY; m. Amy Gardner
Ira, b. 1798; d. 1887, Ohio; m. Charlotte Wilcox
Charlotte, b. 1800
Ezra, b. 1802; d. 1847, Illinois; m. Mary Fuller
Uzal G., b. 1804; d. 1827, NY; m. Almira Wilcox
Noah, b. 1807; d. 1829, NY
Susan, b. 1810; d. Illinois; m. Samuel G. Fuller
Sarah G. b. 1812
Miranda, b. 1814; d. 1911, NY; m. George P. Sterling
Emily, b. 1817; d. 1911, Illinois; m. Albert Sanford

- - - - -

Bond, NOAH   b. (abt. 1763)
(gmnj) (njhs) (lgl)   d. November 12, 1827

This Stone
heads the mortal remains of
Noah Bond
who died
Novr. 12th. 1827
in the 64th year
of his age

wife, KETURAH (Martin)   b. (April 12, 1773)
(gmnj) (njhs) (lgl) (photo)   d. September 3, 1806

In Memory of
Keturah. wife of
Noah Bond
who died Sept. 3rd. 1806
Aged 33 years 4 months
& 21 days

son, PIERSON   b. (abt. February 5, 1803)
(gmnj) (njhs) (lgl) (photo)   d. June 21, 1827

Sacred
(to the memory of)
Pierson Bond
who died
June 21st 1827
aged 24 years.
4 months

& 16 days

How short the race our friend has run,
Cut down in all his bloom,
The course but yesterday begun,
Now finished in the tomb.

Notes:
--Noah, son of William Bond, q.v.; m. July 30, 1793, Keturah Martin, dau of Jeremiah Martin; sister of Enos Martin; Noah m. #2, January 3, 1808, Elsey Southard

Children of Noah Bond and Keturah Martin:
Daniel, b. 1795, d. 1877; bur. St. Mark's Cemetery, Orange
Israel Columbus, b. 1798; d. 1869 South Carolina
Pierson, b. 1803, d. 1827

- - - - -

Bond, SAMUEL   b. (June 5, 1779)
(photo)   d. (January 8, 1865)
     (newer stone, Caldwell Presb.)

wife, ELECTA (Force)   b. December 5, 1780
(gmnj) (lgl) (njhs) (photo)   d. May 27, 1846
     (newer stone, Caldwell Presb.)

Electa Force
widow of Samuel
died May 27, 1846
in her 66th Yr.

daughter, BETSEY	b. February 6, 1814
(photo)	d. June 23, 1815
	(newer stone, Caldwell Presb.)

daughter, BETSY	b. (abt. January 31, 1819)
(gmnj) (njhs) (lgl) (photo)	d. April 25, 1840
	(newer stone, Caldwell Presb.)

Betsy.
daughter of Samuel & Electa Bond
died April 25th. 1840
aged 21 years. 2 months & 25 days

Notes:
--Samuel, son of William Bond, q.v., and Keturah Earl
--Samuel m. July 20,1799, Electa Force, dau. of Isaac Force
--1850 Census; p.83, Caldwell Twp: Samuel Bond, age '50',
b. NJ, no occupation; at res. of Enoch T. Shinn, innkeeper
--1860 Census, p.102 Caldwell: Harvey Harrison,age 62,
farmer; Mary,age 58; Ann Bond, age 22; Samuel Bond, age
81; all b. New Jersey

Children of Samuel Bond and Electa Force:
Alvah, 1800-1869; bur. Prospect Hill Cemetery
Isaac, 1804-1883; bur. Roseland Methodist Cemetery
Lydia W., 1811-1893; m. ..... Canfield; bur. Prospect Hill
Betsey, b. 1814, d. 1815
Betsy, b. 1819, d. 1840

- - - - -

Bond, Smith	b. (1799)

d. (1879)

Bur. Branchville Cemetery,
Sussex Co., New Jersey

1st wife, JANE Cadmus   b. (abt. July 30, 1805)

(gmnj) (njhs) (lgl) (photo)   d. September 20, 1839

In
Memory of
Jane.
Consort of
Smith Bond
who departed this life
Septr. 20th. 1839
aged 34 years. 1 month.
and 21 days

Notes:

--Smith Bond, born Buffalo, New York?

--1822 "Jan'y 17, Smith Bond m. Jain Codmus" (Record of Marriages 1822. Presbyterian Church, Caldwell); dau. of William Cadmus & Betsy Jones; granddaughter of Peter Cadmus, q.v.

--Smith Bond m. #2, Sarah A. .....

--1850 Census; p.263, Frankford, Sussex Co., NJ: Smith Bond, age 55, b. Buffalo, NY, laborer; Sarah A., age 24, b. Sussex Co. NJ: Marcus age 16, b. Sussex Co., NJ, laborer; Almeda, age 3, b. Sussex Co.; Henry, age 1 b. Sussex Co.NJ

--1860 Census; p.0, Image 543, Pehaquarry, Warren Twp., NJ: Smith Bond, age "40" b. NY, tanner; Sarah A., age 33, b. NJ; Almeda, age 13; Henry, age 11; James, age 10; Joseph, age 6; Anna J., age 9 months; all children b. NJ

--1870 Census; p.49, Stillwater, Frankford Twp., Sussex Co. NJ: Smith Bond, age 70, laborer; Sarah A., age 43; Joseph, age 17; James, age 10; all b. 'NJ'

Children of Smith Bond and Jane Cadmus:
Marcus, b. abt. 1834

- - - - -

Bond, STEPHEN   b. (abt. 1801)
(gmnj) (photo)   d. June 25, 1862

To the
Memory of
Stephen Bond
who died
June 25, 1862
Aged 61 yrs.

wife, Sarah (Kent)   b. (abt. 1801)
                                 d. (March 21, 1880)

Notes:
--Stephen Bond m. June 10, 1821, Sarah Kent
--1850 Census; p.88, Caldwell Twp: Stephen Bond, age 47, farmer; Sarah, age 48; Cornelia, age 15; William H., age 8; Charles W., age 4; Jacob Kent, age 62, farmer; Mary Beckhorn, age 15; 1 laborer; all b. NJ
--1860 Census; p.104, Caldwell: Stephen Bond, age 48, farmer; Sarah, age 59; William H., age 19; Charles, age 14; William Bowles, age 62, b.. b. NJ

--1870 Census; p.68&69 Chatham, Morris Co., NJ: Charles Bond, age 24, b. NJ, farm labor; Emma, age 23 b. NJ; Clarence C., age 4 b. NJ; Lindwood, age 1, female, b. NJ; Sarah Bond, age 69, b. NJ

Children of Stephen Bond and Sarah Kent:
Cornelia, b. abt. 1835; m. Nov., 11, 1858, Judson Stiles
William H., b. abt. 1842
Charles W., b. abt. 1844; ?m. Aug. 3, 1865, Emma Irene .....

- - - - -

Bond, William(Capt.?)	b. (abt. 1730)
	d. (abt. 1820)
wife, Keturah (Earl)	b.
	d.
daughter, KETURAH	b. (December 23, 1772)
(gmnj) (njhs) (lgl) (photo)	d. June 6, 1790

In Memory of Keturah
Daughter of William &
Keturah Bond who
Departed this life
June 6, 1790 Aged 17
Years 5 months
& 13 days
Young as I am I've quit the stage
Nor did I know the faults of age

Notes:

?Served: Revolutionary War: (Documents Relating to the Revolutionary History of the State of New Jersey. Vol I. Wm. S. Stryker, Ed. Trenton. 1901.) "William Bond was commissioned Captain November 28th, 1776. He retired from the Army Sept. 26th, 1780. During his military service he was also Captain and later Lieutenant Colonel of the First Regiment of Sussex County." In February 1777 he advertised " Four men deserted from Capt. Bond's Company, in the 4th Battalion of New Jersey Forces" (The Pennsylvania Gazette, Feb. 19th and March 12th, 1777)
--William, son of Samuel Bond; Keturah, dau. of Henry Earl

Children of William Bond and Keturah Earl:
Rachel, m. February 28, 1795, John Chitterling
William,
Noah, q.v., b. abt. 1763; d. 1827; m.Keturah Martin
Abner, q.v., b. October 23, 1766
Keturah, b. 1771; d. 1790
Samuel, q.v., b. 1779; d. 1865

- - - - -

Bond, William H. b. (February 24, 1829)
d. (March 11, 1915)
(bur. Prospect Hill Cemetery)

wife, Eliza (Francisco) b. (February 5, 1833)
d. (June 5, 1883)
(bur. Prospect Hill Cemetery)

son, WILLIS PIERSON b. (abt. May 16, 1856)
(gmnj) d. October 1, 1856

Willis Pierson
Son of William H. Bond
died October 1, 1856
Aged 0.4.15

Notes:
Served: Civil War
--William H. m. Eliza Francisco; dau. of Henry Francisco
--1850 Census; p.84 Caldwell Twp: Jared Beach, age 46
carpenter; Eliza 37; Matthias 12; Erastus 9; Cyrus C. 4; Eliza
Jane 3; Joseph E. age 6 months; John J. Mann, age 20,
carpenter; William H. Bond, age 21, carpenter; all b. NJ
--1850 Census; p.92, Caldwell Twp: Henry Francisco, age
52, farmer; James, age 22, farmer; Mariah, age 19; Eliza, age
17; Euphemia, age 19; all b. NJ
--1860 Census; p.96, Caldwell Twp: Wm. Bond, age 29,
carpenter; Eliza, age 27; both b. NJ
--1870 Census; p.127, Caldwell Twp: William Bond, age 40,
carpenter; Eliza, age 37; both b. NJ; (adj. to Josiah and
Elizabeth Francisco.)
--1880 Census; p.426.3, Caldwell Twp: William H. Bond,
age 48, carpenter; Eliza, age 46, wife; Edwin E., age 8, son;
Sarah E. Stager, age 18, niece; Charles H. Stager, age 10,
nephew; (children of Eliza's sister, Euphemia "Effie" Stager
and her husband, Cornelius Stager); all b. NJ
--1900 Census; p.11B, Caldwell: Edwin Bond b. May 1871,
m.4 yr, b. NJ, physician; Marion, b. Sept. 1873; William H.
b. Feb. 1829, widower, father, carpenter

Children of William H. Bond and Eliza Francisco:
Willis Pierson, b. 1856; d. 1856

Edwin E., b. May 1871; m. abt. 1896, Marion Chitterling

- - - - -

BOWDEN

Bowden, Anthony

b. (1827) (October 22, 1827)
d. (1909)
(bur. Prospect Hill Cemetery)

wife, Eliza (Stagg)

b. (1830)
d. (1927)
(bur. Prospect Hill Cemetery)

son, JABEZ
(gmnj)

b. (abt. April 2, 1858)
d. July 20, 1860

Jabez
Son of Anthony Bowden
died July 20, 1860
aged 2.3.18

Notes:
--Anthony, b. October 22, 1827, son of John Bowden and Mary Sidebotham; (both bur. Prospect Hill Cemetery); m. December 10, 1851, Eliza Stagg, dau. of Nicholas Stagg and Rebecca Jacobus

Children of Anthony Bowden and Eliza Stagg:
Lewis Grover, b.1852 (?)
Sarah S. b. abt 1853; d. 1940; m. Walter C. Bross (bur. Prospect Hill Cemetery)

Mary b. 1856; d. 1932; m. Wilbur Canfield (bur. Prospect Hill)

Jabez, b. abt. 1858; d. 1860

Johnny, b. abt 1858; d. 1860 (bur. Prospect Hill Cemetery)

Josephine b. 1860; d. 1929; m. Edwin E. Taylor (bur. Prospect
Hill Cemetery)

William, b. 1864; d. 1955 (bur. Prospect Hill Cemetery)

Lewis Grover, b. 1871; d. 1934; (bur. Prospect Hill Cem.) m.
1909 Blanche Day Lunger; b. 1876; d. 1967, Little
Falls, NJ

- - - - -

Bowden, John	b. (May 10, 1789)
	d. (January 8, 1856)
	(bur. Prospect Hill Cemetery)
wife, Mary (Sidebotham)	b. (March 12, 1793)
	d. (August 19, 1867)
	(bur. Prospect Hill Cemetery)

Notes:

--John Bowden of Derbyshire m. January 8, 1812, Mary
Sidebotham; at Stockport, Cheshire, England

--In 1825 John had cotton mill at Cedar Grove. In 1826 he
purchased the Van Riper farm from Matthias Williams of
Elizabeth, NJ. For several years he served as organist in the
old Episcopal Church in Newark. His son John was an
organ-maker in New York City. (Biographical and Genealogical
History of the City of Newark)

--1850 Census: Caldwell Twp.: John Bowden, age 61, b.
England, cotton mfr.; Mary, age 57 b. England; Hannah, age

26; Anthony, age 22, cotton mfr.; Alice F., age 19; Edna, age 16; Elizabeth, age 35; Rachel, age 15; Mary, age 13; Henry A. Jacobus, age 35 b. NJ; James Lenox, age 20 b. Ireland; Samuel Roberts, age 19 b. NJ; John Roberts, age 16, b. NJ; (Adj. to John Personett, hatter, at the Personett House) --1860 Census: Caldwell Twp.; Mary Bowden, age 67 b. England, farmer; Mary,age 38 b. NJ; Anna, age 36, b. NJ; Olive J., age 7 b. NJ; Rachel, age 24 b. NJ; Henry A. Jacobus, age 50 b. NJ, laborer; Thomas Botts, age 46, b. England, laborer; Wm. Dexheimer, age 13, b. NJ (adj. to Anthony Bowden, cotton mfr.; near, Joseph Bowden, carpenter

Children of John Bowden and Mary Sidebotham:
John, (? bapt. May 1816, Mellor, Derbyshire, England)
Thomas (? bapt. October 1814, Mellor, Derbyshire, England)
William S.,q.v., b. Oct. 25, 1812, (? bapt. Nov. 1812,
    Mellor, Derbyshire,England); d. Dec. 31, 1839;
    m. Elizabeth Van Riper (1815-1902)
Joseph S., b. 1819, NJ; d. 1901; NJ; m. Esther Jacobus
    Trustee, Little Falls Ref. Church, Passaic Co., NJ
Mary Sophia, b.abt. 1822; d. Apr. 2, 1861; m. Obadiah W.
    Hulbert,q.v.
Hannah, b. March 1824; d. 1902; m. Peter Lee (bur. Prospect
    Hill Cemetery)
Anthony, q.v., b. 1827; d. 1909
Alice Ann, b. 1831; d. 1863; (bur. Prospect Hill) m. Henry J.
    Courter
Edna, b. 1833; d.1916; m. Abram E. Jacobus (bur. Prospect Hill
    Cemetery)

- - - - -

Bowden, MATTHEW b. (May 26, 1750)
(gmnj) (njhs) (lgl) d. November 30, 1820
(NJ Will #11305G 1821)

Matthew Bowden
Son of Matthew and Susan Bowden
of Norwich. County of Norfolk.
Great Britain
died Novr. 30th.1820
aged 70 years. 6 mos.
& 4 days

wife, MARTHA (Corby) b. (April 15, 1765)
(gmnj) (njhs) (lgl) d. March 2, 1846

Martha
widow of
Matthew Bowden
died March 2d. 1846
aged 82 years

Notes:
Served: Revolutionary War: Enlisted at Cherry Valley, NY,
company commanded by Capt. Robert McKeen in the first
NY Regiment, commanded by Colonel VanSchaick;
discharged at Newburgh, NY
In April 1818 Matthew, age 68, res. of Caldwell, applies for
pension 'for persons engaged in the land and naval service of
the United States in the Revolutionary War.'...he is in
reduced circumstances and stands in need of the assistance of

his country for support. Attested to by Leon Bleecker, late Capt. Light Infantry, 1st NY Regiment.

--Matthew, b. Norwich, County of Norfolk, Great Britain; son of Matthew Bowden

--Matthew m. April 22, 1784, First Presb. Church, Hanover, Martha, dau. of Gideon Corby and Martha Riker

Children of Matthew Bowden and Martha Corby:
John, b. abt. 1787; m. Mary Stanley; m. #2, Rachel Doremus
    (bur. Fairmount Cemetery, Newark)
Susan, b. abt 1789; m. John Riker
William, b. abt. 1791; d. 1875; m.#1 Elizabeth .....;
    m. #2 Esther Townley; (bur. South Orange Cemetery,NJ)
Thomas, b. abt 1793; d. aft. 1846 NJ;
Gideon, b. Jan. 1, 1797
Martha 'Patty' Gould, b. 1797; m. #1 John Tice
    m. #2 John .....
Matthew Jr., b. September 16, 1799; bapt. February 23, 1800, Old Dutch Church, Totowa; d. 1849; NJ 1849 Will #13793G
    (paper maker?) (?see Bloomfield Cemetery)
Mariah, b. abt 1802; m. Zadok Corby (1802-1860)
Elizabeth 'Betsy', b. abt 1805; m. Nicholas Tice; m. #2,
    Cornelius Jerolaman (bur. Fairmount Cem. Newark)
Lydia C., b. abt 1807;d. 1887; m. Lucas Carter (NJ 1879 Will
    #19558G?) (bur. Mount Pleasant Cem. Newark)
Sarah, b. abt. 1810; m. Ambrose King

- - - - -

Bowden, WILLIAM   b. (October 25, 1812)
(gmnj) (lgl) (njhs) (photo)   d. December 31, 1839

William
son of
John & Mary Bowden
died Decr. 31st. 1839
aged 27 years. 2 mos.
& 6 days

wife, Elizabeth (VanRiper)   b. (January 1815)
d. (1902)
(bur. Prospect Hill Cemetery)

daughter, JOSEPHINE   b. (abt. October 1838)
(njhs) (gmnj) (lgl) (photo)   d. November 22, 1839

Josephine.
daughter of
William and Elizabeth
Bowden
died Novr. 22d. 1839
aged 1 year. 1 month

Notes:
--William S. Bowden, son of John Bowden and Mary
Sidebotham, both bur. at Prospect Hill Cemetery
--William m. September 6, 1834, Elizabeth VanRiper
--1850 Census; p.74B, Caldwell Twp: John Bowden, age 61,
b. England, cotton mfr; Mary, age 57, b. England; Hannah,
age 26; Anthony, age 22, cotton mfr.; Alice F., age 19; Edna,
age 16; Elizabeth, age 35; Rachel, age 15; Mary, age 13; 4
laborers

Children of William S. Bowden and Elizabeth VanRiper:
Rachel, b. January 1836; d. 1921; (bur. Prospect Hill Cem.)
Mary, b. abt. 1837; m. Joseph G. Stanley, b. 1821
Josephine, b. abt. 1838; d. 1839

- - - - -

BROWN

Brown, John	b.
	d.
wife, Rachel	b.
	d.
son, JACOB	b. (abt. February 16, 1816)
(gmnj)	d. August 27, 1817

Jacob
Son of John Brown and Rachel
Died August 27, 1817
Aged 1.6.11

Note:
--Jacob, on same stone as Mary, wife of David Kent, q.v.
(gmnj)
--1830 Census: Acquackanonk Twp.: p.380, John J. Brown?;
p.408, John A. Brown?; p.409, John Brown?

- - - - -

BRUNDAGE

Brundage, STEPHEN   b. March 14, 1771
(gmnj)   d. July 25, 1820

Stephen Brundage
born March 14, 1771
died July 25, 1820

wife, MARY (Perry)   b. May 11, 1777
(gmnj)   d. January 11, 1864

Mary
Wife of
Stephen Brundage
born May 11, 1777
died January 11, 1864

Notes:
--Stephen, son of James Brundage and Phebe Seaman
--Mary, dau. of John Perry, Sr.
--1850 Census; p.170, Bloomfield, Essex Co., NJ: Mary
Brundage, age 73, b. NJ; Jacob Garrabrant, age 44, b. NJ,
shoemaker
--1860 Census; p.138, Bloomfield, Essex Co., NJ; Mary
Brundage, age 83, b. NJ

Children of Stephen Brundage and Mary Perry:
Elizabeth, b. bef. 1803
Mary Martin, b. bef. 1803
Phebe, b. bef. 1803
Miranda, b. bef. 1803; m. Thomas Harrison
Martin, b. bef. 1803

- - - - -

BULL

Bull. REV. WILLIAM   b. November 26, 1765
(gmnj) (njhs) (lgl)   d. August 23, 1847

Rev. William Bull
born in Kettering. Eng.
Novr. 26th. 1765
died in this place
Aug. 23d. 1847
in his 83d. year

Notes:
--(?)William Bull, b. November 26, 1765; bapt. December 8, 1765, Kettering, Northampton, England, son of Thomas Bull and Elizabeth ......
--(?)"List of Ministers: First Methodist Episcopal Church of Rahway, NJ: 1821-1820: William Bull"
--(?)"William Bull, Methodist minister, m. Elizabeth Haydock, b. 1809 Rahway; dau. of John Haydock and Mary Wright

- - - - -

BURNET

Burnet, CALEB D.   b. (abt. 1786)
(gmnj) (njhs) (lgl)   d. July 26, 1850

Caleb D. Burnet
died July 26th, 1850
in his 64th year

wife, PHEBE (Miller Ward)   b. (abt. January 19, 1793)
(gmnj)   d. June 21, 1861

Phebe Burnet
died June 21, 1861
Aged 68.5.2

son, WILLIAM STILES   b.
(gmnj)   d. March 22, 1850

William S. Burnet
died March 22, 1850
In his 27th year

Notes:
--Caleb Dodd Burnet, son of William Burnet, q.v., and
Annah Dodd
--Caleb m. July 17, 1819, Caldwell Presbyterian Church,
Phebe Ward (?Phebe Miller, widow of ..... Ward);
"lived on the old homestead of Major Caleb Dod, near Pine
Brook, and died about 1849. He married the widow, Phebe
Ward, and had George; William Stiles (died a young man);
Jabez; Mary Eliza; Charles; Justus Smith; John Ransford."
(Genealogies of Male Descendants of Daniel Dod. Bethuel L. Dodd and
John R. Burnet. Newark, NJ. 1864)
--1850 Census; p.88, Caldwell Twp: Caleb D. Burnet, age
64, farmer; Phebe, age 57; Jabez D. age 24, farmer; Anna E.,
age 22; Justus S., age 16, farmer; John R., age 11; all b. NJ

--1860 Census, p.88, Caldwell: John J. Kent, age 30; Ann, age 31; Laura, age 4; Ida, age 3; Clarence, age 1; Phebe Burnet, age 67; all b. NJ

Children of Caleb Dodd Burnet and Phebe Ward:
George Crockett, b. 1821; m. Sarah Jane Nafie
William Stiles, b. 1823; d. 1850
Jabez Dodd, 1825; d. 1899; m. Rachel Jacobus
Ann Eliza, b. 1828; d. 1919; m. John Joseph Kent
Charles, b. 1831; m. Ellen Stagg
Justus Smith, b. 1835; m. Alice Elizabeth Hall
John Ransford, b. 1838; d. 1890

- - - - -

Burnet, William	b. (April 5, 1758)
	d. (February 5, 1807)
wife, ANNAH (Dodd)	b. (abt. 1765)
(gmnj) (njhs) (lgl)(photo)	d. June 26, 1818

Sacred
to the memory of
Annah
widow of
William Burnet
She died June 26th. 1818
In the 53rd year
of her age

Notes:

--William Burnet, son of William Burnet and Mary Miller;
m. Annah Dodd, dau. of Caleb Dodd and Mary Harrison

Children of William Burnet and Annah Dodd:
Annah, b. 1783; dy
Caleb Dodd, q.v., b. April 1786; m. Phebe Miller Ward
Mary, b. 1789; m. Isaac Baldwin
Joanna, b. 1791; m. John Ketcham
Elizabeth Gould, b. 1795; m. Moses Stiles, q.v.
Justus Allen, b. 1798; m. Phebe H. Moore, daughter of
      Joshua Moore, q.v.
Sarah Mead, b. 1801; m. Cornelius VanDuyne, q.v.
John Francisco, b. 1805; m. Christiana Hamma

- - - - -

Burnet, WILLIAM S.   b. (abt. 1754)
(lgl) (njhs)   d. March 15, 1829

William S. Burnet
died March 15th. 1829
aged 75 years

Notes:
--"stone has disappeared or inscriptions illegible" (lgl)
--(??)"Hannah Headley married William S. Headley. Their
daughter Joanna married William S. Burnet, son of Capt.
Jonathan Burnet; and had children, Mary, Martha and
Levi."Genealogies of the First Settlers of Passaic Vaalley. John Littell.
Feltville, N.J. 1851

- - - - -

BUSH

Bush, Absalom
b. (January 31, 1814)
d. (October 13, 1900)
(bur. Ref. Dutch Cemetery,
Montville, Morris Co., NJ)

first wife, ADELIA ANN (Jacobus)
(gmnj)
b. (abt. September 15, 1823)
d. May 15, 1857

Adelia Ann
wife of Absalom Bush
Died May 15, 1857
Aged 33.8.0

daughter, LEAH
(gmnj) (njhs)
b. (abt. August 24, 1846)
d. September 29, 1848

Leah.
daughter of
Absalom and Delia Ann Bush
died Septr. 29th. 1848
aged 2 years. 1 mo.
& 5 days

son, WILLIAM
(gmnj)
b. (abt. May 28, 1851)
d. March 18, 1855

William

son of Absalom Bush
died march 18, 1855
Aged 3.9.21

Notes:
--Absalom, son of Cornelius Bush and Ellen Maseker;
m. #1, bef. 1845, Adelia Ann Jacobus, dau. of John D.
Jacobus and Eliza Ann Oliver
--Absalom m. #2, 1858, Mary Ann Mowerson; widow of
Jacob R. Crane; daughter of Peter Mowerson and Elizabeth
VanHorn
--1850 Census; p.84 Caldwell Twp: Absalom K. Bush age 39
farmer; Delia Ann age 27; Elizabeth age 6; Walter R. age 2;
James L. Estile age 28 shoemaker; all b. NJ
--1860 Census; p.1 Caldwell Twp: Absalom K. Bush age 47
farmer; Mariann age 37; Marcus B. age 11; Maria E. Crane
age 13; Walter R. Bush age 12; Martha A. Bush age 6; John
H. Bush age 3; Cors. M. Bush age 1 month; all b. NJ
--1870 Census; p.208 Montville Twp Morris Co. NJ:
Absalom K. Bush age 56 farmer; Mary A. age 47; Cornelius
M. age 10;
--1880 Census; p.420.4 Caldwell Twp: Absalom K. Bush age
65 farmer; Mary A. age 57
--1900 Census; p.8B Caldwell Twp: Absalom Bush b.
January 1814 farmer; Mary Ann b. August 1822

Children of Absalom K. Bush and Adelia Ann Jacobus:
Leah, b. 1846; d. 1848
Elizabeth, b. abt. 1844
Walter Riddle, b. abt. 1848
Marcus Baldwin, b. 1849; m. Mary Louisa Husk
William, b. 1851; d. 1855

Martha Ann, b. abt. 1854
John Henry, b. abt. 1857

- - - - -

Bush, Jacob	b. (September 2, 1806)
	d. (August 19, 1882)
	d. Aged 76 yrs., widowed
	(bur. Mount Pleasant Cem. Newark)

1st wife, Eliza (Doremus)   b. (abt. 1809)
d. (April 8, 1849)
(bur. Mount Pleasant Cem. Newark)

daughter PRISCILLA   b. (abt. June 8, 1834
(gmnj)   d. September 28, 1836

Priscilla
Daughter of Jacob and Eliza
Died September 28, 1836
Aged 2.3.20

Notes:
--Jacob Bush m. February 1, 1826 Elizabeth Doremus, dau.
of George Doremus and Jannetje Ryerson
--Jacob Bush, age 43 of Caldwell, tobacconist, m. Oct. 9,
1849, Caroline Speer, age 38 of Caldwell.
--1850 Census, Caldwell Township: Jacob Bush, age 43,
tobacco mfg.; Caroline 38; Aaron J., age 23, tobacco mfr.;
George D., age 21; Catherine, age 18; Henry M., age 11; Ann
V. age 8; Charlotte age 3; 3 boarders

--1860 Census, Caldwell Township:Jacob Bush, age 53, farmer; Caroline age 48; Henry, age 26, tobacco packer; Charlotte, age 13;

--1870 Census, Caldwell: Jacob Bush, age 63, farmer; Caroline, age 58

Children of Jacob Bush and Eliza Doremus:
Aaron J., 1827-1859
Catherine E., 1831-1897
Priscilla, 1834-1836
Henry M., 1839-1911
Ann V. , 1841 -
Charlotte 1847 -
son, b. abt. April 8, 1849, d. April 14, 1849. Age 0

- - - - -

BYRAM

Byram, **JOSEPH**   b. (August 22, 1753)
(gmnj) (njhs) (lgl)   d. March 15, 1829
(NJ Will 12040G.1829)

Joseph Byram
died March 15th. 1829
aged 75 years

wife Esther (Douglass)   b. (December 11, 1750)
                                d. (March 28, 1840)
                                (d. New Hurley, Ulster Co., NY)

Notes:

--Joseph, b. Mendham, NJ; son of Ebenezer Byram Jr. and Abigail Alden

--Joseph, m. March 21, 1776, First Presb. Ch., Hanover, Esther 'Dalglish', dau. of Capt.John Douglass and Esther Leach. She d. at Ulster Co. NY

Children of Joseph Byram and Esther Douglass:
Ebenezer, b. 1777; d. .....
John Reed, b. 1779; m. Mary Hudson
Ebenezer Alden, b. 1781; d. 1857, d. Detroit, Michigan; m. Eliza
    Burtsell (1786-1877)
Roletta A., b. 1783; m. James Donnelly
Esther, b. 1787; m. Thomas Cochran q.v.
Elizabeth, b. October 1, 1789; d. August 13 1848
    m. Stephen R. Grover. q.v.
Joseph, b. 1791;d. 1864, Galesburg, Illinois; m. Abigail
    Thompson Harris; had sons Stephen Grover Byram
    and Thomas Cochran Byram
Elias, b. 1793; d. 1874; m. Hettie Marsh (1793-1876) (bur.
    Maple Grove Cem. Waterloo,Seneca Co., NY)
Charles, b. 1798; d. 1870
William, b. 1800; m. Abigail D. Miller

- - - - -

CADMUS

Cadmus, **PETER**   b. 1783 (May 23, 1783)
(gmnj)   d. 1863
(NJ Will 15886G.18664)

wife, **ELIZABETH** (Jones) b. 1784

(gmnj)   d. 1868

Elizabeth Jones
wife of Peter Cadmus
1784-1868

Notes:
--Peter, son of John P. Cadmus and Phebe Crane
--(?)Peter Cadmus m. Dec. 1804, Betsey 'Tobit' of Cedar
Grove
--1850 Census; p.94 Caldwell Twp: Peter Cadmus age 67
farmer; Elizabeth age 65; Margaret age 69?; Sarah C. age 23;
also: William age 35 farmer; Sarah age 32; Elizabeth age 12;
Louisa age 10; Georgianna age 5; James H. age 3; Abby Jane
age 3 months; Peter C. Condit age 16 farmer; Martha J.
Bond? age 12; all b. NJ; adj. to Henry and Sarah Cadmus
--1860 Census; p.97&98 Caldwell Twp: Peter Cadmus age
78 farmer; Elizabeth age 74; William age 43 farmer; Sarah
age 42; Elizabeth age 21; Charlotte age 18; James H. age 13;
Abba J. age 9; Peter E. age 6; Ella age 4; George A. age 3;
Ida age 9 months; Martin Jacobus age 21 laborer

Children of Peter Cadmus and Elizabeth Jones:
Eliza, b. 1808; d. 1868;
     m. July 25 1832, William Smith Condit q.v.
Henry, b. abt. 1810; m. Sarah (VanNess?)
Margaret, b. abt. 1812; d. 1882; (bur. Prospect Hill Cemetery) m.
     George Sindle
William, q.v., b. 1816; m. Sarah .....

- - - - -

Cadmus, William   b. (December 25, 1816)
                                 d. (July 23, 1898)
                                 (bur. Prospect Hill Cemetery)

wife, Sarah (Courter)   b. (February 11, 1819)
                                 d. (January 15, 1897)
                                 (bur. Prospect Hill Cemetery)

daughter, **GEORGIANNA**   b. (abt. May 2, 1845)
(gmnj)   d. January 25, 1857

Georgiana
Daughter of
William & Sarah Cadmus
died January 25, 1857
Aged 11.8.23

son, **RICHARD**   b. (abt. December 2, 1842)
(gmnj) (njhs) (lgl)   d. November 11, 1846

Richard. son of
William & Sarah Cadmus
died Novr. 11th. 1846
aged 3 years. 11 mos.
& 9 days

Notes:
--William, son of Peter Cadmus, q.v., and Elizabeth Jones;
m. Sarah Courter, dau. of Thomas C. Courter and Elizabeth
Gould
--1850 Census: see Peter Cadmus
--1860 Census: see Peter Cadmus

--1870 Census; p.122 Caldwell Twp: William Cadmus age
51 farmer; Sarah age 50; James H. age 21 farm labor; Abby
J. age 19 seamstress; Peter E. age 17 farm labor; Rachel E.
age 14; George H. age 11; Ida age 9; all b. NJ
--1880 Census; p.424.3 Caldwell Twp: William Cadmus age
62 farmer; Sarah age 63; Ella R. age 24 dau.; Ida age 19 dau.;
Abby Ryerson age 30 dau. dressmaker; Henry C. Ryerson
age 30 son-in-law wheelwright; Nellie E. Ryerson age 4
granddaughter; Lucy B. Ryerson age 1 granddaughter;
Margaret Sindle age 69 sister widow; all b. NJ

Children of William Cadmus and Sarah Courter:
Sarah Elizabeth, b. 1837; d. 1912; (bur. Prospect Hill Cem.) m.
    Martin Jacobus
Charlotte Louisa, b. 1840; d. 1915 (bur. Prospect Hill Cem.)
Richard, b. 1842; d. 1857
Georgianna, b. 1845; d. 1857
James Henderson, b. 1847; d. 1918; m. Anna E. Dodd; (bur.
    Prospect Hill Cemetery)
Abigail Jane, b. 1850; d. 1932 m. Henry C. Ryerson (bur.
    Prospect Hill Cemetery)
Peter Edward, b. 1853; d. 1936; m. Ella J. Ryerson (bur.
    Prospect Hill Cemetery)
Rachel Ella, b. 1855; d. 1929 (bur. Prospect Hill Cemetery)
George H., b. 1858; d. 1926; m. Emma J. Hallenbeck (bur.
    Prospect Hill Cemetery)
Mary Ida, b. 1859; m. Wilson Hennion Jacobus

- - - - -

CANFIELD

Canfield, **MATTHIAS**   b. March 31, 1775
(gmnj) (njhs) (lgl)   d. April 1, 1847
(NJ Will 13599G.1847)

Matthias Canfield
born
March 31st. 1775
died
April 1st. 1847
aged 72 years

wife, **ELIZABETH CRANE** b. (abt. 1782)
(gmnj) (photo)   d. October 12, 1868

Elizabeth Crane
wife of
Matthias Canfield
Died October 12, 1868
in the 86th year
of her age

Notes:
--Matthias, son of Joseph Canfield and Phebe Baldwin;
m. Mar. 8, 1802,Elizabeth Crane dau. of Samuel Crane, q.v.
"He purchased tanning/currying business of Zadoc Baldwin
and sold it in 1817 to Abram Personett", q.v.
--1850 Census; p.81 Caldwell Twp: Cyrus Canfield age 36
farmer; Eliza age 29; Caroline age 8; Hanford M. age 5; also:
Isaac N. Canfield age 27 farmer; Betsy age 67; Mary age 39;
Matthias S. age 32 school teacher; all b. NJ
--1860 Census; p.93 Caldwell: Elizabeth Canfield age 77;
Isaac N. age 35 farmer; Mary age 49; all b. NJ

Child of Matthias Canfield and Elizabeth Crane:

Mary, b. abt. 1811

Elizabeth, b. 1813; d. 1889; m. Jared Beach, q.v.

Cyrus, b. 1815; d. 1900; m. Eliza Courter; (bur. Prospect Hill)

Matthias S., b. 1817; d. 1888; m. Elizabeth Van Emburg;
(bur. Prospect Hill Cemetery)

Isaac Newton, b.1823; d. 1912; (bur. Prospect Hill Cemetery)
    m. Caroline Cole

- - - - -

CARMAN

Carman, Joseph Gardner   b. (May 1, 1819)

d. (October 7, 1909)

(bur. Memphis Cemetery
Richmond Twp.Macomb Co.
Michigan)

first wife, Susan Louisa (Gould)

b. (January 22, 1819)

d. (November 4, 1856)

(d. Macomb Co., Michigan)

son, **FRANK GOULD**   b. (abt. October 1, 1850)

(gmnj)   d. September 1, 1853

Frank Gould
son of Joseph
and Susan Carman
Aged 2.11.0 (?)

Notes:

--Joseph G. Carman, b. NY, son of Joseph Carman and Mina Leete; or Lydia(?)

--Joseph m. September 15 1846, Susan Louisa Gould; she died at Macomb Co. Michigan

--1850 Census; p.77, Caldwell Twp: Joseph G. Carman age 31 b. NY farmer; Susan L. age 31 b. NY; Joseph age 1 b. NJ adj. to Joseph Carman age 63 b. NY farmer and his wife, Lydia age 51 b. NY

--1860 Census; p.565 Richmond Twp. Macomb Co. MI: Lydia Carman, age 42 b. NY; Joseph G. Carman age 40 b. NY; George Carman age 7 b. NY; Lydia C. Carman age 63 b. NY; Chester Dudley age 35 speculator b. MA

--1870 Census; p.72 Memphis Macomb Co. MI: Gardner Carman age 48 b. NY money lender; George Carman age 15 b. MI; Lydia Dudley age 50 b. NY

--1880 Census: p.521C Memphis Twp. Macomb Co.,MI: George W. Carman age 27 b. NY postmaster; Harriet wife age 24 b. NY; Ruth.. dau. age 1 b. MI; Joseph G. Carman father widower age 60 b. NY father b. NY mother b. CT; Lydia Dudley aunt widow (sister of Joseph) age 64 b. NY father b. NY mother b. CT; 1 servant

Children of Joseph Carman and Susan Louisa Gould:
Joseph, b. December 13, 1848; d. Michigan
Frank Gould, b. 1850; d. 1853 NJ
Oliver, b. bef. 1851; d. 1851 Michigan
George Weson, b. 1852; m. Harriet Hanford Lacy
Clifton, b. abt. 1854; d. abt. 1856.. Michigan

- - - - -

COCHRAN

Cochran, **THOMAS** b. January 18, 1773
(gmnj) (njhs) (lgl) (photo) d. January 28, 1850
(NJ Will 13930G.1850)

In
Memory of
Thomas Cochran
born Jany. 18th. 1773
died Jan. 28th. 1850
aged 77 years & 6 days

wife, **ESTHER** (Byram) b. (abt. May 7, 1787)
(gmnj) (njhs) (lgl) (photo) d. November 26, 1822

Sacred
to the memory of
Esther
wife of
Thomas Cochran
who died Novr. 26th. 1822
aged 35 years. 6 months
& 19 days

daughter, **ANN ELIZA** b. (abt. November 1807)
(gmnj) (njhs) (lgl) d. January 7, 1829

Ann Eliza Cochran
died Jan 7th. 1829
aged 21 years. 2 months

& 20 days

son, **CHARLES THOMAS** b. (abt. May 3, 1821)
(gmnj) (njhs) (lgl) (photo)   d. March 18, 1822

In
Memory of
Charles Thomas
son of
Thomas and Esther Cochran
he died March 18th, 1822
aged 10 months
& 15 days

Notes:
--Thomas Cochran, b. (Paisley?) Scotland; m. June 1806,
Esther Byram, dau. of Joseph Byram, q.v.

Child of Thomas Cochran and Esther .....:
Ann Eliza, b. 1807; d. 1829
Electa Catherine, b. 1809; d. 1863; m. Peter V. Miller, q.v.
Esther, b. 1812; d. 1863; m. Joseph T. Hopping, q.v.
Caroline, b. abt. 1816, d. 1886; m. Lewis C. Grover, son of
      Stephen R. Grover, q.v.
Charles Thomas, b. 1821; d. 1822

- - - - -

COLE

Cole, **JOHN**   b. (abt. December 29, 1765)

(gmnj) (njhs) (lgl) (photo)   d. April 29, 1827
(NJ Will 11824G.1827)

John Cole
died April 29th 1827
aged 61 years. & 4 months

wife, **SOPHIA** (Jacobus)   b. (abt. February 17, 1769)
(gmnj) (photo)   d. October 15, 1852

Sophia
wife of John Cole
died Oct. 15, 1852
Aged 84.7.28

son, **JOHN PARLIAMEN**   b. (abt. May 12, 1800)
(gmnj) (njhs) (lgl) (photo)   d. September 12, 1814

In
Memory of
John Parliamen. son of
John & Sophia Cole
died Septr. 12th. 1814
Aged 14 Years & 4 months
(gmnj: 4.4.0)

son, **WILLIAM**   b.
(gmnj) (njhs) (lgl)   d. February 3, 1817

In
Memory of
William Cole, Son of

John and Sophia Cole
died Feb. 3, 1817
aged 20 years. 1 month
and 25 days

Notes:
--Sophia, dau. of Henry Jacobus
--1850 Census; p.313 Pequannock, Morris Co., NJ: Joel Dayton age 49 farmer; Sarah age 49; Stephen, age 22; Sophia age 16; Sophia age 83; Jonathan H. Mulf age 14; all b. NJ

Children of John Cole and Sophia Jacobus:
William, 1797-1817
Richard, q.v., b. 1799; d. 1835; m. Mary 'Polly' Bush

John Parliamen, b. 1800; d. 1814
Sarah, b. abt. 1801; m. Joel Dayton

- - - - -

Cole, **RICHARD**   b. (abt. June 1799)
(gmnj)   d. September 1835)
(NJ Will 12583G.1835)

Richard Cole
died Sept. 13, 1835
Aged 36.2.25

wife Mary (Bush)   b. (abt. March 10, 1802)
                               d. (October 4 1864)
                               (bur. Hillside Cemetery

Fairfield Essex Co. NJ)

Notes:
--Richard m. January 29, 1820, Mary 'Polly' Bush, dau. of Marcus Bush
--1860 Census, Caldwell: John R. Cole, age 25; Hannah M., age 22; Lauretta, age 0; Mary Cole age 58

Children of Richard Cole and Mary Bush:
Caroline, b. 1821; d. 1891; m. Simeon D. Pier
William, b. abt. 1825
Harriet, b. abt. 1833; m. July 2 1851, Mahlon Munson
John R., b. 1835; d. 1894; m. Hannah Gilliland

- - - - -

COLYER

Colyer, Ezra

b. (1818)
d. (1890)
(bur. Prospect Hill Cemetery)

first wife Sarah S. (Cole)

b. (abt. July 12, 1824)
d. (September 4, 1849)
(bur. Ref. Church Cemetery
Fairfield, Essex Co. NJ)

second wife, Matilda (Bush)

b. (1830)
d. (1907)
(bur. Prospect Hill Cemetery)

son, **JOHN H.**

b. September 21, 1853

(gmnj) (photo)   d. November 3, 1863

John H.
son of
Ezra and Matilda B.
Colyer
born Sept. 21, 1853
died Nov. 3, 1863

son, **CLARENCE E.**   b. October 5, 1862
(gmnj)   d. November 12, 1863

Clarence E. Colyer
son of Ezra and Matilda B.
Born October 5, 1862
Died November 12, 1863
Notes:
--Ezra, son of Henry Colyer
--1850 Census: p.91, Caldwell Twp: Ezra 'Collyer' age 36 b.
NJ; at res of Simeon D. and Caroline Pier
--1860 Census: p. 193 Livingston Essex Co. NJ: Ezra
'Colier' age 41 farmer; Matilda B. age 28; Sarah M. age 17;
Euphemia age 14; John H. age 6; Henry age 31 school
teacher
--1870 Census: p. 299 Livingston: Ezra 'Collier' age 51
farmer; Matilda age 39; Agnes age 3; all b. NJ
--1880 Census: p.433.4 Newark Essex Co. NJ: Ezra
'Collyer' age 60 no occupation; Matilda age 45; Agnes age
12; all b. NJ

--1900 Census p.8A 9Wd Newark: Matilda K. 'Colyer' b.
February 1831 widow; Ethel M. Cummings, b. August 1890,
granddaughter b. NJ

Children of Ezra Colyer and Sarah S. Cole:
Amarintha, b. 1844; d. August 20 1845 age 0.10.17
    (bur. Ref. Church Cemetery... Fairfield .. NJ)
Sarah M., b. 1843; d.1915; m. Abraham P. Williams
(1840-1924) (bur. Prospect Hill Cemetery)
Euphemia, b. 1846; d. 1918; m. Nathanel Nelson Crane
    (1835-1894) (bur. Prospect Hill Cemetery)

Children of Ezra Colyer and Matilda Bush:
John Henry, b. 1853; d. 1863
Clarence E., b. 1862; d. 1863
Agnes, b. 1868; d. 1925; m. James H. Cummins (1863-1919)
    (bur. Prospect Hill Cemetery)

- - - - -

Colyer, **SUSAN**   b. (abt. May 8, 1763)
(gmnj) (njhs) (lgl) (photo)   d. March 29, 1825
(NJ Will 11632G.1825)

In
Memory of
Susan Colyer
who died.
March 29. 1825
aged 61 years.
10 months
& 21 days

Notes:
--?Susan/ Susanna, mother/grandmother of Ezra Colyer, q.v.

- - - - -

CONDIT
CONDICT
Condit, Cunditt,
Conduit

Note: Condit is the spelling used here; as shown on the
gravestones, census and other records of these persons.

Condit, **STEPHEN**   b. (January 1771)
(gmnj) (njhs) (lgl)   d. January 24, 1850

Stephen Condit
died. Jan. 24th 1850
aged 78 years

wife, **BETSY** (Harrison)   b. (abt. 1779)
(gmnj) (njhs) (lgl)   d. February 6, 1849

Betsy.
wife of
Stephen Condit
died Feby. 6th 1849
aged 70 years & 1 month

Notes:
--Stephen, son of Zenas Condit and Phebe Johnson
--Elizabeth 'Betsy', dau. of Reuben Harrison

Children of Stephen Condit and Elizabeth Harrison:
Charlotte, b. abt. 1806; d. 1877; m. Isaac Bond (1804-1883)
    (bur. Roseland Methodist Church Cemetery)
Stephen J., q.v., b. 1808; d. 1869
    m. #1 1829, Elizabeth E. Morrison
    m. #2 1854, Catherine Tappan
William Smith, q.v., b. 1811; m. Eliza Cadmus

- - - - -

Condit, Stephen J.   b. (November 19, 1808)
                     d. (October 9, 1869)
                     (Bur. Prospect Hill Cemetery)

first wife, **BETSEY E.** (Morrison)
(gmnj)   b. (abt. February 1802)
                     d. March 23, 1851

Betsey E.
Wife of Stephen J. Condit
died March 23, 1851
aged 50.1.1

Notes:
--Stephen J. Condit, son of Stephen Condit, q.v., and
Elizabeth Harrison
--Stephen m. #1 abt. 1829, Elizabeth E. Morrison
--Stephen m. #2 1854, Catherine Tappan Matthews; (bur.
    Prospect Hill Cemetery)
--1850 Census; p.109 Livingston Twp. Essex Co. NJ:
Stephen J. Condit age 41 shoemaker; Betsey age 48; William

H. age 20 shoemaker; Cortland age 1 shoemaker; Georgianna
ageg 13; Francis ...age seven; all b. NJ
--1860 Census: p.195 Livingston: Stephen J. Condit age 50
farmer; Catherine age 33; Francis age seventeen...
shoemaker; Andrew F. age 3; Stephen W. age 1; Josephine
age 15; 2 boarders;

Children of Stephen J. Condit and Elizabeth E. Morrison:
William Henry, b. 1830; d. 1916; m. Mary Allen
Cortlandt, b. 1833; d. 1903; m. Sarah Cobb
Georgianna, b. 1837; d. 1912; m. Charles W. Kent
Francis, b. 1843; m. Mary E. Davenport (1846-1895)
?Josephine, b. abt. 1845

Children of Stephen J. Condit and Catherine Tappan:
Fillmore Andrews, b. 1855; d. 1939, California; (bur. Prospect
    Hill Cemetery)m. Ida Frances Rafter; m. #2 Mrs.
    Helen MacKinnon
Charles S., b. 1857
Stephen Willis, b. 1859; d. 1909; m. Mary M. E. Trelease
(1862-1937) (bur. Evergreen Cemetery, Hillside, N.J.)

- - - - -

Condit, William Smith   b. (1811)
                             d. (1889)
                             (bur. Prospect Hill Cemetry)

wife, Eliza (Cadmus)   b. (1808)
                             d. (1888)
                             (bur. Prospect Hill Cemetery)

daughter, **SARAH E.**   b. (abt. February 24, 1844)
(gmnj)   d. April 18, 1850

Sarah E.
Daughter of
William S. Condit
died December 2, 1846
Aged 1.9.6

son, **CHARLES C.**   b. (abt.1849)
(gmnj)   d. April 18, 1850

Charles C.
Son of
William S. Condit
Died April 18, 1850
Aged 0.4.10

son, **GEORGE S.**   b. (abt. March 29, 1851)
(gmnj)   d. May 17, 1857

George S.
son of William S. Condit
Died May 17, 1857
Aged 6.1.20

Notes:
--William, son of Stephen Condit, q.v.; m. July 25 1832,
Eliza Cadmus, dau. of Peter Cadmus, q.v., and Elizabeth
Jones
--1850 Census; p.83 and 84, Caldwell Twp: William S.
Condit age 39 wheelwright; Eliza age 36; Peter C. age 16;

Zenas E. 14; Stephen G. age 12; William age 10; Reuben M. 8; Margaret J. age 3; Mary Mann age 17;all b. NJ
--1860 Census; p.95 Caldwell: William S. Condit age 49 wheel wright; Eliza age 50; William H. age 20 carpenter; Reuben M. age 17; Margaret J. age 12; all b. NJ
--1870 Census; p.111&112 Caldwell: Wm. S. Condit age 59 wagon maker; Eliza age 61; Wm. H. H. age 29 carpenter; Margaret J. age 23 seamstress
--1880 Census; p.429.2 Caldwell: William S. Condit age 69 carpenter; Eliza age 71; Wm. H. H. age 39 carpenter; Agatha L. age 32; Charles Berry age 7; Della May age 5; William Clifford age 2

Children of William Smith Condit and Eliza Cadmus:
Peter Cadmus, b. 1834; d. 1910; m. Mary E. Henion, b.1840
Zenas E., b. 1836;d. 1906, Fredonia, Kansas; m. Anna Eliza
    Buckingham
Stephen G., b. 1838; m. Sarah W. Morris (1840-1914)
William Henry Harrison, b. 1840; m. Agatha L. Canniff
Reuben Munson, b. 1842; m. Emma Courter, b. 1849
Sarah E., b. 1844; d. 1846
Margaret J., b. 1847; m. John S. Gilbert. He d. 1905
Charles C., b. 1849; d. 1850
George S., b. 1851; d. 1857

- - - - -

CONOVER

Conover, **STEPHEN**   b. August 23, 1783
(gmnj)   d. December 6, 1876

Stephen Conover
born August 23, 1783
died December 6, 1876

wife, **MARY** (Jones)   b. January 25, 1781
(gmnj)   d. April 14, 1867

Mary Jones
wife of Stephen Conover
born January 25, 1781
died April 14, 1867

daughter, **ADELINE**   b. (January 3, 1813)
(gmnj) (njhs) (lgl) (photo) d. August 16, 1830

Adeline. daughter of
Stephen and Mary Conover
died Aug. 16th 1830
aged 17 years. 7 months
& 13 days

Notes:
Served: War of 1812; Captain 1st Artillery
--(?)Capt. Stephen Conover, aka, Stephen Covenhoven Sr.,
b. Monmouth Co. NJ, son of Tunis Conover and Hannah
VanBrackle. Stephen, 5th great-grandson of Wolphert
Gerretse Van Kouwenhoven
--Stephen m. March 28 1806, Mary Jones dau. of Phineas
Jones and Jemima Green.
--In 1810 Stephen established Conover & Co. a successful
hardware business in New York City

--1850 Census; p.283 6Wd NYC NY: Stephen 'Conour' age 67 b. NJ; hardware; Mary age 68 b. NJ; Sarah Andrews age 32 b. NY; George Andrews age 44 clerk b. CT; Mary Andrews age 12 b. NY; George Andrews age 8 b. NY; Helen Andrews age 4 b. NY; 3 other persons

--1860 Census; p.66.. 6 Wd.. NYC NY: Geo. Andrews age 54 bookkeeper; Sarah age 42; Ellen age 14; Stephen "Carver' age 77; Mary "Carver" age 79; 2 servants

--1870 Census; p.247 11Wd Brooklyn: Stephen Conover age 87 b. NJ retired merchant; Sarah Andrews age 50 b. NY; Sarah Ward age 70 b. NJ; 1 domestic

Children of Stephen Conover and Mary Jones:

Anna Maria, b. 1810; d. 1830; m. Aaron B. Heath, q.v.

Malvina, m. Aaron B. Heath, q.v.

Eliza,

Adeline, b. 1813; d. 1830

Sarah, b. abt. 1818; m. George Andrews, b. 1805; d.1864; (bur. Winchester Cemetery, Litchfield Co., CT) He was choir director of the Broadway Tabernacle, Brooklyn She was a soloist there.

Stephen Jr., b. April 1 1822; d. Jan. 5, 1899 at East Orange NJ m. 1846, Lucy Turner Hale (1826-1904). (Both bur. Rosedale Cemetery, Orange) He was ass't choir director, Broadway Tabernacle, Brooklyn; She was a soloist there.

- - - - -

CONSELYEA

Conselyea, **AARON S.**   b. (abt. 1803)

(gmnj) (njhs) (lgl)   d. January 30, 1837

Aaron S. Conselyea
died Jan. 30th. 1837
aged 34 years

first wife...Ann (Powers)   b.
                                 d. (July 14 1831)
                                 (bur. Methodist Burying Ground,
                                 Belleville Essex Co. NJ)

Notes:
--Aaron, son of John Conselyea and Sarah Courter
--Aaron m. #1 June 5 1830, Ann Powers
--?Aaron m. #2 1832, Hannah D. Ross

- - - - -

Conselyea, **MARY**   b. (abt. April 1796)
(gmnj) (njhs) (lgl) (photo)   d. January 1, 1828

In
Memory of
Mary Conselyea
who died Jan. 1st. 1828
aged 31 years. 8 months
& 4 days

Notes:
--Mary, dau. of John Conselyea and Sarah Courter
--Mary, sister of Aaron S. Conselyea, q.v.

- - - - -

COOK

Cook, Joseph   b. (February 2, 1806)
                                d. (August 8, 1891)
                                (bur. Prospect Hill Cemetery)

wife, **PHEBE** (Harrison)   b. August 28, 1807
(gmnj)   d. August 21, 1865

Phebe Harrison
wife of Joseph Cook
born August 28, 1807
died August 21, 1865

Notes:

--Joseph, son of Francis Brant Cook and Mary Cook; m. July 2, 1835, Phebe Harrison, dau. of Zenas Harrison, q.v.

--1850 Census; p.107 Livingston, Essex Co. NJ: Joseph Cook, age 44 farmer; Phebe age 42; Hannah M. age 13; Zenas F. age 11; Abby L. age 8; Cyrus A. age 5; Joseph H. age 1; Phebe Harrison age 77; all b. NJ

--1860 Census; p.200 Livingston: Joseph Cook, age 53 farmer; Phebe age 52; Hannah M. age 23; Abby L. age 18 school teacher; Cyrus A. age 15; Joseph H.M. age 10; Phebe Harrison age 88; 2 farm hands

--1870 Census; p.239 Livingston: Joseph Cook age 64 farmer; Anna M. age 30; Joseph H.M. age 21 farmer

--1880 Census; p.575.2 Livingston: Joseph Cook age 74 farmer; Anna dau. age 40; Joseph H. son age 31 home; Henry

Crane age 38 son-in-law; Abbey L. Crane age 38 dau; Fredk
H. D. Crane age 7 grandson; Imogene age 2 granddaughter

Children of Joseph Cook and Phebe Harrison:
Hanna Mariah, b. 1836; d. 1919; unm.
Zenas Francis, b. 1839; d. abt. 1855, age 16
Abby Lurana, b. 1842; d. 1920; m. Henry Duryea Crane,
    son of Caleb S. Crane, q.v.
Cyrus Alexander, b. 1845; m. #1, 1876, Mary Imogene Peck
    m. #2, 1880, Louise Whitehead Crane, sister of Henry
    Duryea Crane, dau. of Caleb S. Crane, q.v.
Joseph Henry Martin, b. 1849; d. 1925; m. Lillias Collins

- - - - -

CORBY

Corby, **DANIEL**   b. (July 6, 1783)
(gmnj)   d. September 11, 1855

Daniel Corby
Died Sept. 11, 1855
Aged 72.2.15

wife, **DORCAS** (Williams)   b. (November 5, 1788)
(gmnj)   d. January 17, 1860

Dorcas
wife of Daniel Corby
Died Jan. 17, 1860
Aged 71.2.12

Notes:
--Daniel, son of Gideon Corby and Martha "Patty" Riker;
m. December 24,1806, Dorcas Williams, dau. of Simeon
Williams and Mary Smith
--1850 Census; p.110 Livingston Essex Co. NJ: Daniel
Corby age 66 shoemaker; Dorcas age 61; George age 30
shoemaker; 3 other persons

Children of Daniel Corby and Dorcas Williams:
George, b. abt. 1820; d. aft. 1880; unm.
Phebe, b. 1822; m. 1837, John Sayre (1812-1886)
Simeon Thompson, b. 1825; d. 1892, PA; m. #1 1848 Mary
    A. .....; b. abt 1833 NJ; d. 1870/77; m. #2
    1870-1877, Margaret C. Williams, dau. of A.
    Williams, Esq. of Binghamton, NY;

- - - - -

Corby, **EZEKIEL**	b. (June 30, 1778)
(gmnj)	d. January 30, 1860

Ezekiel Corby
Died Jan. 30, 1860
Aged 81.7.0

wife, Rebecca (Day)	b. (abt. 1781)
(NJ Vital Records)	d. (January 1, 1867)
	In her 86th year

son, **ISRAEL B.**	b. (abt. March 18, 1804)
(gmnj)	d. August 21, 1833

Israel B.
Son of Ezekiel Corby
Died August 21, 1833
Aged 29.5.3

Notes:

--Ezekiel, son of Gideon Corby and Martha 'Patty' Riker

--Ezekiel m. November 1798, Rebecca Day

--1850 Census: p.70, Caldwell Twp: Ezekiel Corby, age 72, farmer; Rebecca, age 69; both b. NJ (adj. to Yehoncris Corby, age 69)

--1860: Rebecca, living with son, Ezekiel Leonard Corby

Children of Ezekiel Corby and Rebecca Day:

Thomas Day, b. abt. 1800; d. July 1875, Susquehanna Co PA
    m. #1 September 1825, Lucinda Wheaton, dau. of
    Bethuel Wheaton; m. #2. bef. 1855, Phebe L.
    .....(1828-1905)

Matthew Bowden, b. abt. 1802; d. abt. 1867, Luzerne Co.,PA
    m. 1825, Elizabeth Williams, dau. of Joseph and
    Mary (Ward) Williams

Israel Brundage, b. 1804; d. 1833, Caldwell; m. 1829,
    Margaret Kent, daughter of Jacob Kent,q.v.
    Sarah Parmelia, b. abt. 1806; d. 1882 PA,
    Susquehanna Co. PA; m.1824, David L.Meeker
    (1805-1866)

Esther D.; b. July 1809; d. Mich.; m. abt.1825, Harvey Gregg

Ezekiel Leonard, b. abt. 1813; d.1888 NJ; m. Margaret Kent
    Corby, widow of his brother Israel B. Corby

Cyrus, b. 1814-15; d. 1899. m. 1845, Johanna (Meeker)
    Smith, dau. of Joseph Meeker and widow of Israel
    Smith; sister of David Meedker who m. Cyrus' sister

Sarah Parmelia; (both bur. Glenwood Cemetery, Dickinson, Broome Co., NY)

Mahala, b. abt. 1816; d. Oct. 1848, Caldwell; m. .... Fritz Squire G., b. 1819-20;d. aft. 1860, Broome Co.NY; m. July, 1841, Esther McDermott

- - - - -

COURTER

Courter, Henry J. b. (March 8, 1824)
d. (November 8, 1901)
(bur. Sidney,Montcalm, MI)

Courter, **ALICE** (Bowden) b. May 15, 1831
(gmnj) d. December 3, 1863

Alice Courter
Daughter of John and Mary Bowden
born May 15, 1831
Died December 3, 1863

Notes:

--Henry, son of John Courter and Sarah Francisco

--Henry m. 1850, Alice Ann Bowden, dau. of John Bowden and Mary Sidebotham; Henry m. twice before 1850

--1850 Census; p.74 Caldwell Twp: John Bowden age 61 b. England cotton mfr.; Mary age 57 b. England; Hannah age 26; Anthony age 22; Alice F. age 19; Edna age 16; Elizabeth age 35; Rachel age 15; Mary age 13; 4 laborers

--1860 Census; p.110 Caldwell: Henry J. Courter age 34 farmer; Alice age 29; Joseph W. age 8; Franklin age 6; Theodore age 4; 1 laborer

Children of Henry J. Courter and Alice Ann Bowden:
Joseph Watson, b. 1852; d. 1935, Michigan; m.1877, Alice
    Crane, dau. of Frank Crane and Annie M. Courter;
    (both bur. Sheridan Cem., Montcalm Co., Michigan)
Franklin C., b. 1854; m. Minnie A. Foote
Theodore, b. 1856; m. #1 Sarah Renfrew; #2 Hannah White
Anthony Bowden, b. 1861; d. 1940; m. Mary VanWyck
    (both bur. Sidney Twp., Cemetery, Montcalm Co. Michigan)
Albert Courter, b. 1863

- - - - -

Courter, **JACOB**	b. (abt. November 6, 1771)
(gmnj)	d. November 6, 1855
(NJ Will 14831G. 1856)	

Jacob Courter
died November 6, 1855
Aged 84 years

wife, **ELLEN** (Jacobus)	b. (abt. 1779)
(gmnj)	d. November 7, 1856

Ellen
Wife of Jacob Courter
Died Nov. 7 1856
Aged 84 years

Notes:

--Jacob, son of Peter Courter; m. Ellen Jacobus, dau. of James Jacobus

--1850 Census; p. 73 Caldwell Twp: Jacob Courter age 78 farmer; Ellen age 72; Peter age 32 farmer; Jane Freeman age 40; Catherine Jacobus age 93; all b. NJ (adj. to George P. Martin)

Children of Jacob Courter and Ellen Jacobus:

Jacob, b. abt 1800; m. Ellen Alice Freeman

John J., b. 1804; m. #1 Sarah Crane; #2 Ellen VanRiper
m.#3 Nancy VanNess

Isaac J., b. 1809; m. Hannah Powlesson

Richard Jacob, b. 1811; d. 1898; m. #1 Ellen Ann Paxton (1811-1873) (Richard and Ellen both bur. Winfield Scott Twp. Cem., Henry Co., Iowa) m. #2 Elizabeth Jacobus

Henry J., b. 1814; d. 1872; m. Amanda D'Arcy (both bur. Prospect Hill Cemetery)

Peter, b. 1817; d. 1892

Eleazer W., b. 1820; m. Sarah Maria Jacobus

Joseph, b. 1823; d. abt. 1833

- - - - -

Courter, **JOHN M.**   b. (June 11, 1820)
(gmnj)   d. November 30, 1860
(NJ Will 15333G. 1860)

John M. Courter
Died Nov. 30, 1860
Aged 40.5.19

wife Martha M. (Stratham)   b. (September 1821)
d. (July 15, 1901)

Notes:
--John Mead Courter, son of John C. Courter and Jane Mead; m. Martha M. Stratham; b. Manchester England; dau. of Jonathan Stratham
--1860 Census: p.91 Caldwell Twp: John Courter age 40 farmer; Martha age 37 b. England; Mary J. age 9; John D. age 5

Children of John Mead Courter and Martha M. Stratham:
Mary Jane, b. 1851; m. George C. Covintree
John Dodd, b. 1855; m. Laura Rebecca Braker

- - - - -

CRANE

Crane, Asher   b. (November 30, 1809)
d. (March 4, 1888)
(bur. Prospect Hill Cemetery)

first wife, **EUNICE**(Baldwin) b. (abt. February 24, 1810)
(gmnj) (njhs)   d. April 14, 1849

Eunice
wife of
Asher Crane
died April 14th.1849
aged 39 years. 1 month
& 18 days

second wife, Joanna (Harrison)
>
> b. (June 20, 1811)
>
> d. (March 20, 1888)
>
> (bur. Prospect Hill Cemetery)

Notes:

--Asher Crane, Board of Trustees, First Presbyterian Church, Caldwell, 1847

--Asher, son of Col. Cyrus Crane, q.v.,; m. #1 1840, Eunice Baldwin; m. #2 1850, Joanna Harrison; she, b. 1811, d. 1888; dau. of Samuel Harrison

--1850 Census; p.79 Caldwell Twp: Asher Crane age 40 farmer; Cyrus age 7; Joseph age 4; Sarah age 30; all b. NJ

--1860 Census; p.93 Caldwell Twp: Asher Crane age 50 farmer; Joanna age 48; Cyrus B. age 16; Joseph E. age 13; Mary E. age 7; Marcus S. age 6; 1 servant; 1 laborer

--1870 Census; p. 107 Caldwell Twp: Asher Crane age 60 farmer; Joanna age 58; Cyrus age 26 farm labor; Joseph age 23 without occupation; Marcus age 17 at home; 1 servant

--1880 Census; p.424.4 Caldwell Twp: Asher Crane age 70 farmer; Joanna age 68; Cyrus B. age 36 farmer; Marcus S. age 27 works on farm

Children of Asher Crane and Eunice Baldwin:
Cyrus Baldwin, b. 1843; d. 1930; (bur. Prospect Hill Cemetery)
>
> m. #1 Phebe Eliz. Stiles; m. #2 Julia Meeker Stiles

Joseph Emmons, b. 1846; m. #1 Annie Sears

Children of Asher Crane and Joanna Harrison:
Mary Elizabeth, b. 1851; d. 1863 (bur. Prospect Hill Cem.)
Son, b. 1852; d. bef. 1860

Marcus Spencer, b. 1853; d. 1942; (bur. Prospect Hill Cem.); m.
#1 Magdalene P. Ostrander; m. #2 Mabel Bonnell
Oliver

- - - - -

Crane, **AZARIAH**   b. (January 19, 1754)
(gmnj) (njhs) (photo)   d. March 15, 1814
(NJ Inv. #12803C-1814)

Sacred
to the
Memory of
Azariah Crane
who died March 15th, 1814
Aged 60 years 1 month
and 24 days

wife, **HANNAH** (Tucker)   b. (abt.1761)
(gmnj) (njhs) (photo)   d. January 3, 1835

Sacred
to the memory of
Hannah Crane
who departed this life
Jany. 3d. 1835
aged 73 years. 11 months
& 4 days

Notes:
--Azariah, son of Stephen Crane and Rhoda Holloway;
Stephen Crane's will proved Nov. 1794: Wife Rhoda; son

Azariah to have "6 acres off the farm; 20 acres over the mountain adjoining what he already possesses and 1 and 1/2 acres salt meadow at Wheeler Point."
--Azariah m. (Hannah) Tucker (note: similar inscriptions)
--Unrecorded Estate Papers of Azariah Crane, dec'd.
Caldwell. names his children: Nancy Brown; Rhoda Baldwin; Thankful Price; Elizabeth Brown; Ralph Crane; Keturah Pierson; Margaret; Benjamin; Rebecca; Sally (the last 3 being under age) Commissioners: Philemon Bates,q.v., and George P. Martin, Recorded Dec. 30, 1820 (Abstracts of Wills. Book III p.399)
--April 1814 Inventory of Azariah Crane of Caldwell. Intestate includes tailor's goose and spoon moulds. Sworn to by Ira Crane, one of the administrators April 1815. (File 10896G Will Book III, p.399. Unrecorded estate papers Dec. 1820)

Children of Azariah Crane and Hannah Tucker:
(?)Ira, b. abt. 1780; signed the Inventory 1814; not named in the will of Azariah
Nancy, b. 1785; d. 1854; m. Stephen H. Brown (1780-1857) (both bur. Wellsburg Baptist Cemetery, Chemung Co., NY)
Rhoda, m. ..... Baldwin
Thankful, b. 1789 d. 1862 Chemung; m. Samuel Price, q.v.
Elizabeth/Betsey, b. August 1791; d. 1841; m. Aram Brown (1790-1851) (both bur. Wellsburg Baptist Cem. Chemung Co)
Ralph
Keturah, m. ..... Pierson
Margaret 'Chevise Peggy', b. June 2,1797 (bapt. at Caldwell, October 1797, dau. of Azariah and Hannah) d. March 24, 1866; m. #1, 1822, Essex Co. NJ,Thomas B. Dayley, who d. bef. October 1833 when she m. #2, Benjamin Freeman Bird, b. 1778, widower of Meribah

Reeves. (Margaret is bur. Ashland Cemetery, just to the left of
the old   Baptist Church, Wellsburg, Chemung Co. NY)

Benjamin,

Rebecca (?) (b. 1801; d.1853; *Rebecca T. Crane* bur. Wellsburg
Baptist Cemetery, Chemung)

Sarah/Sally

- - - - -

Crane, **CALEB**   b. (August 28, 1769)
(gmnj) (njhs)   d. June 10, 1844
(NJ Will 13341G. 1844)

Caleb Crane
died June 10th 1844
aged 74 Years 4 months
& 12 days

wife, **LYDIA**(Personett)   b. (October 3, 1767)
(gmnj) (lgl)   d. May 12, 1863

Lydia Personett
Wife of Caleb Crane
Died May 12, 1863
Aged 95 yrs.,7 mo. 9 days

eldest daughter, **MARIA**   b. (April 29, 1794)
(gmnj) (njhs)   d. October 14, 1830

Maria.
Eldest Daughter of
Caleb & Lydia Crane

died Octr. 14th 1830
in her 37th year
(njhs says "*adopted daughter*")

Notes:
--Caleb Crane, Deacon, First Presbyterian Church, Caldwell
--Caleb, son of Samuel Crane, Esq. and Mary Baldwin; m.
April 6, 1793 Lydia Personett, dau. of George Personett,
Esq., q.v., and Mary Condit
--1850 Census; p.79B, Caldwell Twp., Essex Co., NJ: Lydia
Crane, age 82; Lydia S. Crane, dau-in-law, age 50
--1860 Census; p.92A, Caldwell Twp, Essex Co., NJ: Zenas
C. Crane, age 55, farmer; Mary H., age 46; Marcus, age 17;
Caleb age 15; Ann M., age 13; Mary H., age 1; Lydia age 93;
2 servants

Children of Caleb Crane and Lydia Personett:
Maria, b. 1794; d. 1830
Samuel Gibson, q.v., b. 1797; m. Lydia S. Crane
Elizabeth Baldwin, b. 1800; d. 1858; (bur. 1st Presb.,Orange)
    m. Gershom Williams Freeman
Moses Personett, q.v., b. 1801; m. Sarah Baldwin Hedges
Zenas C., q.v., b.1804; d.1883; m. Mary Harrison
Lydia Personett, b. 1809; d.1899; m. George C. Steele, q.v.

- - - - -

Crane, **CALEB S.**   b. July 30, 1815
(gmnj)   d. August 29, 1851
(NJ Will 14192G. 1852)

Caleb S. Crane

born July 30, 1815
died August 29, 1851

first wife, **RHODA MARIA** (Dodd)
(gmnj) (njhs) (lgl)   b. (January 5, 1816)
                    d. March 21, 1848

Rhoda Maria
wife of
Caleb S. Crane
& only child of
Aaron & Tamar Dodd
died March 21st 1848
aged 32 years

Notes:
--Caleb Samuel Crane, Elder, First Presbyterian Church
--Caleb S. Crane, son of Nathaniel S. Crane, q.v., and Jane
Lee Duryea; m. #1, 1838, Rhoda Maria Dodd, dau. of Aaron
Dodd, q.v.,d. after birth of twins; m. #2, 1849, Henrietta
Marsh
--1850 Census, p.218, Jersey Twp., Licking Co., Ohio: Caleb
S. Crane age 35 b. NJ, teacher; Henrietta M. age 23 b. NJ;
Aaron D. age 10, b. NJ; Mariah, age 9 b. NJ; Henry, age 7, b.
NJ; Louisa W., age 2, b. NJ
--1851: "her husband, returning from Ohio to sell his
father-in-law Dodd's farm, was killed by a kick of his horse,
August 30, 1851, aged about 36" (Gen. of the Male Descendants
of Daniel Dodd. p.170)

Children of Caleb S. Crane and Rhoda Maria Dodd:

Aaron Dodd, b. 1839; d. 1895;m. #1, Sarah Campbell; m.
#2, Maria Crane Steele; m. #3, Martha A. Cooper
Mariah, b. abt. 1841
Henry Duryea, b. June 1842; d. 1906; m. Abby L. Cook.
daughter of Joseph Cook, q.v.
Louisa Whitehead, twin, b. Jan 1848; d. 1902; (bur. Prospect
Hill Cemetery) m. Cyrus A. Cook, son of Joseph Cook,
q.v.
Maria, twin, b. Jan 1848; d. 1892 (bur. Prospect Hill Cemetery)
m. Francis A. Wheeler

- - - - -

Crane, **CALVIN S.**   b. (abt. 1796)
(gmnj) (njhs) (lgl) (photo)   d. March 4, 1837
(NJ Inv. 12861G. 1838)

In
Memory of
Calvin S. Crane
who died
March 4th. 1837
in the 41st year
of his age

first wife, **NANCY** (Day)   b. (abt 1794)
(gmnj) (njhs) (lgl) (photo)   d. January 9, 1827

Nancy
the consort of
C. S. Crane
died Jan 9th 1827

in the 34th year
of her age

By the side of the
mother's grave,
lie the
remains of her infant
son.
aged 6 weeks & 4 days

second wife, **JULIA A.** (Douglass)
(gmnj) (njhs) (lgl) (photo)   b. (abt. 1800)
                          d. January 22, 1835

Julia
wife of
Calvin S. Crane
& daughter of Nathaniel
& Sarah Douglass
who died Jany. 22d. 1835.
aged 35 years

Notes:
--Calvin Smith Crane, son of Jonas Crane, q.v.
--Calvin m. #1, 1818, Nancy Day; m. #2, 1829, Julia
Angelina Douglass, dau. of Nathanial Douglass,q.v.; Calvin
m. #3, 1836, Mary Hier, dau. of John Hier
--Calvin W. Crane, Postmaster, Caldwell
--1822 "The old Parsonage was sold to Calvin S. Crane of
Parsippany, who conducted a boy's boarding school therein,
until the time of his death in 1837." (lgl. p.71)

Children of Calvin Smith Crane and Nancy Day:
Son, b. 1826; d. 1827
Phebe Ann, m. 1851, Stephen M. Sayre

Children of Calvin Smith Crane & Julia Angelina Douglass:
Delia, b. abt. 1831; m. Charles G. Campbell
Walworth Douglass, b. abt. 1834; m. Eliza 'VonLeer'

Children of Calvin Smith Crane and Mary Hier:
Catherine Augusta, b. abt. 1836

- - - - -

Crane, **CYRUS, Col.**   b. (October 23, 1779)
(gmnj) (njhs) (lgl) (photo)   d. November 17, 1827
(NJ Will 11035G. Inv.1828)

Cyrus Crane
died Novr. 17th. 1827
in his 49th year

wife, **HANNAH** (Crane)   b. (abt 1781)
(gmnj) (njhs) (photo)   d. May 1, 1850
(NJ Will #11935G)

In
Memory of
Hannah Crane
consort of Cyrus Crane
who died
May 1st 1850
in her 69th year

son, **JOSEPH B.**   b. (abt. 1816)
(njhs) (lgl)   d. March 25, 1832

Joseph B. Crane
son of
Col. Cyrus & Hannah Crane
died March 25th 1832
in his 16th year

Notes:
--Served: War of 1812: ..."colonel of the state militia; served
War of 1812 having a command at Brooklyn'
--1826, Dec. 22: "Cyrus Crane requested leave to resign his
commission as Colonel of the ... (blank) Regiment of the
Essex Brigade."
--Col. Cyrus Crane, son of Samuel Crane and Mary Baldwin;
m. 1807, Hannah Crane, dau. of William Crane and Lydia
Baldwin

Children of Col. Cyrus Crane and Hannah Crane:
Hannah, b. 1807
Dorcas, b. 1808; d.1894;(bur. Prospect Hill) m. Demas Harrison
Marcus Emmons, b. 1811; d. 1843
Joseph Baldwin, b. 1816; d. 1832
Asher Baldwin, q.v., b. 1809; d. 1888
Mary B., b. 1814;d.1883;(bur. Prospect Hill) m. Geo. A. Pierson
Elizabeth Maria, b. 1818, d.1895; (bur. Prospect Hill) m. Aaron
        G. Baldwin
Sarah, b. 1820; m. Cyrus Freeman Harrison, q.v.

- - - - -

Crane, **CYRUS**   b. (abt. 1803)
(photo) (gmnj)   d. December 31, 1828
(NJ Will 11935G.1828)

*The Grave
of
Cyrus Crane
who died
Dec. 31, 1828
Aged 25 years (23?)
and 9 days*

wife, Sarah   b.
                         d.

son, **ELIJAH PIERSON**   b. (abt. October 3, 1826)
(gmnj) (njhs) (photo)   d. May 21, 1833

*Elijah Pierson
son of Cyrus
and Sarah Crane
died May 21st 1833
aged 6 years. 7 momths
and 18 days*

Notes:
--Cyrus Crane, son of Timothy Crane, q.v.

- - - - -

Crane, **EDWARD J.**   b. (abt. February 22, 1802)

(gmnj) (njhs) (lgl)   d. October 6, 1831

Edward J. Crane
died Oct. 6th 1831
aged 24 years. 7 months
& 14 days

Notes:
--Edward (Jones?) Crane

- - - - -

Crane, George M.   b. (abt. 1803)
                                    d. (June 20, 1873)
                                    (bur. Mahwah Cem. Bergen Co.)
                                    (Aged 70.5.8, husband of Ellen)

wife, Ellen (Sindle)   b.
                                    d. (April 4, 1884)
                                    (bur. Mahwah Cem. Bergen Co.)

daughter, **ELIZA**   b. December 6, 1821
(gmnj) (njhs)   d. May 5, 1846

daughter **LYDIA**   b. November 15, 1832
(gmnj) (njhs)   d. May 1, 1834

son, **HARLEY W**.   b. June 7, 1836
(gmnj) (njhs)   d. August 28, 1838

Lydia. born Nov. 15th 1832. died May 1st 1834
Harley W. born June 7th, 1837. died Augst. 28th 1838

Eliza. born Decr. 6th 1821. died May 5th 1846
Children of George M. & Ellen Crane

Here lies our little son,
Died in his tender age,
By his two little sisters young,
All were delightsome babes.
In deep and silent graves
They are in numbers three,
And while we mourn their loss on earth,
In heaven we hope they be.
(Epitaph: lgl p. 471)

son, George A.   b. (abt. 1834)
                                   d. (May 20, 1865)
                                   (bur. Mahwah Cem. Bergen Co.)

Notes:
--?1840 Census, p.328, Caldwell Twp: George M. Crane

- - - - -

Crane, James Harvey   b. (January 7, 1824)
                               d. (January 24, 1903)
                               (bur. Cemetery Park, Ventura,CA)

wife, Abby D. (Harrison)   b. (abt. 1829)
                               d. (June 24, 1903)
                               (bur. Cemetery Park, Ventura, CA)

son, **WILLIE M.**   b. (abt. June 4, 1850)
(gmnj) (njhs) (photo)   d. May 4, 1850

William M.
son of James H. & Abby D. Crane
died May 4th, 1850
age 11 months

Notes:
--James Harvey Crane, son of Nathaniel Samuel Crane, q.v.
and Jane Lee Duryea; m. Abigail Dodd Harrison. dau. of
Caleb Dodd Harrison and Phebe Steele
--1850 Census; p.78 Caldwell Twp: James H. Crane, age 25,
farmer; Abby D., age 21 b. NJ; Thomas (last name unknown)
age 12, b. NJ
--1860 Census; p.89 Caldwell Twp: James H. Crane, age 36,
farmer; Abba D., age 31; Ella C. age 7; all b. NJ
--1870 Census; p.109 Caldwell Twp: James H. Crane, age
46, farmer; Abby, age 42; Ella, age 17
--1880 Census; p.422.4, Caldwell Twp: James H. Crane, age
56 farmer; Abbey D., age 51; Ella E. Gould, age 27,
daughter; Thomas Gould, age 29, son-in-law, farmer; all b.
New Jersey
--1900 Census: Ventura City,Ventura Co., California:
Thomas Gould, b. April 1851, m. 20 yrs; florist & seedman;
Ella E. b. July 1852; Olive C. b. May 1881; Thomas C. b.
Dec. 1886; James H. Crane, father-in-law b. Jan. 1824, m. 52
years, capitalist; Abbie D. Crane, mother-in-law b. may
1827, 2 born 1 living

Children of James Harvey Crane and Abby D. Harrison:
Willie, b. 1850; d. 1850
Ella Elizabeth, b. 1852; d. 1945; m. Thomas Gould,
          (1851-1934) son of Amos C. (both d. Ventura, California)

- - - - -

Crane, **JONAS**   b. (abt. July 29, 1750)
(gmnj) (njhs) (lgl) (photo)   d. October 17, 1806
(NJ Will 10400G.1806)

In
Memory of
Jonas Crane
who died Octr. 17th
1806 aged 56
Years. 2 months
& 18 days

wife, **PHEBE** (Munn)   b. (February 14, 1755)
(gmnj) (njhs) (lgl) (photo)   d. June 26, 1821

The Widow of
Jonas Crane
died June 26th 1821
In the 67th year
of her age

Notes:
--Jonas, son of William Crane; m. Phebe Munn, dau. of Benjamin Munn
--1812: Children of Jonas Crane, dec'd. mentioned in Will of Jonas' sister, Rachel, who m. Simeon Baldwin

Children of Jonas Crane and Phebe Munn:
Bethuel, b. abt 1780; d. 1854; m. 1803, Abigail Harrison

Lydia, b. abt. 1782
Rachel, b. abt. 1784
Phebe, b. abt. 1786
Abigail, b. abt 1788
Amos, b. abt. 1791; d. aft. 1850; m. Mary Ryerson
William, b. abt. 1793
Calvin Smith, q.v., b. 1795; m. #1, 1818, Nancy Day;
     m. #2 1829 Julia Douglass; m.#3, 1836 Mary Hier

- - - - -

Crane, Moses Personett   b. (August 19, 1801)
                              d. (1887)
                              (bur. Mandarin Cemetery,
                              Jacksonville, Duval Co., FL)

wife, Sarah B. (Hedges)   b. (July 2, 1802)
                              d. (December 29, 1874)
                              Aged 72 years
                              (bur. Prospect Hill Cemetery)

son,**WILLIAM WALLACE** b. (October 14, 1836)
(gmnj) (njhs) (lgl) (photo)   d. April 28, 1837

William Wallace
died
April 28th 1837
aged 6 months & 14 days

son, **EDWARD NELSON**   b. (July 16, 1839)
(gmnj) (njhs) (lgl) (photo)   d. January 11, 1840

Edward Nelson
died
Jan. 11th 1840
aged 5 months & 27 days

Sons of Moses P. & Sarah B. Crane
Sleep sweet babes, and take thy rest,
God called thee home. He thought it best.

Notes:

--Moses, son of Caleb Crane and Lydia Personett

--Moses m. 1831, Sarah Baldwin Hedges, dau. of Elias Hedges and Mary Baldwin

--1850 Census; p. 184 Caldwell Twp: Moses P. Crane, age 49, farmer; Sarah B., age 48; Caleb G. age 17, clerk; Edward N., age 7; 3 laborers

--1860 Census; p.93A, Caldwell Twp: Moses P. Crane, age 57, farmer; Sarah B., age 57; Wallace E., age 17; all b. NJ 3 laborers

--1870 Census; p.106A, Caldwell Twp: Moses P. Crane, age 67 farmer; Sarah, age 67; Edward W., age 26, merchant; Almira, age 24 (dau-in-law); Edward L., age 1 (grandson); 1 servant; 1 laborer

--1880 Census; p.428.3, Caldwell Twp: Moses P. Crane, age 78, farmer; E. Wallace age 36, paper mfr; Elmira, dau-in-law, age 30 b. NJ; Edward L. age 10, grandson; Oscar Maynard, age 24, b. NY, electrician; Hiram Maynard, age 21 b. NY, fish merchant; 1 laborer

--1885 Florida State Census: p.510, Mandarin, Duval Co., FL: C. G. Crane age 54 b. NJ, farmer; Eva D., age 33 wife b. NY; M. E. age 19, dau, b. NJ; M. P. father b. NJ; W. Arnold, age 23, boarder, b. NY, father b. England, mother b. NY; H.

Patterson, age 25, boarder, b. England; N. Merry, age 32, boarder, b. NY, salesman; Ella Merry, age 30 boarder, b. NJ; Edith Merry, age 1, boarder b. Florida, father b. NY, mother b. NJ

Children of Moses Personett Crane and Sarah B. Hedges:
Caleb Gibson, b. 1833; d. 1888 m. #1, 1853, Mary Jane
    Maynard; m. #2, 1875, Eva D. Leverich; (bur. Mandarin
    Cemetery, Jacksonville, Florida)
Wallace William, b. 1836; d. 1837
Edward Nelson, b. 1839; d. 1840
Edward Wallace, b. 1843; d. 1934 (bur. Prospect Hill); m.
    Elmira Maynard

- - - - -

Crane, **NATHANIEL S.**   b. (February 24, 1789)
(gmnj) (photo)   d. July 9, 1870
(NJ Will 17030G. 1870)

Nathaniel S. Crane
died July 9, 1870
Aged 82 years

first wife, **JANE LEE** (Duryea)
(gmnj) (njhs) (lgl)   b. (abt. 1791)
                 d. January 16, 1820

Jane Lee Duryea
wife of Nathaniel S. Crane
and daughter of
John & Mary Duryea

died Jan. 16th 1820
in her 28th year

second wife, **JULIA** Ann Ford (Hedges)
(gmnj) (njhs)   b. (abt. 1797)
                              d. December 14, 1852

Julia F. Hedges
died December 14, 1852
Aged 55 years

third wife, Janette Cook   b.
                                  d.

son, **DELPHINE EDGAR**   b. (abt. July 25, 1820)
(gmnj) (njhs) (lgl)   d. February 13, 1825

Delphine Edgar. son of
Nathaniel S. & Julia F. Crane
died Feb. 13th 1825
aged 4 yrs. 6 mos.
& 19 days

son, **JOSEPH**   b. (abt. August 7, 1838)
(gmnj) (njhs) (lgl)   d. January 14, 1840

Joseph
son of Nathaniel S.
& Julia F. Crane
died Jan. 14th. 1840
aged 1 year. 5 months

& 7 days

Notes:
See: <u>Sayre Family by Theodore Melvin Banta.</u> NY. 1901
--Nathaniel Samuel "Lord North" Crane, son of Samuel
Crane, Esq., q.v., and Mary Baldwin
--Nathaniel m. #1, 1810, Jane Lee Duryea, dau. of Rev.
John Duryea, q.v.
--Nathaniel m. #2, 1821, Julia Ann Ford Hedges
--Nathaniel m. #3, 1854, Janette E. Cook, dau. of Ellis Cook
--1850 Census; p.92, Caldwell Twp: Nathaniel S. Crane age
61, farmer; Julia, age 52; John D., age 37, farmer; Phebe M.,
age 23; Julia, age 15; Joseph, age 7; 3 laborers
--1860 Census; p.89 Caldwell Twp: Nathaniel S. Crane, age
71, farmer; Janette, age 56; Ellis Cook, age 76; 1 servant; 4
laborers
--1870 Census; p.109, Caldwell Twp: Nathaniel S. Crane,
age 81, farmer; Janet age 65; 1 laborer; 1 servant

Children of Nathaniel Samuel Crane and Jane Lee Duryea:
Samuel S., b. abt. 1810; d. 1874; (bur. Prospect Hill) m. 1834,
  Maria Pierson
John Duryea,b. 1813;d. 1888;(bur. Prospect Hill) m. Ann E. Day
Caleb Samuel, q.v., b. 1815; d. 1851; m. Rhoda M. Dodd
Henry Wilson,b. 1817; d.1890 (bur. Prospect Hill) m. Sarah
  Ann Duryea
Jane Eliza, b. Oct. 1819;

Children of Nathaniel Samuel Crane and Julia A. F. Hedges:
Delphine Edgar, b. 1820; d. 1825
James Harvey, q.v.,b.1824;d.1903; m.Abigail Dodd Harrison

Phebe Maria, b. 1827; d. 1910; m. William Gould (bur.
  Prospect Hill Cemetery, Caldwell)
Cyrus Edgar, b. 1829; d. 1904; m. Josephine Field
Julia Hedges, b. 1835; d. 1913; m.Rev. Lemuel S. Potwin
  (1832-1907) (both bur Lakeview Cemetery, Cleveland, Ohio)
Joseph Adolphus, b. 1838; d. 1840;"scalded to death by falling
  into a caldron"
Joseph Wilmouth, b. 1842; d. 1908; m. Anna E. Parkhurst

- - - - -

Crane, **NEHEMIAH**   b. (April 5, 1778)
(gmnj) (njhs) (lgl)   d. September 5, 1821
(NJ Will 11396G.Inv.1822)

Nehemiah Crane
died Septr. 5th 1821
aged 43 years & 4 months

wife, **PHEBE** (Jones)   b. (abt. May 4, 1779)
(gmnj)   d. October 29, 1834

Phebe
Wife of Nehemiah Crane
(married 2nd Timothy Gould) (q.v.)
Died October 29 1834
Aged 54 years

son, **PHILIP**   b. (April 5, 1804)
                         d. September 5, 1828

also Philip Crane

died on his passage from
Santiago de Cuba to New Orleans
Sept. 5th 1828
aged 24 years & 5 months

Notes:
--Nehemiah, son of John R. Crane and Elizabeth Crane; m.
1801, Phebe Jones, dau. of Joseph? Jones and Phebe
Harrison

Children of Nehemiah Crane and Phebe Jones:
Edward, b. 1802; d. 1802
Philip, b. 1804; d. 1828
Noah H., b. 1808; m. Catherine A. Matthews

- - - - -

Crane, **OLIVER**, Deacon   b. (abt. September 29, 1765)
(gmnj) (njhs)   d. August 31, 1817
(NJ Will 11042G.1817)

Deacon Oliver Crane
who was killed by the kick of a horse on Sabbath Day.
August 31st 1817
as he was repairing to the house of divine service
aged 51 years. 11 months
& 21 days

wife, **SUSANNA** (Baldwin) b. (abt. March 30, 1768)
(gmnj) (njhs) (lgl) (photo)   d. November 11, 1838

Sacred

to
the memory of
Susanna
Relict of
Deacon Oliver Crane
who departed this life
Novr. 11th A.D.1838
aged 70 years. 7 mos.
& 12 days

O ye mourners! cease to languish,
O'er the grave of her we love,
Far removed from pain and anguish,
She is chanting hymns above

Notes:
--Oliver Crane, son of William Crane and Mary/Mercy....
m. Susannah Baldwin, dau. of David Baldwin
--1812: Oliver received $200 in the Will of his sister, Rachel,
wife of Simeon Baldwin
--Will (noncupative) Aug. 31, 1817: "Oliver Crane of Bloomfield. Aged
abt. 53 years. Having received a mortal wound in the breast from the kick
of a horse near the Presbyterian Meeting House in Caldwell, was carried
to the house of Rev. Mr. Grover, where he recovered his recollection and
bade persons present to take notice while he made his will: to married
daughter, Lydia Crane, $100; son Fordham, his horse; all real estate to be
divided equally between his sons; wife, household goods and 2 cows;
next two oldest sons (Amos and Zophar) the rest of the horses and cattle;
Having thus made his will the testator 'died in a few minutes apparently in
possession of his senses'." Witnesses: Mrs. Sarah Fordham; Joanna Crane
(Mrs. Zadoc); Joseph S. Dodd. Recorded Dec. 1817 by Philemon Bates.
(File 11042G)

Children of Oliver Crane and Susannah Baldwin:

Sarah, b. 1787; d. 1835

Lydia, b. 1789; d. 1848; m. Josiah Eliakim Crane (bur. Bloomfield Cemetery, Bloomfield, NJ)

Stephen Fordham, b. 1791; m. Matilda Howell Smith

Rachel, b. 1794;d. 1855; (bur. Prospect Hill) m. 1818, Amos Baldwin

Amos, b. 1799; d. 1882; m. 1861, Rhoda Caroline Ward (?bur. Rosedale Cemetery, Orange)

Zophar Baldwin, b. 1803; d. 1877; m. Julia Freeland (bur. Bloomfield Cemetery)

Nathaniel Marcus, b. 1805; d. 1859; m. 1836, Julia A. Ostrander

Isaac Wheeler, b. 1808; d. 1864; m. Elizabeth Burrows; m. #2, Mary L. Turnbull

- - - - -

Crane, **SAMUEL, ESQ.** b. (abt. 1747)
(gmnj) (njhs) (lgl) d. February 28, 1811
(NJ Will 10665G. 1811)

Founding Elder and Deacon

Samuel Crane, Esq.
died Feb. 28th 1811
in his 64th year

A prudent Magistrate
An active and useful officer of the Church
an exemplary Christian,
and affectionate Parent

wife, **MARY** (Baldwin)   b. (abt. 1748)
(lgl) (gmnj) (njhs)   d. January 26, 1817

> *Mary.*
> *relict of Samuel Crane.*
> *died Jan.26th 1817*
> *in her 69th year*

son, **CYRUS**   b. (abt. 1772)
(photo)   d. (abt. 1772)

> *Cyrus*
> *Infant son of*
> *Samuel and Mary B.*
> *Crane*

Notes:
Served: Revolutionary War
--Samuel, son of Noah Crane and Mary Baldwin;
m. Mary Baldwin, dau. of John Baldwin

Children of Samuel Crane, Esq. and Mary Baldwin:
Caleb Crane, q.v., b. 1769; m. Lydia Personett
Cyrus, b. 1772; d. 1772
Zenas, q.v., b. 1776; m. Abigail Grover
Dorcas Maria, b. 1777; m. Timothy Crane, q.v.
Cyrus, q.v., b. 1778; m. Hannah Crane
Elizabeth, b. 1782; m. Matthias Canfield, q.v.
Mary, b. 1784; m. Samuel Harrison, q.v.
(?)Abigail, b. abt. 1785; m. John Sturdevant(?)
Nathaniel Samuel, q.v., b. 1789; m. #1, Jane Lee Duryea
    m. #2, Julia Ann Ford Hedges; #3, Janette E. Cook

- - - - -

Crane, **SAMUEL GIBSON** b. (February 14, 1797)
(gmnj) (lgl) (njhs) d. August 21, 1821

Samuel Gibson Crane
died Augt. 21st 1821
in his 24th year
He has left a dear and afflicted Widow.
Affectionate Parents, Brothers, and Sisters.
To mourn the great and unexpected loss.
But cease my friends the falling tear,
A God of mercy, calls you. 'Hear'
It is his will, do not complain,
And you my little orphan dear,
Who never knew a father's care,
May God your friend and father be.
Thro' life, and in eternity.
Youth! a solemn call to three;
O! prepare to follow me

wife, **LYDIA S.** (Steele) b. (June 27, 1800)
(gmnj) (njhs) (photo) d. October 10, 1855

In
Memory of
Lydia S.
widow of
Samuel G. Crane
Died October 10, 1855
Aged 55.3.13

daughter, **ANNA MARIA G.** b. (September 15, 1820)
(gmnj) (njhs) (lgl) (photo)   d. May 1, 1839

> *Ann Maria Gibson*
> *only child of*
> *Samuel G. & Lydia S. Crane*
> *died May 1st. 1839*
> *aged 18 years. 7 months*
> *&16 days*

Notes:
--Samuel Gibson Crane, son of Caleb Crane, q.v., and Lydia
Personett; m. 1819, Lydia Steele
--1850 Census, p.79B, Caldwell Twp., Essex Co., NJ: Lydia
Crane, age 82; Lydia S. Crane, age 50

Child of Samuel Gibson Crane and Lydia Steele:
Anna Maria Gibson, b. 1820; d. 1839

- - - - -

Crane, Simeon, Capt.   b.
                            d. (1835) Wayne Co., NY

wife, Eunice (Baldwin)   b. (abt. 1776)
                            d. (1842) Calhoun Co., MI

son, **AMBROSE**   b. (abt. January 20, 1798?)
(gmnj) (njhs) (photo)   d. March 12, 1810 (1812?)

> *Sacred*

to the memory of
Ambrose Crane
son of
Capt. Simeon and Eunice
Crane
died March 12, 1810
aged 12 years. 1 month (10 years?)
& 21 days

Notes:
Served: War of 1812; Capt. Rifle Co., 3rd Reg't.
--Simeon, son of Gamaliel Crane and Susanna Dodd;
m. Eunice Baldwin, dau. of Caleb Baldwin
--Simeon d. Wayne Co., New York (His brother, Zebina, b.
1772; d.1823 Marion, Wayne Co. NY, (bur. Upper Corners
Cemetery, Wayne Co.)
--1840 Census: Sheridan Twp., Calhoun Co.,Michigan:
Eunice Crane; adj. to Caleb J. Crane

?Children of Simeon Crane and Eunice Baldwin:
Lydia,
Phebe, b. 1789 NJ; d.1877, Macomb Co.MI; m....Thompson
Ambrose, b. 1800; d. 1810 NJ
David B., b. abt. 1803, NJ; d. Michigan
Isaac
Caleb J. b. abt 1808, NJ; d. Michagan
Harriet
Jane
Elizabeth
Marcus Horatio, b. abt 1820 NJ; d. 1905, Albion, Calhoun
        Co. Michigan
Maria, b. abt. 1823 NJ; d. 1903 Albion MI; m. ...Blanchard

Lewis Dodd, b. abt. 1833 NJ

- - - - -

Crane, Stephen Fordham   b. (1791)
                                    d. (bef. 1870)

wife, Matilda H. (Smith)   b. (March 15, 1791)
                                    d. (January 18, 1871)
                                    (bur. Sussex Co., N.J.?)

daughter, **SARAH URANIA** b. (January 17, 1825)
(gmnj) (njhs) (lgl) (photo)   d. December 28, 1834

Sarah Urania
daughter of Stephen E.
& Matilda H. Crane
who was called from this earthly abode.
Dec. 28th 1834
in her 10th year

Notes:
Served: War of 1812
--Stephen Fordham Crane, eldest son of Oliver Crane, q.v.;
m. 1816, Matilda Howell Smith, dau. of Peter Smith
--1870 Census, Montclair, Essex Co.: Matilda Crane, age 79;
Sarah Baldwin, age 40, no occup.; Matilda Roster age 56,
music teacher; Stephen S. Crane, age 40, no occup.; John
Mulkehany, age 55 b. Ireland, laborer (near Timothy Crane,
age 84 and Matilda, age 85)

Children of Stephen F. Crane and Matilda Howell Smith:

Emeline Huldah, b. 1817; d. 1857, Philadelphia
Susan Philetta, b. 1820, d. 1864; m. Lemuel F. Corwin
Oliver, (Rev. Dr.) b. 1822; d. 1896, Boston (bur.Rosedale Cem);
    AM Yale; DD, LLD; missionary to Turkey; house at
    Winter Park, FL; m. 1844, Marion Dunn Turnbull, d.
    1890 (bur. Rosedale Cem.); m. #2, 1891, Boston, Sibylla
    Adelaide Bailey of Boston
Sarah Urania, b. 1825; d. 1834
Hannah Maria, b. 1827, d.1855
Stephen Smith, b. 1830, d. 1872 (bur. Rosedale Cemetery)

- - - - -

Crane, Timothy	b. (abt. 1777)
	d. (1846) (Ohio)

first wife, **DORCAS** (Crane)	b. (abt. 1777)
(gmnj) (njhs) (lgl)	d. January 4, 1805

Dorcas
wife of
Timothy Crane
died Jany. 4th. 1805
in her 29th year

son, **CYRUS**	b. (abt. December 22, 1804)
(gmnj) (njhs) (lgl)	d. December 31, 1828

Cyrus Crane
died Dec. 31st. 1828
aged 25 years & 9 days
(gmnj: "23.0.9")

Notes:

--Timothy, son of Jonathan Crane and Mary Ward

--Timothy m. 1799, Dorcas Maria Crane, dau. of Samuel Crane, q.v.

--Timothy, son of Jonathan Crane, mentioned in will of Jonathan's sister, Rachel Crane Baldwin

--1850 Census, p.212, Jersey Twp., Licking Co., OH: Zenas Crane, age 49, b. NJ, farmer; Elizabeth, age 45, b. NJ; 2 children b. NJ; 4 children b. Ohio

Children of Timothy Crane and Dorcas Crane:
Zenas Personett, b. 1802; d. 1875; bur. Jersey Presb. Cem. Pataskala, OH; m. 1826, Elizabeth Poole Speer, she d. 1881, OH
Elizabeth, b. 1804
Cyrus, b. abt. 1804; d. 1828. q.v.

- - - - -

Crane, Uzal A.   b. (1807)
                           d. (August 22, 1884)Brooklyn
                           ('bur. place, Caldwell')

wife, Lucetta Banks (Gould) b. (abt. 1805)
                           d. (October 8, 1889) Brooklyn
                           ('bur. place, Caldwell')

son, **DAVID BANKS**   b. (abt. December 31, 1838)
(gmnj) (njhs) (lgl)   d. September 22, 1839

*David Banks
son of Uzal A.*

& Lucetta B. Crane
died Sept. 22. 1839
aged 8 months & 22 days

daughter, **MARY BANKS**   b. (abt. April 10, 1843)
(gmnj) (njhs) (lgl)   d. March 20, 1844

Mary Banks.
daughter of
Uzal A. & Lucetta B. Crane
died March 20th 1844
aged 11 months & 10 days

Notes:
--Uzal, son of Abijah Crane; m. 1830, Lucetta B.
daughter of Stephen Gould, q.v., and Sarah Banks
--Lucetta, "widow of Uzal A. Crane, died October 8, 1889, in
her 84th year; services to be held at the home of her
son-in-law, John Tiebout, Brooklyn, NY" (*New York Times)*
--Uzal "learned the art of printing in the Law Publishing
House of Stephen Gould,(q.v.) formerly of Gould Banks &
Co. NYC. Mr. Crane started out editing the *Paterson
Courier*."
(Genealogy of the Crane family. p.408)
--1850 Census: 7Wd. NYC: U. A. Crane, age 43 b. NJ; 'Rosa'
wife age 44 b. NY; Alexander age 15 b. NY, clerk; Uzal, age
5, b. NY; Henry B., age 2, b. NY; 2 boarders
--1860 Census: Indianapolis, Marion Co. IN: Alexander
Crane, age 24, b. NY clerk; Mary age 20 b. IN; Cary, age 3 b.
IN; Willie, age 2 b. IN; Tillie, age 1 b. IN; (adj. to in-laws)
--1875 NY Census: Brooklyn: Alexander G. Crane, age 40;
Mary J. wife age 37; Wm. G. son age 17; Tillie G. dau. age

16; Lucetta B. dau., age 10; Theron J., son, age 14; Theron Park, age 69, father-in-law; Matilda Park, age 63, mother-in-law

Children of Uzal A. Crane and Lucetta Banks Gould:
Caroline Holmes, b. abt. 1831;d. 1890; m.1850, John
Tiebout (bur. Green-Wood Cemetery, Brooklyn, NY)
Alexander Gould, (Mjr.); b.abt.1835; d. 1876; m. Mary Park
David Banks, b. 1839; d.1839
Mary Banks, b. 1843; d. 1844
Uzal Ogden, b. abt. 1845; d. 1902; m. Sarah Eliz. Mundell
Henry Paxton, b.abt. 1848, d. 1919, Brooklyn; unm. ('bur. place Caldwell')

- - - - -

Crane, William G.	b. (December 26, 1794)
	d. (August 13, 1871)
	(bur. Belvidere Cemetery Warren Co., N.J.)
wife, **SARAH A.** (Condit) (gmnj)	b. January 24, 1800
	d. March 22, 1851

Sarah A.
wife of William G. Crane
born January 24, 1800
died March 22, 1851

daughter, **HENRIETTA** (gmnj) (njhs) (photo)	b. (abt. 1826)
	d. March 20, 1836

Henrietta. daughter of
William G. & Sarah A. Crane
died March 20th 1836
in her 11th year

Notes:
--William Gould Crane m. Sarah A. Condit, dau. of Stephen Condit and Elizabeth Harrison
--1850 Census; p.330 West Ward, Newark: William G. Crane, age 55, spice merchant; Sarah, age 50; Wickliffe, age 22; Phebe, age 20; Elizabeth, age 16; Stephen Condit, age 11;
Mary Ann Taylor, age 26; Elenor Taylor, age 18; all b. NJ
--1860 Census; p.371, 4Wd, Newark: Hettie Crane, age 50; Wm. G. Crane, age 64, wool carder; Sarah B. Stagg, age 70; all b. New Jersey
--1870 Census; p.10, Belvidere, Warren Co., NJ: Edwin R. Crane, age 51 b. NJ, dentist; Jane N., age 48 b. NY; Jennie H., age 12 b. NY; Wm. G. age 75, b. NJ; 1 servant; 1 apprentice dentist

Children of William G. Crane and Sarah A. Condit:
Edwin R., b. abt. 1819; m. Jane Nodine; (bur. Belvidere Cem.)
Charles, b. abt. 1825 (d. Phildelphia?)
Henrietta, b. 1826; d. 1836
Wickliffe N. , b. 1828; m. Ella F. .....; (d. New York?)
Elizabeth Phebe, b. abt. 1834 (d. Iowa?)
Adeline, b. ....; m. October 1841, Ward Martin (d. Iowa?)
Stephen Condit, b. abt. 1839

- - - - -

Crane, **ZADOC**   b. (abt. 1758)
(gmnj) (njhs) (lgl)   d. February 14, 1841
(NJ Will #13115G)   (February 11, 1841?)

Zadoc Crane
died Feb. 14th 1841
in his 83rd year

wife, **JOANNA**   b. (abt. 1766)
(gmnj) (njhs) (lgl) (photo)   d. October 22, 1849

In
Memory of
Joanna
Relict of
Zadoc Crane
she died Octr. 22d. 1849
in the 83rd year
of her age

Notes:
Served: Revolutionary War: 'he was a waiter in the
bodyguard of the Commander In Chief but his name does not
appear on the rolls'(source unknown)
--Zadoc, son of William Crane; brother of Jonas Crane,q.v.
--Zadoc "took care of (Gen.) Washington's horse when he
was at Cranetown...Zadoc, a son of William, who had been
lame from boyhood offered to assume the difficult job even
though one leg was shorter than the other." (Gen. of the Crane
Family. E. B. Crane. p.314)
--1812: Zadoc received $100 in the will of his sister, Rachel,
wife of Simeon Baldwin

- - - - -

Crane, **ZENAS,** Capt. b. (abt. 1772)
(gmnj) (njhs) (lgl) d. November 19, 1801
(NJ Will Int. 10040G. 1801)

Sacred
the the memory of
Capt. Zenas Crane
who was drowned in crossing the ferry
from Brooklyn to New York
on 19th of November A.D. 1801
in the 30th year of his age

wife, Abigail (Grover) b. (January 2, 1777)
 d. (March 22, 1862)
 (bur. Jackson Presbyterian
 Cemetery, Wayne Co., Ohio)

Notes:

--Zenas, son of Samuel Crane, q.v.; m. April 29, 1795, Abby Grover, dau. of Joseph Grover and Sarah Howell; Abigail m. #2, 1803 at Caldwell, John Sturdevant, b. 1776 d. 1854, Prattsburgh, Steuben Co., New York.

--An earlier 1801 account of a ferry accident between New York and Brooklyn: "We started from Fulton Market...some passengers talked about taking the boat themselves...the boatman owing to intoxication...but we allowed them to proceed. ...the boat was upset several of the passengers were immediately lost. ...one woman and five men were drowned, six of us were saved after having been upset. These incidents are of value as the barge or scow that carries the passenger at the risk of his life between New York and Brooklyn."

Published in: The American Citizen. May 27, 1801: (History and Commercial and Industrial Record of Brooklyn. Henry R. Stiles. Vol. I, NY 1884)

--1850 Census: Canaan, Wayne Co., Ohio: Abigail Sturdevant, age 76; John David Sturdevant, age 34; Oliver Sturdevant, age 21; adjacent to son Zenas Z. Crane w/ wife and 8 children

--?1850 Census: Prattsburgh, Steuben Co., NY: John Sturdevant, age 75 b. CT, farmer; Abby Sturdevant, age 33 b. NJ, daughter (wife Abby, not listed)

--?1860 Census: Prattsburgh, NY: Abby Sturdevant, age 45, at res. of (brother) Joseph G. Sturdevant age 53, b. NJ, farmer (Abby b. 1777, not listed)

Children of Zenas Crane and Abigail Grover:
Clarinda, b. 1796; m. Collin Haslett
Sarah, b. 1799; m. 1819, Ichabod B. Ward, q.v.
Esther, b. 1801
Caleb L.,
Zenas Z., b. April 10, 1802;d. March 21, 1886; (bur. Jackson Presbyterian Cem., Wayne Co., OH); m. 1830, Mary 'Polly' Stiles

- - - - -

Crane, Zenas C.   b. (1804)
                             d. (July 7, 1883)
                             (bur. Prospect Hill Cemetery)

wife, Mary (Harrison)   b. 1813
                             d. 1889
                             (bur. Prospect Hill Cemetery)

Note:

--Zenas C. Crane, son of Caleb Crane and Lydia Personett.

--Zenas C. Crane "had been a member of the church forty-six years, an elder for four terms of five years each, and a trustee for many years." (lgl, p.230)

--"Zenas C. Crane attended the Academy, (founded by Calvin S. Crane, q.v.) in his youth...his desk made by slave labor on his father's farm." (lgl p. 71)

--Memorial Window at First Presbyterian, Caldwell

In Memory of
Zenas C. Crane
1804 and 1883
Mary Harrison Crane
1813 and 1889
His Wife

- - - - -

CROWELL

Crowell, **JOSEPH FREEMAN**
(gmnj) (njhs) (lgl) (photo)   b. (abt. July 28, 1793)
                                     d. September 20, 1821

Joseph Freeman Crowell
died
Septr. 20th 1821
aged 28 years. 1 month
& 23 days

wife, **ROSALINDA GROVER**

(gmnj) (photo)   b. October 15, 1795
                                   d. November 27, 1873

Rosalind Grover
wife of
Joseph F. Crowell
Born October 15, 1795
Died November 27, 1873

Notes:

--Joseph, son of John Crowell and Mary Marsh

--Rosalinda, daughter of Rev. Stephen Grover, q.v.

--1850 Census; p.359, Newark: Stephen G. Crowell age 34 dry goods; Sarah age 29; Joseph age 6; David age 3; Stephen age 1; Rosalinda age 55; all b. NJ; 1 servant

--1850 Census; p.181 Bloomfield: Albert Morris age 36 farmer; Margaret age 35; Harriet G. age 14; Joseph age 12; Robert age 8; George age 7; Henry age 4; Harriet Crowell age 31; all b. NJ

--1860 Census; p.162&163 Bloomfield Essex Co. NJ: Albert Morris age 47 sawyer; Margaret age 45; Joseph age 22 bending work for carriages; Robert age 18; Anna age 7; Rosa Crowel age 60; Harriet Crowel age 40; all b. NJ; laborers

--1870 Census p.89&90 Bloomfield: Albert Morris age 57 saw mill; Margaret M. age 55; Robert A. age 28 clerk; Annie M. age 17; Rosalind Crowell age 74 no occup.; Harriet B. Crowell age 50; all b. NJ;Hattie Oakes age 34; George A. Oakes age 2

Child of Joseph Freeman Crowell and Rosalinda Grover:
Margaret, b.1815, d. 1885; m. Albert Morris (1813-1885)
both buried Mount Pleasant Cemetery, Newark

Stephen Grover, b. 1817, d. 1854; m. Sarah W. Smith; bur.
Mount Pleasant Cemetery, Newark
Harriet, b. abt 1819; unm. in 1870

- - - - -

DAVENPORT

Davenport, Ezra   b. (September 12, 1803)
                                   d. (March 24, 1889)
                                   (bur. Fairfield Reformed
                                   Church Cemetery)

wife, **MARY** (Beach)   b. (abt. October 12, 1807)
(gmnj)   d. March 23, 1871
                                   (also on monument at Fairfield
                                   Reformed Church)

Mary
Wife of Ezra Davenport
died March 23, 1871
Aged 63.5.11

Notes:
--Ezra, son of Leonard Davenport and Catherine Stiles;
m. November 2 1827; Mary Beach, dau. of Jonathan Beach
and Rachel Jacobus
--1850 Census: p.79 Caldwell Twp.; Ezra Davenport age 46
farmer; Mary age 42; Jonathan B. age 19 farmer; Sarah F.
age 16; Catherine age 74; all b. NJ
--1860 Census: p.111 Caldwell Twp: Ezra Davenport age 56
farmer; Mary age 52

--1870 Census: p. 127 Caldwell; Ezra Davenport age 66 farmer; Mary age 63; Jonthan B. age 38 farmer; Mary age 37; Clara age 9; Emma age 7; all b. NJ

Children of Ezra Davenport and Mary Beach:
Salenna Elizabeth, b. abt. 1828; m. Sardius Stewart, b. 1827; d. Aug. 1910, Burning Springs, Wirt Co.,WVA, res. Parkersburg, Wood Co., WVA
Sarah F., b. abt. 1834 m. George Speer
Jonathan Beach, b. 1831; m. Mary E. Speer

- - - - -

DAVIDSON

Davidson, Henry P.   b. (abt. 1799)
                           d.

wife, CHARITY (Wade)   b. (abt. 1800)
(gmnj) (njhs) (lgl)   d. August 16, 1850

Charity
wife of
Henry P. Davidson
& daughter of
Obadiah and Nancy Wade
died Augst. 16th 1850
aged 50 years

Notes:

--Henry, son of William Davidson and Elizabeth Clark; m.
Charity Wade, dau. of Obadiah Wade,q.v., and Nancy
Edwards

--1830 Census: Livingston Twp., Essex Co., NJ: Henry P.
Davidson

--1850 Census; p.105 Livingston Twp. Essex Co. NJ: Henry
P. 'Davison' age 51 wheel wright b. NJ; Charity age 50 b.
New Jersey

- - - - -

DAY

Day, Moses	b. (abt. 1776)
	d. (May 8, 1837)
	(bur. Fairfield Ref. Church Cem.)
	In 61st year

wife, **REBECKAH** (Berry)	b. (abt. October 1, 1783)
(gmnj) (njhs) (lgl)	d. March 22, 1817

Sacred
to the Memory of
Rebeckah
wife of
Moses Day
died March 22d. 1817
aged 53 years

Notes:
--Moses, son of David Day and Mary Denman; m.1803
Rebecca Berry, dau. of Jacob Berry and Margaret Mead

Children of Moses day and Rebecca Berry:
Martin B. Day, b. 1814, d.June 21, 1875. Age 61
Rebecca B. day, b. 1817, d. Dec. 31, 1876; m. .... Mains

- - - - -

DE CAMP

DeCamp, Aaron	b. (abt. 1741)
	d. (bef. March, 1827)
wife, Keturah (Clark)	b. (abt. 1745)
	d. (aft. 1827)
son, **JOHN**	b. (abt. September 3, 1785)
(gmnj) (njhs) (lgl) (photo)	d. September 9, 1804

In Memory of
John Decamp. Son
of Aaron & Keturah
Decamp died Sept. 9th
1804. aged 19 years
& 6 days

Notes:
--Aaron, son of Aaron DeCamp of Staten Island; m. April 22,
1771: Keturah, dau. of Daniel Clark and Abigail Shipman
--Will of Aaron DeCamp, proved March 1827 (Lib.D, p.465)
Ment: wife Ketura; sons Moses, Benjamin, Daniel; dau.
Sarah Riker, Abigail Beach, Mary Shippen, Deborah
DeCamp. Executors: Zenas Harrison and William Gould.

Witnesses: Josiah Steele, Abram Personett and Nathaniel M. Gould (neighbors?)

Children of Aaron DeCamp and Keturah Clark:
Moses, q.v, b. 1771; m. Catherine Williams of Orange
Sarah, b. 1774; m. John Riker
Daniel, b. 1776
Benjamin, q.v, b. 1778; Dorcas Williams
Abigail, b. 1780; m. Timothy Beach
Mary Ely, b. abt. 1783; m. John Blair Shippen
John, b. 1785; d. 1804
Deborah, b. abt. 1788; m. Warren VanName

- - - - -

De Camp, **BENJAMIN**   b. (August 18, 1778)
(gmnj) (njhs) (lgl) (photo)   d. August 11, 1838
(NJ Will:12868G. Lib. G. p.95)

In memory
of
Benjamin De Camp
who died
Augst. 11th 1838
in the 60th year
of his life

wife, **DORCAS** (Williams)   b. (December 21, 1781)
(gmnj)   d. December 4, 1866

Dorcas Williams
Wife of Benjamin DeCamp

Died December 4, 1866
Aged 86.0.2

Notes:
--Benjamin, son of Aaron DeCamp, q.v.; m. 1804: Dorcas
Williams, dau. of Jonathan Williams and Nancy Squire
--1850 Census; p.108 Livingston Twp. Essex Co. NJ: Dorcas
DeCamp age 68; Jonathan D. age 29 shoemaker; Margaret
age 28; Mary Ann age 7; Martha age 5; Benjamin age 3;
Timothy age 11 months; Henry Lyon age 63 shoemaker
--1860 Census; p.193 Livingston: Widow Dorcas DeCamp
age 79; Timothy DeCamp age 50; both b. NJ
--Will: signed 1837; proved 1838: Liber G.,p.95; Ment: wife,
Dorcas; sons: Aaron, Timothy, Jonathan and Zenas Harrison;
daughters: Phebe, Mary and Keturah; Executor son Aaron;
Witnesses Zenas Harrison, Grimes Bolton, Wm. Moore

Children of Benjamin DeCamp and Dorcas Williams:
Phebe, b. 1804; m. John Conselyea
Mary, b. 1807; m. Cornelius Kent
Aaron,
Timothy B., b.1815; d. 1889; (bur. Roseland Meth. Ch. Cem)
Aaron, b. 1814;d. 1901 m. Mary E. (Tomkins?)
    (bur. Roseland Meth. Ch. Cemetery)
Keturah, b. 1817
Jonathan D., b. 1821; m. 1842...Margaret Vincent
Zenas Harrison, b. 1823; d. 1897 m. Electa Catherine Bond
    (bur. Roseland Meth. Ch. Cemetery)

- - - - -

DeCamp, **MOSES**   b. (June 24, 1771)

(gmnj)   d. Feburary 18, 1852

Moses DeCamp
died February 18, 1852
Aged 82.8.0

wife, **CATHARINE** (Williams)
(gmnj) (njhs)   b. (abt. 1785)
                                d. January 28, 1849

Catharine
wife of
Moses Decamp
died Jan. 28th 1849
in her 64th year

Notes:
--Moses, son of Aaron DeCamp, q.v.; m. Catherine
Williams, dau. of Jonathan Williams and Mary Squier
--1850 Census; p.82 Caldwell Twp: John DeCamp age 45
farmer; Jane age 42; Amanda age 17; Daniel age 15
tobacconist; Jane L. age 8; Samuel age 3; Moses age 80
farmer; all b. NJ

Children of Moses DeCamp and Catherine Williams:
John, b. abt. 1795; m. Jane .....
Daniel, b. abt 1800
Abigail, b. abt. 1802

- - - - -

DEXHEIMER

Dexheimer, Jacob   b. (abt. 1815)
                                    d.

wife, Susan Catherine (Kling)b. (abt. 1826)
                                    d.

son, **JOHN M.**   b.(abt. November 1841)
(njhs) (lgl)   d. January 1, 1842

John M.
son of Jacob
and Susan Dexheimer
died Jan. 1st 1842
aged 8 weeks. & 2 days

Notes:
--Jacob, born in Germany (?Jacobus bapt. March 28, 1815
Rheinhessen Hessen; son of Johannis Dexheimer and
Catharine Hahn)
--m. Susan Catherine Kling, born in New York
--1850 Census: p.70 Caldwell Twp: Jacob Dexheimer age 35
farmer b. Germany; Susan C. age 24 b. NY; Catherine age 7
b. NJ; William age 4 b. NJ; Joseph C. age 2 b. NJ; Peter age
22 b. Germany coal carter; 1 laborer
--1860 Census: p.118 Caldwell Twp: Jacob 'Dexhamorne'
age 46 b. Germany butcher; Susan age 34 b. NY; Catherine
age 16; William age 14; Joseph age 11; George age 10; Jacob
age 8; Alfred age 6;Eugene age 2 b. NY; older children b. NJ
--1870 Census: p.753 Tusten, Sullivan Co. NY: Jacob
Dexheimer age 56 b. Bavaria farmer; Susan age 46 b. NY;

Joseph age 21 b. NJ; Jacob age 17 b. NJ; Alfred age 15 b. Nj; Eugene age 13 b. NJ; Benjamin age 2 b. NY

Children of Jacob Dexheimer and Susan C. .....:
John M., b. 1841; d. 1842
Catherine, b. abt. 1843
William, b. abt. 1846; m. Elizabeth .....
Joseph C., b. abt 1848
George, b. abt. 1850
Jacob, b. abt. 1852; d. 1900; m. Alice L. Tyler
      (bur. Beaver Brook Cem. Narrowsburg, Sullivan Co., NY)
Alfred, b. abt. 1854;d. 1908; m. 1879; Esther Davenport
      (bur. Beaver Brook Cem. Narrowsburg,Sullivan Co. NY)
Eugene, b. abt. 1858
Benjamin, b. abt 1868; d. 1957; (bur. Montoza Cem., Barryville, Sullivan Co., New York)

- - - - -

DOBBINS
DOBBIN

Dobbins, David   b. (May 4, 1762)
(?NJ Will 11250G. Inv.1820)   d. (July 12, 1812)

wife, **MARY** (Soveril)   b. (abt. October 14, 1768)
(gmnj) (njhs) (lgl)   d. March 14, 1849

Mary Dobbins
died March 14th 1849
aged 80 years. 4 months
&20 days

Our grandmother

daughter, **ANN C.**   b. (bef. 1799)
(gmnj)   d. June 23, 1860

> *Ann C. Dobbins*
> *died June 23, 1860*
> *aged 60.6.8*

Notes:
--1840 Census, Caldwell Twp; Mary Dobbins

Children of David Dobbins and Mary Soveril:
John Gordon, b. 1785; d. 1868
Isaac Soveril, b. 1787; d. 1868; m. Rachel Harrison
David Lodwich, q.v., b. 1789; d.1830 m. #1, Hannah
    Williams;m. #2, 1822, Susannah Harrison
Elizabeth, b. 1791; d. 1865
Samuel Soveril, b. 1795; d. 1824
Joseph Wilbur, b. 1797; m. Abigail Williams
Ann Canfield, b. 1799; d. 1860
Jane Robinson, b. 1802; m. Isaac Condit
Matthias Canfield, b. 1806; d. 1874; m. Sabina .....

- - - - -

Dobbins, **DAVID L.**   b. (April 21, 1789)
(gmnj) (njhs) (lgl) (photo)   d. May 11, 1830
(NJ Will 12227G.1830)

Sacred

to the memory of
David L. Dobbins
who died
May 11th A.D. 1830
aged 41 years
and 20 days

first wife, **HANNAH** (Williams)
(gmnj) (njhs) (lgl)   b. (March 6, 1794)
d. August 13, 1821

Hannah
wife of
David L. Dobbins
died Augt 13th 1821
aged 27 years. 5 months
& 6 days

second wife, Susan (Harrison)
b. (1796)
d.

daughter, **MARY WILLIAMS**
(gmnj) (njhs) (lgl)   b. (abt. March 11, 1817)
d. February 4, 1824

Mary Williams
daughter of
David L. & Hannah Dobbins
died Feb. 4th 1824
aged 6 years. 11 months
& 13 days

son, **DAVID HARRISON**   b. (abt. May 1826)
(gmnj) (njhs) (lgl) (photo)   d. October 5, 1827

Sacred
to the
Memory of
David Harrison
infant son of
David L.
and
Susan Dobbins,
who died
Octr. 5th 1827
aged 10 months

Notes:
--David Lodwich, son of David Dobbins, q.v.; m. #1, Hannah Williams, dau. of Jonathan Williams and Mary Squier; m. #2 1822, Susannah Harrison, dau. of David Harrison

Children of David Lodwich Dobbins and Hannah Williams:
Mary Williams, b. 1817; d. 1824

Children of David Lodwich Dobbins and Susannah Harrison:
Hannah Williams, b. abt. 1825
David Harrison, b. 1826; d. 1827

- - - - -

Dobbins, **ISAAC**   b. (March 27, 1787)
(gmnj)   d. April 15, 1868

Isaac Dobbins
died April 15, 1868
Aged 81.0.19

wife, **RACHEL** (Harrison)   b. (August 21, 1793)
(gmnj) (njhs) (lgl)   d. March 20. 1846

Rachel
wife of
Isaac Dobbins
died March 20th 1846
aged 52 years. 6 months.
& 29 days

son, **JUSTUS SOVERILL**   b.
(gmnj) (photo)   d. September 12, 1853

In
Memory of
Justus Soverill
son of
Isaac and Elizabeth
Dobbins
Died
September 12, 1853
Aged 28.4.22

Notes:
--Isaac Soveril Dobbins, son of David Dobbins, q.v.;
m. 1813, Rachel Harrison

--1850 Census: p.68 Caldwell Twp: Isaac Dobbins age 63, farmer; Elizabeth, age 30; Susan H. age 27; Justus S. age 25; Isaac N., age 20, farmer; George VanOrden, age 16, wagon maker; Rachel A. VanOrden, age 12; all b. NJ
--1860 Census, p.113, Caldwell: Isaac Dobbins, age 73, farmer; Elizabeth, age 40 b. NJ; Susan, age 35 b. NJ; 1 laborer

Children of Isaac Soveril Dobbins and Rachel Harrison:
Emeline C., b. abt. 1817; m. #1, Ira Baldwin
    m. #2, 1879, James J. Randall, Jr.
Samuel Soveril, b. 1819; d. 1895; m. Hannah Maria
    Baldwin (bur. Prospect Hill Cemetery)
Elizabeth, b. abt. 1820; unm. in 1880
Susan Harrison, b. 1823; unm. in 1880
Justus Soveril Dobbins, b. 1825; d. 1853
Isaac Newton, b. abt. 1830

- - - - -

Dobbins, **JOHN**   b. (abt. January 28, 1785)
(gmnj)   d. June 29. 1868
(NJ Will 16641G,1868)

John Dobbins
died June 29, 1868
Aged 83.5.1

first wife, **ABIGAIL** (Allen) b. (abt. May 19, 1790)
(gmnj) (photo)   d. June 29. 1837

Abigail

Wife of John Dobbins
died June 29, 1837
Aged 47.1.10

second wife, **SARAH**(Sindle) b. (abt. August 30. 1791)
(gmnj) (photo)   d. June 28. 1868

Sarah
wife of John Dobbins
died June 28, 1868
Aged 76.9.29

Notes:
--John G. Dobbins m. #1, Dec.1809, Abigail Alling/Allen
--John G. Dobbins m. #2, 1839, Sarah Sindle
--1850 Census, p.84 Caldwell Twp: John G. Dobbins, age
65, farmer; Sally, age 58; John H., age 25; William H.
Martin, age 13; all b. NJ
--1860 Census, p.104, Caldwell: John G. Dobbins, age 75;
Sarah, age 67;

Children of John G. Dobbins and Abigail Alling:
John Harvey, b. 1825; d.1909; m. Sarah Augusta Mann
    (bur. Prospect Hill Cemetery)

- - - - -

Dobbins, **JOSEPH**   b. (abt. August 15, 1797)
(gmnj)   d. February 23, 1855
(NJ Will 14688G.1855)

Joseph Dobbins

died February 23 1855
Aged 57.6.8

wife, **ABIGAIL** (Williams)   b. August 11, 1803
(gmnj) (photo)   d. March 30, 1879

Abigail Williams
wife of
Joseph Dobbins
Born August 11, 1803
Died March 30, 1879

daughter, **ANN ELIZA**   b. September 25, 1823
(gmnj)   d. May 2, 1852

Ann Eliza
daughter of
Joseph Dobbins
Born September 25, 1823
Died May 2, 1852

Notes:
--Joseph Wilbur Dobbins, son of David Dobbins, q.v.; m.
Abigail Williams, dau. of Nathan Williams and Catherine
Wade
--1850 Census:p.85, Caldwell Twp: Joseph Dobbins, age 53,
farmer; Abby, age 48; Eliza Ann, age 26; Catherine E., age
22; all b. NJ; 1 laborer
--1860 Census, p.105 Caldwell: Marcus Y. Baldwin, age 37,
farmer; Electa C. age 32; Joseph W., age 4; Emma C., age 6;
Abby Dobbins, age 56; 1 laborer

--1870 Census, p.110 Caldwell: Marcus Y. Baldwin, age 46, farmer; Emma C., age 16; Joseph W., age 14; Abby Dobbins, age 66; August Kling, age 40, b. Germany, wheel wright

Children of Joseph Wilbur Dobbins and Abigail Williams:
Elizabeth Ann, b. 1823; d. 1852
Electa Catherine, b. 1828 m. Marcus Young Baldwin, q.v.

- - - - -

DODD
DOD

Dodd, **AARON**   b. (August 7, 1772)
(gmnj) (njhs) (photo)   d. January 18, 1839
(NJ Will 12964G.1839)

Aaron Dodd
died Jan. 18th 1839
aged 66 years. 5 months
& 11 days

wife, **TAMAR H.** (Harrison) b. (August 14, 1775)
(gmnj) (njhs) (lgl)   d. May 6, 1835

Tamar H. wife of Aaron Dodd
died May 6th 1835
aged 59 years. 8 months & 22 days

Notes:
--Aaron, son of Adonijah Dodd, q.v., and Mary Ogden; m. 1795, Tamar Harrison, dau. of Joseph Harrison, Esq., q.v.

"he was mortally hurt by a blow from the handle of a windlass in digging a well"(Gen. of the Male Descendants of Daniel Dodd. p.170)

Child of Aaron Dodd and Tamar Harrison:
Rhoda Maria Dodd, b. 1816;
 m. 1838, Caleb Samuel Crane Jr., q.v.
 Rhoda's " husband, (Caleb S. Crane, Jr.) returning
 from Ohio to sell his father-in-law Dodd's farm, was
 killed by a kick of his horse, August 30, 1851, aged
 about 36"(Gen. of the Male Descendants of Daniel Dodd.
 p.170)

- - - - -

Dod, Abel	b. (abt. 1751) d. (abt. 1821) ("bur. at Caldwell")
wife, Martha (Osborn)	b. (abt. 1742) d. (abt. June, 1820) ("bur. at Caldwell")
son, **JOHN** (gmnj) (njhs) (lgl) (photo)	b. (abt. May 7, 1773) d. September 20, 1795

In Memory of John
Son of Abel and
Martha Dod He
died Sept. 20th 1795
aged 22 years. 4
months & 13 days

son **WILLIAM**   b. (abt. December 3, 1774)
(gmnj) (njhs) (lgl) (photo)   d. November 23, 1789

In Memory of
William, Son of Abel
and Martha Dod. He
Died Nov. 23d,1789
Aged 14 years
11 months and
20 days

Notes:
--Abel, 5th child of John Dodd and Jemima Harrison; m.
Martha Osborn
--"Abel, of John the carpenter lived near his brother
Adonijah and his family were also buried at Caldwell."
--"The children (of Adonijah Dodd, q.v.) were born in
Orange but the family early removed to Swinefield now
Centerville in Livingston Township and their graves are at
Caldwell." (Genealogies of the Male Descendants of Daniel Dodd.
Bethuel Lewis Dodd. Newark. 1864. p. 174)

Children of Abel Dodd and Martha Osborn:
John, b. 1773; d. 1795; age 22
William, b. 1775; d. 1789; age 14
William, b. 1789; d. 1774
Jemima, d. 1833; unm.
Rachel, m. Delphiat Carlock
Mary/Polly, b. 1790; m. Hiram Williams (1787-1825)
Betsy, m. Isaac Williams
Phebe,

- - - - -

Dodd, Adonijah   b.
                          d.
                          ("graves are at Caldwell")

wife, Mary (Ogden)   b.
                          d.
                          ("graves at Caldwell")

Notes:
--Adonijah, third son of John Dodd and Jemima Harrison:
--"The children (of Adonijah Dodd) were born in Orange but
the family early removed to Swinefield now Centerville in
Livingston Township and their graves are at Caldwell."
(Genealogies of the Male Descendants of Daniel Dodd. Bethuel Lewis
Dodd. Newark. 1864. p. 174)
--"Abel, q.v., of John the carpenter lived near his brother
Adonijah and his family were also buried at Caldwell."

Children of Adonijah Dodd and Mary Ogden:
Aaron, q.v.
Catherine, b. 1768; d. 1843; m. Dec. 1788, Aaron
        Tompkins,1766-1846, son of Aaron Tompkins,q.v.
        (bur. Roseland Methodist Churchyard)
Samuel, q.v.
Matthew

- - - - -

Dodd, **CALEB Capt.**   b. (May 18, 1775)

(gmnj) (njhs) (lgl) (photo)   d. January 9, 1811
(NJ Will 10666G. 1811)

Sacred
to the memory of
Capt. Caleb Dodd
who died
January 9th, 1811
In the 35th year
of his age.

wife, Mary (Bates)   b. (abt 1778)
                                 d. (September 20, 1852. Ohio)
                                 (bur. Wakeman Cem.,
                                 Waterville, Lucas Co., Ohio)

Notes:
Served: Capt., Militia
--Caleb Dodd, Jr., son of Caleb Dodd and Mary Foster
Harrison; m. Mary Bates, dau. of David Bates and Phebe
Tappan; sister of Capt. William Bates
--1850 Census, p.128, Waterville Twp., Lucas Co., Ohio:
Elijah Dodd, age 44 b. NJ, merchant; William age 16, b. NJ;
Amanda age 11 b. OH; Adaline age 7 b. OH; Clarence age 1
b. OH; Mary (Bates) Dodd, age 70 b. NJ; J. M. Stiles, age 22,
b. NJ, clerk; Betsey Broadsmore age 23 b. PA

Children of Caleb Dodd and Mary Bates:
Phebe, b. 1797, m. Richard Shaw (Openshaw) q.v.
Philemon Bates, b. 1799; m. Rachel Van Duyne
Sarah, b. 1801; m. Robert Reston
Ezra Squier, b. 1803; m. Sarah Ann Pearce
Elijah, b. 1806; m. Mary Jane Wardley

Lucius, b. 1808
William, b. 1810; m. Mary Thompson

- - - - -

Dodd, Elijah	b. (June 6, 1806)
	d. (October 24, 1876)
	(bur. Wakeman Cemetery, Waterville, Lucas Co., Ohio)
first wife, Malvina (Stiles)	b. (January 21, 1812)
	d. (October 12, 1849)
	(bur. Wakeman Cem. Ohio)
second wife, Mary Jane Wardley	b.
	d. (1908)
	(bur. Wakeman Cemetery, Ohio)
son, **WALTER**	b. (September 24, 1847)
(gmnj) (njhs) (lgl)	d. August 12, 1848

Walter.
son of Elijah & Malvina Dodd
died August 12th 1848
aged 10 months & 18 days

Notes:
--Elijah, son of Caleb Dodd, q.v.; m. #1, 1831, Malvina Stiles, dau. of William Stiles and Mary Morrison; m. #2, 1851, Mary Jane Wardley, dau. of Thomas Wardley

--1850 Census, p.128, Waterville Twp., Lucas Co., Ohio:
Elijah Dodd, age 44 b. NJ, merchant; William age 16, b. NJ;
Amanda age 11 b. OH; Adaline age 7 b. OH; Clarence age 1
b. OH; Mary Dodd, age 70 b. NJ; J. M. Stiles, age 22, b. NJ,
clerk; Betsey Broadsmore age 23 b. PA
--1860 Census, p.314, Waterville Twp.Lucas Co., Ohio: E.
Dodd, age 54 b. NJ, farmer; Mary, age 38, b. NY; Amanda,
age 20 b. OH; Clemens age 10 b. Oh; Elijah, age 8 b. OH;
Clifford, age 7 b. OH; Fred, age 3 b. OH; Mary, age 1, b.
OH; 1 laborer; 1 servant

Children of Elijah Dodd and Malvina Stiles:
Caleb, b. 1831; m. Catherine Ann Leonard
William, b. abt 1836; d.1842 Ohio (Wakeman Cemetery)
Oscar, b. 1837; d. 1842
Amanda Malvina, b. 1839; d. 1848 (Wakeman Cemetery)
John(James?) Steedman, b. 1842; d. 1843; (bur. Wakeman
Cem.)
Adaline, b. 1844; m. Samuel Rathbone Adams
Walter, b. 1847; d. 1848
Clarence E., b. 1849; d. 1930; m. Mary Elizabeth Casler

Children of Elijah Dodd and Mary Jane Wardley:
(for all below, see Wakeman Cem. Waterville, Lucas Co., Ohio)
Theodore Wardley, b. 1851; d. 1851
Elijah Jr., b. 1853; d. 1917; m. Frances Jane Downing
Thomas Clinton b. 1854; d. 1856
Clifford Philemon, b. 1855; d. 1918
Frederick Charles b. 1857; d. 1955; m. Mary L. Gunn
Mary Evelyn b. 1859; d.1942; m. Frederick Jaeger Banks

- - - - -

Dodd, Linus

b. (June 18, 1765)
d. (August 3, 1825
(bur. Old Burying Ground,
Presb. Church, Orange, NJ)

first wife, Elizabeth (Pierson) b. (April 28, 1767)
d. (May 1, 1793)
(bur. Old Burying Ground,
Presb. Church, Orange, NJ)

second wife, **MARY** (Baldwin)
(gmnj)   b. (abt. 1773)
d. April 10, 1855

Mary Baldwin
wife of Linus Dodd
died April 10, 1855
in her 82nd year

Notes:
--Linus, son of John Dodd and Jane Smith
--Linus m. #1, Elizabeth Pierson, dau. of Caleb Pierson and
Joanna Baldwin; m. #2, 1802, Mary Baldwin, dau. of Joseph
Baldwin and Esther Crane
--1850 Census, p.88&89, Caldwell Twp: Naomi Baldwin,
age 64; Mary Dodd, age 76;Hannah Baldwin, age 59; Joseph
V. Baldwin, age 41, farmer; Noah O. Baldwin, age 35,
farmer; Esther Baldwin, age 33; Louisa Baldwin, age 25;
Mary D. Baldwin, age 2; all b. NJ; 1 laborer

Children of Linus Dodd and Elizabeth Pierson:

Achsah, b. 1789; m. Daniel Day Condit
Calvin, b. 1792; m. 1820, Elizabeth Harrison

- - - - -

Dodd, **PHEBE**   b. (abt. February 22,
1747)
(gmnj) (njhs) (lgl)   d. April 2, 1814

Phebe Dodd
died April 2d. 1814.
aged 67 years. 1 month
& 11 days

Notes:
--Phebe, possible daughter of Timothy Dodd
--(?)"of this branch of the family less is known than of any
other. Rev. Stephen Dodd states that Timothy married ,
whom he had married not known: children: Jesse, Phebe, and
Timothy. The last two did not marry. A head stone in the
grave yard at Caldwell next to that of Phebe, wife of Josiah
Steele, records that Phebe Dodd died in 1814 aged 67 years.
This makes her birth 1747. From an old newspaper we learn
that Timothy Dodd, a soldier of the Revolution distinguished
for his pleasing manners died at Caldwell October 7, 1831 at
the age of 80. This makes his birth 1751. If Jesse was the
oldest he was probably born about 1745."(Genealogies of the
Male Descendants of Daniel Dodd. Bethuel Lewis Dodd. Newark. 1864.
p. 174)

- - - - -

Dodd, **SAMUEL**   b. (Mary 11, 1776)
(gmnj) (njhs)   d. May 11, 1848
(?NJ Will #13822G. 1849)

Samuel Dodd
died
May 11th 1848
aged 72 years

wife, Amy (Peffer)   b. (abt. 1778)
                          d. (February 11, 1823)

Notes:
--Samuel, son of Adonijah Dodd, q.v., and Mary Ogden
--Samuel m. 1801, Amy Peffer

Children of Samuel Dodd and Amy Peffer:
Hiram, b. 1802; m. 1832, Mary W. Condit
Ambrose, b. 1803; d. 1840

- - - - -

Dodd, Timothy   b. (abt. 1751)
                          d. (October 7, 1831)
                          ("died at Caldwell, Age 80")

wife   b.
                          d.

Notes:
Served: Revolutionary War: Capt. Dodd's Co; State Troops;
and Continental Army

--"Of this branch of the family less is known than of any other. Rev. Stephen Dodd states that Timothy married to 'not known' and had Jesse, Phebe, and Timothy --" ...from an old newspaper we learn that Timothy Dodd, a soldier of the Revolution distinguished for his pleasing manners died at Caldwell October 7, 1831 at the age of 80. This makes his birth 1751. (Genealogies of the Male Descendants of Daniel Dodd. Bethuel Lewis Dodd. Newark. 1864. p. 174)

- - - - -

DOUGLASS

Douglass, **LUCIUS F.**   b. (abt. 1782)
(gmnj) (njhs) (lgl)   d. February 25, 1813

Lucius F. Douglass
died
Feb. 25th 1813
in his 31st year

wife, Phebe Baldwin (Gould) b. (1782)
d. (1879)
(age 97)

Notes:
--Lucius Franklin, son of Nathaniel Douglass, q.v.; "Lucius,son of Nathaniel and Sarah Dalglish, bapt. Sept. 4, 1785, First Presb. Chuch, Hanover"; m. 1807, Phebe Baldwin Gould, dau. of Gen. William Gould, q.v.; she also m. Jacob Vreeland and m. 1817, Edward Faitoute

- - - - -

Douglass, Marcus Brutus   b. (December 27, 1784)
       d. (February 21, 1864)
       (bur. Mount Pleasant Cem. Newark)

first wife, Nancy Crane Gould b. (November 11, 1781)
       d. (December 21, 1849)
       (bur. Mount Pleasant Cem.Newark)

second wife, Caroline Cook   b. 1803
       d. 1892
       (bur. Mount Pleasant Cem.)

daughter, **ELIZABETH**   b. (abt. 1816)
(gmnj) (njhs) (lgl) (photo)   d. December 3, 1837

In
Memory of
Elizabeth
daughter of Marcus B.
and Nancy Douglass
who died
Decr. 3d. 1837
aged 21 years

Notes:
Served: Sgt. 2nd Regt. Essex County Militia
--Marcus Brutus, bapt. Sept. 4, 1785, First Presb. Church,
Hanover; son of Nathaniel Douglass, q.v.; m. July 12, 1807,
Nancy Crane Gould, dau. of Timothy Gould, q,v,;

m. #2, 1851, Caroline Cook
--1830: Judge, Bergen Co., NJ
--1850 Census, p.347, West Ward, Newark: Marcus B.
Douglass, age 65, boots&shoes; James D. Orton,age 26, bank
teller; Hetty Orton, age 24; Anna Orton, age 3; Delia Crane,
age 23; all b. New Jersey
--1860 Census, p.50, 2Wd, Newark: Marcus Douglass, age
68, b. 'NY' no occup.; Caroline, age 55, b. 'NY'; 1 servant

Children of Marcus Brutus Douglass and Nancy Crane Gould
Sarah Ann, b. 1809; d. 1838
Elizabeth, b. abt. 1816; d. 1837
Esther M. 'Hetty', b. abt. 1826; m. James D. Orton

- - - - -

Douglass, **NATHANIEL**   b. (January 24, 1760)
(gmnj) (njhs) (lgl)   d. May 15, 1824

> *Nathaniel Douglass*
> *died*
> *May 15th 1824*
> *in his 65th year*

wife, **SARAH** (Bates)   b. (abt. 1762)
(gmnj) (njhs) (lgl)   d. January 22, 1816

> *Sarah. wife of*
> *Nathaniel Douglass*
> *died Jan. 22d, 1816*
> *in her 54th year*

Notes:
--Nathaniel, son of David Douglass and Esther Reed; m. January 1, 1782, Sarah Bates, dau. of Capt. David Bates and Phebe Tappan; Nathaniel: Deacon; Ruling Elder 1811-1814, 2nd. Presb. Church, Newark
Partner: Vanderpoel & Douglass, leather manufacturers

Children of Nathaniel Douglass and Sarah Bates:
Lucius, q.v., b. abt 1782; "bapt. Sept. 4, 1785, First Presb. Church, Hanover, son of Nathaniel and Sarah Dalglish"; m. Phebe Gould
Marcus, q.v., b. 1784; "bapt. Sept. 4, 1785, First Presb. Church, Hanover, son of Nathaniel and Sarah Dalglish" m. Nancy Crane Gould
Mjr. David Bates, b. 1790; d.1849; m. Ann Eliza Ellicott
  Grad. Yale College; Capt. of Engineers War of 1812; professor U.S. Military Academy, West Point; engineer the Erie Canal; Chief Engineer on the Morris Canal; 1838-1841 designed the renowned Green-Wood Cemetery, Brooklyn; and 2 other cemeteries. LL.D, Yale College 1841 (bur. Green-Wood Cem.)
?Julia Angelina, b. abt. 1800; d. 1835; m. Calvin S. Crane

- - - - -

DURYEA
(Duryee)

Duryea, **GEORGE**   b. (April 18, 1768?)
(gmnj) (njhs) (lgl) (photo)   b. (August 20, 1767?)
                             d. February 24, 1842

The

Grave of
George Duryea
He died
Feb. 24th 1842
in the 74th year
of his age

wife, Mary (Sharpe Sutphen) b.

d.

Notes:

--George, son of Joost Duryee and Catherine Schenck;

--George, brother of Rev. John Duryea, q.v.

--George, m. ("Mary 'Polly' Sharpe,widow of John Sutphen")

Children of George Duryea and Mary Sharpe Sutphen:
George, b. February 4, 1797
John/Jacob, b. April 19, 1798; ?m. Fanny Sutphen
Peter Wilson, b. April 21, 1800
Abraham, b. July 12, 1801
Peter Sharpe, b.1807 d. 1877; m. Newark, Susan,
      (1816-1886) daughter of William Rankin; parents of
      Rev. William Rankin Duryea, (1838-1897)
Anna Sabina, m. John H. Brower ' of Bn'
(Documentary History of the Dutch Congregation of
Oyster Bay) (Inscriptions: Mount Pleasant Cemetery, Newark, NJ)
(Inscriptions at Newark: say DURYEE)

- - - - -

Duryea, **JOHN, Rev.**   b. (August 1, 1752)
(gmnj) (njhs) (lgl)   d. October 2, 1836

(NJ Will 12682G. 1836)

Rev. John Duryea
died
Oct. 2d 1836
aged 84 years (84.1.1)

He was for nearly 50 years, a faithful
Minister of the Gospel of Christ, serving
as a Pastor of the Reformed Churches of
Somerville, Preakness, and Fairfield

1st wife, **MARY LEE** (Brinkerhoff)
(gmnj) (njhs) (lgl)   b. (September 4, 1749)
                              d. November 10, 1825

Mary Lee
wife of
Rev. John Duryea
died Novr. 10th. 1825
aged 75 years. 2 mos.
& 8 ds.

2nd wife, Eleanor   b. (October 22, 1767)
(Riker) Kierstead   d. (aft. October 1836)

Notes:

Served: Revolutionary War: *"That shortly after the commencement*
of the war he entered as a volunteer, as a soldier in the company of
militia under the command of Captain Outwater in the Regiment of
Colonel Dey of the New Jersey Militia. That shortly after he enlisted he
was with the regiment ordered to New York where he continued in actual
service with the regiment until the enemy captured New York and Long

Island and they were evacuated by the American troops. After the retreat, the company of Captain Outwater was stationed on the line at Hackensack in Bergen County. While there they assisted in covering the retreat of the American baggage from New York across to Hackensack. And was once sent to escort Mrs. Washington, the wife of General Washington from Newark through Hackensack to Tappan. The exact date when he entered and left this service he cannot recollect.

He was afterwards in actual service, a volunteer in the same company. In March 1781 on the 23 of which month while in an engagement with the enemy at .....he was taken prisoner and carried to the Sugar House in New York where he remained until the month of September following having been kept as a prisoner of war for six months when he was released by an exchange of prisoners. ...Sylvester Marius whose affidavit is hereto...is a living witness of his service. ...at Hackensack he had property destroyed and plundered by the enemy to the value of (five?) thousand dollars. (National Archives Microfilm Publications.Non selected Records. p.327-p.337)

--"It is the prevalent impression that Rev. John Duryea was the first resident pastor of the Ref. Church at Fairfield; he preached in the old and the new church. The present edifice was completed during his pastorate. He owned a quarry and contributed the stone for the building." (History of Essex and Hudson Counties, N.J. 1884)

--John, b. August 1, 1752, Bushwick, Kings Co., NY, son of Joost Duryee (1715-1793) and Catherine Schenck (b. 1721); d. Little Falls, Passaic Co.

--Will (July 22, 1793)of Joost Duryee, Bushwick: "to <u>my son Johannas four hundred pounds one year after my decease</u>"

--<u>John m. #1</u>, March 30, 1777, Ref. Dutch Ch., Acquackanonk, <u>Mary Lee Brinkerhoff</u>, b. New York, Sept. 4, 1749, dau. of John Lee and Jane DeGroot; widow of Henry Brinkerhoff

--"John Duryee is married to Mary Brinckerhoff the 30th of March 1777" (Duryee Family Bible)

--"March 31, 1777 Ref. Church Acquackanonk: Mari
Brinkerhoff married Johannes Duryee by decree." (Dutch Ref.
Church Records) (NY License:Jan. 7, 1767, Vol 11, p.5)
--"March 24, 1777. Acquackanonk. Johannes Duryee b. Long
Eyland. res. Hackensack: to Maria (Lee) Brinckerhoff,
widow, b. New York, res. Hackensack (Dutch Ref. Ch. Records.
Holland Society of New York)
--"Death of my Dear Companion Mary. on the 10th of Nov.
1825. Aged 76 years & 2 months & 8 days" (Duryee Family
Bible)
--John m. #2: "March 25, 1828. Married on the 25th ult. near
the Little Falls, NJ by the Rev. John G. Tarbele: Rev. John
Duryea to Mrs. Eleanor (Riker) Kierstead." (Paterson
Intelligencer) (poss. dau. of John Riker; widow of John
Kierstead, (c.1757-c.1826)
--"Revd. John Duryee departed this life Sunday morning
October 2nd, 1836. Age 84 years, 1 month and 1 day."

The gospel was his joy & song
Even to his latest Breath
The truth he had proclaimed so long
Was his support in death
(Duryee Family Bible)

Will: Signed Sept. 5, 1828 Proved October 29, 1836
NJ #12682G. (NJ Probate Records, Essex. Vol. F. Image 569)
--"all my property to be sold at public or private sale within
one year excepting a coloured woman named Dinah which I
bequeath to my daughter Elizabeth; also a silver set
--"fifty dollars to my beloved wife Eleanor
--"remainder in equal shares to my six children"
--Executors: George J. Duryea and Jared F. Harrison

Children of Rev. John Duryea and Mary Lee Brinkerhoff:
Catherine, b. 1778; d. 1815; m. Philip Isaac Schuyler
John Lee, b. 1781; d.1854; m. Catherine Vroom
George John, b. 1783; d.1871; m. Nancy Perry
Henry Brinkerhoff, b. 1786; d. 1854; m. Hester Dey,
      granddaughter of Col. Theunis Dey
Elizabeth, b. 1789 d 1882; m. Jared Freeman Harrison
Jane Lee, b. 1791 d. 1820; m. Mjr. Nathaniel S. Crane, q.v.

- - - - -

FAIRCHILD

Fairchild, **WILLIAM**   b. (abt. June 23, 1779)
(gmnj)   d. September 23, 1854
(NJ Will 14516G. 1854)

William Fairchild
died September 23, 1854
Aged 75.3.0

wife, **MARY B.** (Williams)   b. (abt. November 24, 1799)
(gmnj)   d. February 7, 1856

Mary B.
wife of William Fairchild
died February 7, 1856
Aged 56.2.14

Notes:

--William, son of Moses Fairchild and Mary Gardner; m. 1819, Mary B. Williams, dau. of Jeniah Williams, q.v., and Charlotte Pierce

--1850 Census, p.83&84, Caldwell Twp: William Fairchild, age 67, b. NJ, tailor; Mary Fairchild, age 50, b. NJ; Charlotte Williams, age 75 b. NJ; Phebe Ann Williams, age 30 b. NY; 'Warner' H. Williams, age 7 b. NY; David Williams, age 5 b. NY; Robert Williams, age 3, b. NY; Florence Williams, age 1, b. NY

- - - - -

FORDHAM

Fordham, **STEPHEN**   b. (abt. January 5, 1754)
(gmnj) (njhs) (photo)   d. November 29, 1829
(NJ Will 12059G. 1829)

Stephen Fordham
died Novr. 29th 1829
aged 75 years. 10 months.
& 24 days

wife, **SARAH** (Crane)   b. (abt. March 6, 1755)
(gmnj) (njhs)(lgl) (photo)   d. August 16,1825

In memory of
Sarah
Consort of
Stephen Fordham
died August 16th 1825
aged 70 years.

5 months
& 10 days

Notes:
Served: Revolutionary War; Capt. Abraham Lyons Co., 2nd Reg't, Essex Co., NJ
--Stephen,of Fordham family, Southampton, L.I., New York?
--Sarah, dau. of William Crane; sister of Rachel Crane who m. Simeon Baldwin; sister of Hannah Crane who m. Major Nathaniel Crane; sister of Jonas Crane; sister of Zadoc Crane
--1789 Census: Newark Twp., Essex Co., NJ: Stephen Fordham
--1812: Sarah (and all children of Stephen Fordham) named in the will of her sister, Rachel wife of Simeon Baldwin

- - - - -

FRANCISCO

Francisco, Andrew

b. (abt. 1798)
d. (January 17, 1853)
(bur. Fairfield Ref. Church Cem.)

wife, Maria (Speer)

b. (abt. 1801)
d. (June 19, 1849)
Aged 48.3.18
(bur. Fairfield Ref. Church Cem.)

son, **JOHN HENRY**
(gmnj) (njhs) (lgl)

b. abt. 1824)
d. December 17, 1845

John Henry

son of Andrew
& Maria Francisco
died Dec. 17th 1845
aged 22 years

Notes:

--Andrew, son of John Francisco and Margaret Stager; m. Maria Speer

Children of Andrew Francisco and Maria Speer:
John Henry, b. 1824, d. 1845
Richard Speer, b. 1827; m. Maria Husk
George, b. abt. 1832; m. Caroline Sindle
Josiah A., q.v., b. 1834; m. Elizabeth Francisco

- - - - -

Francisco, **HENRY**   b. (abt. 1797)
(gmnj)   d. October 17, 1863
(NJ Inv. 15740G. 1863)

Henry Francisco
died October 7, 1863
Aged 66 years

wife, **SARAH H.** (Husk)   b. (abt. 1799)
(gmnj) (njhs) (lgl)   d. May 1837

Sarah H.
wife of
Henry Francisco
died May 1837

aged 38 years

Notes:
--Henry, son of John Francisco and Margaret Stager; m. #1, Sarah Husk, dau. of John Husk; ?m. #2, Maria .....
--1850 Census; p.92, Caldwell Twp: Henry Francisco, age 52 farmer; James, age 22; Mariah, age 19; Eliza, age 17; ia, age 19; all b. NJ
--1860 Census; p.89 Caldwell Twp: Henry Francisco, age 62, Maria, age 54; Harriet Jacobus, age 20

Children of Henry Francisco and Sarah Husk:
James, b. abt. 1828
Euphemia, b. abt. 1831
Mariah, b. abt 1831
Eliza, b. 1833; m. 1854, William H. Bond, q.v.

- - - - -

Francisco, Josiah

b. (February 5, 1833)
d. (June 5, 1883)
(bur. Prospect Hill Cemetery)

wife, Elizabeth (Francisco)

b. (September 24, 1833)
d. (1919)
(bur. Prospect Hill Cemetery)

son, **PETER A.**
(gmnj)

b. (abt. June 20, 1857)
d. September 1, 1863

Peter A.
Son of Josiah Francisco

died September 1, 1863
aged 6.2.12

Notes:

--Josiah, son of Andrew Francisco, q.v.; m. 1855, Elizabeth Francisco, dau. of Peter Francisco and Abigail Gould

--1850 Census; p. 92, Caldwell Twp: Andrew Francisco, age 50, farmer; Richard, age 23 farmer; Mariah, age 21; George, age 18 farmer; Josiah age 16, farmer; William, age 13, farmer; John H., age 1

--1860 Census; p.26, Caldwell Twp: Josiah Francisco, age 26, farmer; Elizabeth, age 26; Peter A., age 3; William, age 1; Sally Gould, age 68; all b. NJ; 1 laborer

--1870 Census; p. 109, Caldwell Twp: Josiah Francisco, age 36, farmer; Elizabeth, age 36; William H., age 10; Bernice age 6; Richard, age 3; all b. NJ

--1880 Census, p.422.4, Caldwell Twp: Josiah A. Francisco, age 46, farmer; Elizabeth, age 46; William H., age 19; Berniece age 16; Richard S., age 13; Lloyd J., age 6; all b. NJ

Children of Josiah Francisco and Elizabeth Francisco:
Peter A., b. 1857; d. 1863
William H. b. abt 1859
Bernice, b. abt. 1864; m. 1901, Theodore M. Grey
Richard Speer, b. abt. 1867
Lloyd J., b. abt. 1874 m. Elizabeth Kierstead

- - - - -

Francisco, **THOMAS**   b. (abt. 1805)
(gmnj) (njhs) (lgl)   d. March 2, 1846
(NJ Will 13527G.1846)

Thomas Francisco
died March 2d. 1846
in his 41st year

wife, **NANCY F.**
(gmnj) (njhs) (lgl)

b. (abt. 1810)
d. June 25, 1856

Nancy F.
widow of
Thomas Francisco
died June 25th 1856
aged 46 years

son, **CALVIN A.**
(gmnj) (njhs) (lgl)

b. (abt. June 9, 1834)
d. June 27, 1835

Calvin A.
son of Thomas
& Nancy F. Francisco
died June 27th 1835
aged 1 year & 18 days
(gmnj: "aged 1.0.16")

Notes:
--Thomas, son of John Francisco and Margaret Stager
--1850 Census: p.92, Caldwell Twp: Nancy Francisco, age 36; Ann E., age 14; Thomas, age 6; all b. NJ

Children of Thomas Francisco and Nancy F. ......:
Calvin A., b. abt 1834; d. 1835
Ann E., b. abt. 1836

Thomas, b. abt. 1844; m. 1866, Charlotte Bush

- - - - -

FRENSON

Frenson, **LOUIS AUGUST** b. (abt. June 15, 1836)
(gmnj)   d. December 15, 1865

Louig August Frenson
died December 15, 1865
aged 29.6.0

wife, Martha   b.
                                     d.

son, **LOUIS AUGUST**   b. (abt. September 7, 1865)
(gmnj)   d. December 7, 1865

Louis August
Son of Louis August Frenson
died December 7, 1865
aged 0.3.0

Notes:
See: (?)Louis E. Franzen, 1898-1979; bur. Prospect Hill
Cemetery

- - - - -

GOODING

Gooding, **FRED G.**   b. (abt. 1828)
(gmnj)   d. May 29, 1857

A Memento
died in Newark
aged 29 years

- - - - -

Gooding, **WILLIAM W.**   b. (abt. 1831)
(gmnj)   d. May 1, 1855

A Memento
on his way to Kansas
aged 24 years

Notes:
--1850 Census, p.42&43, North Ward, Newark: William M.
Gooding, age 52 b. England, pattern maker; Anna, age 52;
William, age 19 b. NY, carpentry tools; Mary, age 12 b. NY;
Caroline, age 10, b. NY

- - - - -

GOULD

Gould, Alexander Stephen   b. (abt. 1809)
    d. (May 15, 1877)
    ("burial place Caldwell" NY Death
    Record)

wife, Mary Jane (Reid)   b. (abt. 1814)

d. (September 28, 1887)
(bur. Woodlawn Cem., NYC)

daughter, **LUCETTA BANKS**
(gmnj) (njhs) (lgl)   b. (abt. 1841)
d. March 1844

Lucetta Banks
daughter of Alexander S.
and Mary Jane Gould
died March 1844
aged 3 years

Notes:
--Alexander, son of Stephen Gould, q.v., and Sarah Banks;
m. Newark, 1833, Mary Jane Reid, daughter of David Reid
and Margaret Hessin (d. 1862)
--Owner: Alexander S. Gould Press, NYC; "as a young man
he was proprietor of the *Paterson Courier*"
--1860 Census, p.110, Caldwell Twp: Alexander S. Gould,
age 51, farmer; Mary J.,age 46; Margaret R., age 21; Lucetta
B., age 16; Alexander P. age 12; Mary, age 10; Sarah, age 4;
Emma, age 1
--1870 Census, p.123, 16 Wd, NYC: Alexander Gould, age
62, b 'NY, printer (Banks & Gould); Mary J. b. 'NJ';
William R., age 34, b. NJ, stationer; Margaret, age 32 b. NY;
Lucetta age 25 b. NY; Alexander, age 20, b. NJ, store clerk;
Mary, age 18 b. NJ; Sarah, age 14 b. NJ; Emma, age 11 b. NJ
One title page: "*Published by Stephen Gould and Son. 1824; Printed*
at Coke Law Press, Caldwell, NJ"; "Published (1824) by Stephen Gould
and Son. Law Booksellers, at the old stand, Sign of Lord Coke, corner of

Wall and Broad Streets, opposite the Custom-House and Joseph P. Gould, Genessee Street, Utica.Printed at the Coke Law Press, Caldwell"
--For a time he was in the envelope manufacturing business with his son W. Reid Gould, law blank manufacturer at Beekman and Nassau Streets, New York City.
--1880 Census, p.240.1, Manhattan, NY: Mary J. Gould, age 66, b. NJ, parents b. Ireland, widow; Wm. R., age 45 b. NJ, stationer; Margaret R., age 42 b. NY; Louzetta B., age 35 b. NY; Alexander P., age 30 b. NY, dry goods clerk; Mary L., age 28, b. NJ; Sarah I., age 24 b. NJ; Emma E., age 21, b. NJ

Children of Alexander Stephen Gould and Mary J. Reid:
William Reid, b. abt. 1834; d.1883; (bur. Woodlawn Cem. NYC)
    manager Gould & Bell Stationery, NYC
Margaret Reid, b. abt. 1839; d. 1907 NYC
Lucetta Banks, b. abt. 1841; d. 1844
Lucetta Banks, b. abt. 1845; d, 1905. NYC; wid. of ...Tiebout
    (bur. Woodlawn Cemetery, NY)
Alexander Paxton, b. abt. 1848; d. 1892; manager Gould &
    Bell Stationery, 1889 to 1914; m. Adeline C. Woods
Mary Louise b. abt. 1850; unm. in 1920
Sarah Irene, b. abt. 1856; unm. in 1920
Emma E., b. abt. 1859; unm. in 1915?
    (?)1915 Census: E. Providence RI: Emma E. Gould, age 58; Olive M. Bowden, age 17 niece, office clerk

- - - - -

Gould, **ANTHONY**
(gmnj) (photo)
(NJ Will 14851G. 1856)

b. October 22, 1774
d. March 6, 1856

Anthony Gould
Born
October 22, 1774
Died
March 6, 1856
Aged 81 years,
4 months and 12 days
As you pass by remember me,
As I am now,
So you must shortly (one day) *be*

wife, **MARY SANDFORD**   b. (October 27, 1772)
(gmnj) (njhs) (lgl) (photo)   d. February 23, 1844

In
Memory of
Mary Sandford
wife of
Anthony Gould
who departed this life
Feb. 23rd 1844
aged 71 years. 3 mos.
and 26 days

son, **SANDFORD**   b. (abt. 1815)
(gmnj) (njhs) (lgl)   d. April 17, 1830

Sandford Gould
Son of
Mary S. & Anthony
Gould
died April 17th 1830

Aged 15 years

Notes:
--Anthony, son of Joseph Gould, q.v.; m. January 15, 1799, Mary Sandford
--1850 Census, p.81, Caldwell Twp: Anthony Gould, age 75, farmer; Rebecca 'Nash', age 41; Mary E. 'Nash' age 18; Ann Augusta, 'Nash', age 16; 1 laborer

Children of Anthony Gould and Mary Sandford:
Betsey, b. bef. January 11, 1801
Ann, b. 1802; m. Ambrose Condit
Rebecca, b. abt 1809; m. Israel Ward
Sandford, b. abt 1815; d. 1830
?other children

- - - - -

Gould, **CORNELIUS**   b. (abt. 1803)
(gmnj) (njhs) (lgl)   d. March 1, 1847
(NJ Will 13617G. 1847)

Cornelius Gould
died March 1st 1847
aged 44 years
(gmnj: "41 years")

wife, **ELIZA BEACH**   b. (abt. 1808)
(gmnj) (njhs) (lgl)   d. July 19, 1848

Eliza Beach.
wife of Cornelius Gould

died July 19th 1848
aged 40 years

Notes:
--Cornelius, son of Samuel? (Stephen? Gould); m. January 23, 1828, Eliza Beach

- - - - -

Gould, Encrease, Esq.   b. (November 27, 1759)
                                     d. (January 11, 1815?)
                                     d. (January 5, 1839)
                                     (prob. bur. Sandy Hill Cemetery and reinterred Cedar Lawn Cemetery, Paterson, NJ)

first wife **MARY** (Personett) b. (March 24, 1764)
(gmnj) (njhs) (lgl)   d. April 22, 1798

Mary
wife of
Encrease Gould, Esq.
died April 22d 1798
in her 34th year

Notes:
Served: 1793: Essex County, Militia
--Encrease, son of John Gould, q.v., and Anna Cobb; m. #1, Nov. 1783, Caldwell, Mary Personett, daughter of George Personett, Esq. q.v.; m. #2, Oct. 1798, Agnes Nichols Helme, b. Nov. 23, 1827; d. Sept. 1851
--Encrease, Justice of the Peace

--Encrease: 1803: appointed to 'Judges and Justices' Essex County

--See: Gould/VanHouten Bible Records. Passaic Co. Historical Society. Note Book No. 42

Children of Encrease Gould, Esq. and Mary Personett:
Elizabeth 'Betsy',b.Apr.19, 1784; m. John Gerrit VanHouten
Nathaniel, b. April 12, 1787; d. 1811
Mary 'Polly', b. Oct. 12, 1789; d. 1794
Julia, b. Dec. 16, 1792; d. May 1812
Moses Encrease, b. July 8, 1795; d. August 1883; m.
    Rebecca Gould; (Moses, and relatives, bur. First
    Presbyterian Section, Sandy Hill Cemetery, Paterson, closed
    1840; reinterred Cedar Lawn Cemetery, Paterson)

Children of Encrease Gould, Esq. and Agnes N. Helme:
Sarah H., b. Aug. 10, 1799 d. abt. 1890) (Cedar Lawn Cemetery)
Benjamin Helme, b. Nov. 3, 1805; d. Dec. 1882;
    m. Sarah McCloud (1814-1891(Cedar Lawn Cemetery)

- - - - -

Gould, Ezekiel   b. (October 17, 1783)
                             d.

wife, Phebe (Kitchell)   b. (November 11, 1787)
                             d.

daughter, **ROSINA**   b. (abt. 1816)
(gmnj) (njhs) (lgl)   d. February 15, 1831

Rosina.

daughter of
Ezekiel & Phebe Gould
died Feb. 15th 1831
in her 15th year

Notes:
--Ezekiel, son of Timothy Gould, q.v.; m. October 11, 1808, Phebe Kitchell, dau. of David Kitchell and Rachel Bates

Children of Ezekiel Gould and Phebe Kitchell:
Rosina, b. 1816; d. 1831

- - - - -

Gould, **HENRY**   b. (October 30, 1771)
(gmnj) (njhs) (photo)   d. December 23, 1817

In
Memory of
Henry Gould
Who died
Decr. 23d. 1817
Aged 45 years

wife, Sarah (Dunn)   b.
                               d.

Notes:
--Henry, son of Stephen Gould, q.v., and Rachel Speer
--Henry m. October 5, 1795, Sarah Dunn

- - - - -

Gould, **JOHN**   b. (October 3, 1735)
(gmnj) (njhs) (lgl)(photo)   d. August 25, 1807

*In
memory of
John Gould
who died the 25th of
August 1807 A D
in the 71st year
of his age*

*As his life was Pious so his
death was tranquil
and resigned.*

*I've seen yon weary winter sun
Full seventy times pass by
And every year has added proof
That man was born to die*

first wife, Ann (Cobb)   b. (June 27, 1738)
                                d. (May 3, 1780)

second wife, Dorcas (Baldwin)
                          b. (1744)
                          d. (1799)

Notes:
Served: Revolutionary War
--John Gould, b. Staten Island, New York

--John m. #1, March 3, 1757, First Presb. Ch., Hanover, Ann Cobb; b. Taunton, Bristol Co., Mass., daughter of Ebenezer Cobb and Mehetable Robinson; John m. #2, Dorcas Baldwin --1782 Sept. 2; "John Gould collector of the township of Acquackanonk was robbed of a large sum of money by a party of Tories from Staten Island. ...August 16, 1784, an act was passed relieving him from responsibility for the loss." (History of Paterson. The Silk City. Nelson)

Children of John Gould and Ann Cobb:
Julia, b. 1756; d.1757
Encrease, q.v., b. 1759; d. 1839; m. Mary Personett
Sarah/Sallie, b. 1761
John Robertson, b. 1764; d. 1853; m. 1797, Nancy Sandford,
        b. 1781; d. 1859 (both bur. Cedar Lawn Cem. Paterson)
Julia, b. 1770
Mehetable, b. 1772; d. 1857; m. Stephen Dod, (1770-1855)
        surveyor, judge; son of Lebbeus Dod (bur. Mount
        Pleasant Cemetery, Newark)
Ann, b. 1774; d. 1846, (bur. Big Woods Cem. DuPage Co.,Ill) ; m.
Zebina Crane b. 1772; d. 1823 (bur. Upper Corners Cem., Wayne
Co., New York)

Child of John Gould and Dorcas Baldwin:
Moses Encrease, b. 1782; d. 1825; m. Feb. 1803, Catherine
        Vreeland (1785-1870) (both bur. Cedar Lawn Cemetery)

- - - - -

Gould, **JOHN**   b. (December 3, 1767)
(gmnj) (njhs) (photo)   d. January 5, 1839

John Gould
died
Jan. 5th 1839
Aged 71 years

Sophia (VanGiesen)   b. (abt. 1763)
                           d. (July 20, 1858)

Notes:
--John Paxton Gould, son of Joseph Gould, q.v., and
Rebecca Paxton; November 24, 1789, Sophia Van Giesen
--1850 Census, p.340, Acquackanonk Twp., Passaic Co., NJ:
Thomas Gould, age 50, farmer; Jane C., age 37 b. NJ;
Sophia, age 86, b. NJ; 2 laborers

Children of John Gould and Sophia VanGiesen:
Lydia, b. 1789; m. Jacob Post
Lemuel, b. abt. 1791; m. Ellen C. .....
Jane, b. abt. 1793; m. 1811, Caleb Harrison
Rebecca, b. 1798; m. 1819, Moses E. Gould
Thomas G., b. 1800; m. Jane C. Bruen
Anthony, b. 1802; m. Martha Jennet Bellous

- - - - -

Gould, **JOSEPH**   b. (July 16, 1737)
(gmnj) (njhs) (lgl)   d. December 7, 1810)
(NJ Will 10677G.Inc.1811) (gmnj) "in 78th yr.")

Joseph Gould
died Decr. 7th 1810
in his 74th year

As a Husband
Parent. Neighbor
Friend and Christian
he was affectionate
tender and obliging .
honest and devout
Farewell my wife, my children, friends,
And all who for me weep
I have surpassed three score and ten
Then weary, fell asleep

wife, **REBEKAH** (Paxton)   b. (December 16, 1738)
(gmnj) (njhs)   d. March 4, 1816

Rebekah Paxton
wife of
Joseph Gould
deid March 4th 1816
in the 78th year
of her age
May she rest in peace

son, **DANIEL**   b. February 12, 1762
                                      d. 1765

daughter, **MARY**   b. (September 28, 1785)
(gmnj) (photo)   d. September 22, 1836

Mary Gould
died
Sept. 22d 1836
Aged 51 years

son, **THOMAS** b. (abt. April 13, 1770)
(gmnj) (njhs) d. December 14, 1802

In memory of
Thomas. son of
Joseph & Rebekah Gould
who died
with the Epilepsy
on Dec. 14th, 1802
Agd 32 years
8 months & 1 day

Notes:
Served: Revolutionary War: Capt. Squire's Co., 2nd Regt.,
Essex Battalion, private
--Joseph Gould, son of John Gould; m. 1762, Caldwell,
Rebecca Paxton, dau. of Daniel Paxton
--Will: Signed Sept. 1808; Proved March 1811: wife,
Rebekah; daughters: Abigail Jacobus; Sarah Jacobus, Polly
Gould; sons: Stephen, William, Anthony, Joseph; grandson,
Zenas Smith Gould, son of Thomas, dec'd. Executors: son
John and nephew Encrease Gould, (son of his brother John
Gould)

Children of Joseph Gould and Rebecca Paxton:
Daniel, b. 1762; d. 1765
Abigail, b. 1763; m. Cornelius H. Jacobus, q.v.
Sarah, b. 1765; d. 1846; m. Peter Jacobus, q.v.
John, q.v., b. 1767; d. 1839; m. Sophia Van Giesen
Thomas, b. 1770; d. 1802; m. Mary Smith

William, b. 1772; d. 1840; m. 1817, Albany, Mary Banks (1777-1846?)(bur. Albany Rural Cemetery, Manands, NY)
Anthony, q.v., b. 1774; m. Mary Sandford
Stephen, q.v., b. 1777; m. Susan Banks
Son, b. 1780; d. 1780
Joseph Paxton, b. 1782; m. Elizabeth Condit (bur. Prospect Hill)
Mary/Polly, b. 1785; d. 1836

- - - - -

Gould, Joseph	b. (February 24, 1745/46)
	d. (August 24, 1820)
wife, Sarah (Ward)	b. (March 17, 1746/47)
	d. (November 14, 1810)
son, **ZEBEDEE**	b. (August 4, 1784)
(gmnj) (njhs) (lgl) (photo)	d. July 18, 1794

In memory of
Zebedee, son of
Joseph and Sarah Gould
who departed this life
July 18th, 1794 aged
aged 9 years. 11 mos
& 14 days

Notes:
--Joseph, son of Thomas Gould and Sarah Johnson; m. September 12, 1768, First Presb. Ch., Hanover, Sarah Ward

Children of Joseph Gould and Sarah Ward:
Caleb, b. 1770; d. 1777
Sarah, b. 1771; m. John Smith
Mary Elizabeth, b. 1773; m. Abner Bond, q.v.
Hannah, b. 1775; m. Abner Dodd; he m. #2, Phebe Bates,
    wid. of Ezra K. Squire, q.v.; he m. #3, Abby Wade
    Squier; dau. of Samuel Squier of Livingston
Catherine, b. 1779; m. David Mills; m. Jacob Smith
Susan, b. 1781; d. 1801
Thomas, b. 1783; m. Mary Smith
Zebedee, b. 1785; d. 1794
Aaron, b. 1791; d. abt. 1864
Uzal, b. 1791; d. 1823

- - - - -

Gould, **JOSIAH**   b. (abt. May 20, 1761)
(gmnj) (njhs) (lgl) (photo)   d. May 25, 1845
(NJ Will 13435G. 1845)

Josiah Gould
died May 25th 1845
aged 84 years & 5 days

wife, **ELIZABETH** (Colyer) b. (abt. August 2, 1761)
(gmnj) (njhs) (photo)   d. July 17, 1821

In
Memory of
Elizabeth Gould
wife of
Josiah Gould

who died
July 17th 1821
aged 59 years.
11 months.
& 15 days

Notes:

--Josiah, son of Stephen Gould, q.v., and Rachel Speer; m. October 6, 1782, Elizabeth Colyer, dau. of Henry Collier
--Elizabeth given 98 acres in her father's 1788 will of which Josiah Gould was an executor with her brother, Isaac.
--(?)Josiah m. #2, 1827, Leah Brown

Children of Josiah Gould and Elizabeth Colyer:
Elizabeth, b. 1783; m. #1, 1800, Thomas C. Courter; m. #2, 1834, Francis Cook
Rachel, b. 1787; m. 1811, Francis Post
Susanna, b. 1790; m. 1812, Richard Gould
Sarah, b. 1794; Elinor, b. 1797; m. Marcus Jacobus
Abigail, b. 1809, m. 1829, Peter Francisco (see Fairfield Ref. Church Cemetery)
Stephen J., q.v., b. 1801, m. 1822, Joanna Beach

- - - - -

Gould, Nathaniel Marcus   b. (November 17, 1799)
(photo)   d. (March 23, 1880)
                                 (bur. Prospect Hill Cemetery)

first wife, **MARGARET** (Francisco)
(gmnj) (njhs) (photo)   b. (February 7, 1803)
                                 d. September 20, 1840

Margaret
wife of
Nathaniel M. Gould
died Septr. 20th 1840
aged 37 years. 7 months
& 13 days

second wife, **NANCY D.** (Ward)
(gmnj) (photo)   b. February 18, 1806
                                  d. May 15, 1862

In
Memory of
Nancy D.
wife of
Nathaniel M. Gould
Born February 18, 1806
Died May 15, 1862
Aged 56 years 2 months.
and 27 days

son, **MARCUS JOHNSON** b. (abt. July 13, 1831)
(gmnj) (njhs) (lgl) (photo)   d. May 16, 1832

Marcus Johnson
died May 16th 1832
aged 10 months
& 3 days
Children of Nathaniel M. and Margaret Gould

daughter, **ABBY FAITOUTE** b. (abt. February 29, 1828)

(gmnj) (njhs) (photo)   d. June 29, 1831

Abby Faitoute
died June 29th 1831
aged 3 years & 4 months
Children of Nathaniel M. & Margaret Gould

son, **GEORGE WHEELOCK** b. (abt. November 18, 1821)
(gmnj) (njhs) (lgl)(photo)   d. September 25, 1838

George Wheelock
son of
Nathaniel M. and Margaret
Gould
died Sept. 25th 1838
aged 16 years. 10 months
& 7 days

Notes:
--Nathaniel Marcus Gould, son of William Gould, q.v.
--Nathaniel m. #1 1821, Margaret Francisco; m. #2 1842,
Nancy D. Ward; m. #3 , Sarah A. ....
--1850 Census: p.82 Caldwell Twp: Nathaniel M. Gould age
50 farmer; Nancy D. age 44; William age 24 farmer; Marcus
N. age 15 farmer; Henry D. age 12; Margaret age 10; Silas
W. age 7; George W. age 5; all b. NJ
--1860 Census: p.95 Caldwell Twp: Nathl. Gould age 60
farmer; Nancy M. age 54; Margaret age 20; George age 14
--1870 Census: p.120 Caldwell Twp: Nathaniel M. Gould
age 70 farmer; Margaret age 29; George W. age 24 farmer; 1
laborer; 1 servant

Children of Nathaniel Marcus Gould and Margaret Francisco:
George Wheelock, b. 1821; d. 1838
John Francisco, b. 1823
Mary Elizabeth, b. 1825; m. Philander Pierson
William, b. 1826; d. aft 1880; m. 1858, Phebe Marie Crane
Abigail, b. 1828; d. 1831
Marcus Johnson, b. 1831; d. 1832
Abigail Faitout, b. 1832
Marcus Johnson, b. 1835
Henry Darcy, b. 1838; m. Harriet Eliz. Reuck;see Aaron
     Reuck
Margaret, b. 1840; m. David Montanyea

Children of Nathaniel Marcus Gould and Nancy D. Ward:
Silas Ward, b. 1843
George Wheelock. b. 1845; m. 1872...Abby Gould..(dau. of
     Stephen J. Gould, q.v., and Joanna Beach)

- - - - -

Gould, **ROBERT**   b. (August 25, 1754)
(gmnj) (njhs) (lgl) (photo)   d. July 23, 1825
(NJ Will 11657G. 1825)

In
Memory of
Robert Gould
who died
July 23rd 1825
aged 71 years
10 months

& 26 days

first wife, **MARY** (Denman) b. (April 20, 1754)
(gmnj) (njhs) (lgl) (photo)   d. June 4, 1820

In
Memory of
Mary Gould
wife of
Robert Gould
died
June 4th 1820
aged 66 years
1 mo. & 15 days

son, **WILLIAM WHEELOCK**
(gmnj) (photo)   b. (May 8, 1796)
                           d. July 12, 1818

In
memory of
William Wheelock
son of Robert and
Mary Gould
who died
July 12, 1818
Aged 22 years
2 months
and 4 days

Notes:
Served: Revolutionary War

--Robert J. Gould, son of Thomas Gould; m. #1 1776, Mary Denman Bond; m. #2 1820, Rhoda Force

Children of Robert Gould and Mary Denman:
Martha Speer, b. 1781
Thomas Denman, b. 1785; m. Nancy ...; m. Caroline....
William Wheelock, b. 1796; d. 1818

- - - - -

Gould, **SAMUEL**   b. (June 20, 1764)
(gmnj) (njhs) (photo)   d. August 26, 1821
(NJ Will 11328G. 1821)

In
Memory of
Samuel Gould
who died
August 26th 1821
aged 57 years

wife, **ELLEN JACOBUS**   b. (abt. 1760)
(gmnj) (njhs)(lgl) (photo)   d. May 28, 1832

In
Memory of
Ellen Jacobus
wife of
Samuel Gould
died
May 28th 1832
aged 72 years

Notes:
--Samuel, son of Stephen Gould, q.v.; m. Elizabeth Courter
b. abt. 1767; m. Ellen Jacobus, b abt 1760

Children of Samuel Gould and Elizabeth Courter:
Benjamin Gould, b. abt. 1787; m. Rachel.....
Stephen, b. abt 1789
John, b. abt. 1791
Samuel, b. abt. 1793

- - - - -

Gould, Stephen	b. (April 18, 1741)
(gmnj)	d. (June 16, 1777)
	(?bur. Caldwell Presbyterian)

wife, Rachel (Speer)	b. (May 18, 1740)
(gmnj)	d. (1784)
	(?bur. Caldwell Presbyterian)

| son, **CORNELIUS** | b. (abt. 1775) |
| (gmnj) (njhs) | d. January 31, 1793 |

Cornelius. son of Stephen & Rachel Gould
died Jan. 31st 1793
in his 18th year

Notes:
--Stephen, son of John Gould and Abigail Woodruff; m.
1760, Caldwell, Rachel Speer, b. 1740, dau. of Teunis Speer

Children of Stephen Gould and Rachel Speer

Josiah, q.v., b. 1761; m. Elizabeth Colyer
Samuel, q.v., b. 1764; m. Elizabeth Courter; m. Ellen
    Jacobus
Henry, q.v., b. 1771; m. Sarah Dunn
Cornelius, b. August 7, 1775; d. January 31, 1793; m. 1792,
    Caldwell, Eliza Beach

- - - - -

Gould, **STEPHEN**, Esq.   b. (June 30, 1777)
(gmnj) (photo)   d. May 20, 1839

Stephen Gould
Died
May 20th 1839
Aged 62 years

first wife, **SARAH** (Banks)   b. (December 25, 1779)
(Historical Soc. of W. Caldwell)   d. (February 26, 1817)

second wife, **SUSAN** (Banks Holmes)
(gmnj) (njhs) (lgl) (photo)   b. (October 17, 1782)
                    d. February 11, 1849

Susan Gould
Died
Feb. 11th 1849
Aged 66 years

Notes:
--Stephen, son of Joseph Gould, q.v., and Rebecca Paxton;
m. #1, Nov. 1801, Sarah Banks, dau. of David Banks, q.v.

m. #2, May 1818, Susan Banks (Holmes), dau. of David Banks, q.v.; widow of Samuel Rathburn Holmes
--"At New York, Sunday evening, the 26th inst., Mrs. Sally Gould, wife of Mr. Stephen Gould, Bookseller of that City, aged 37 years, last Christmas.."(Sentinel of Freedom. Feb 25,1817)
--Stephen Gould: printer, publisher, bookseller, e.g., Gould, Banks & Gould, Co., with William and Anthony Gould and David Banks. He was publisher of the *Sentinel of Freedom* 1799-1803. (American Antiquarian Society) In 1807 a copy of "A sermon preached July 22, 1807 at the funeral of the Rev. Alexander MacWhorter DD senior pastor of the Presbyterian Church in Newark" was "*Printed and Published by S. Gould*".
--In 1824 he opened a printing office in Verona which he called the *Coke Law Press*. He closed that in 1830. (Today, 2018, an 1824 Coke Law Press copy of *Cottage Economy* by William Cobbett is offered for $850 from Joseph J. Felcone, antiquarian bookseller at Princeton, New Jersey.)
--1822 Title: "*Published by Stephen Gould. Law Bookseller (Sign of Lord Coke) Corner of Wall and Broad Streets*"
--For more see: Legal Publishing in Antebellum America. M. H. Hoeflich, Cambridge. 2010

Children of Stephen Gould and Sarah Banks:
Edward Banks, b. 1802; m. Caroline C. Abel
Joseph Paxton, b. 1804; d.1880; m. 1831, Eloise E. Tuttle
       (1808-1860) (bur. Mount Pleasant Cemetery, Newark)
Lucetta Banks, b. 1806; m. Uzal A. Crane, q.v.
Alexander Stephen, q.v., b. 1808; m. Mary Jane Reid
James Ogden, b. 1811; d. 1847

Children of Stephen Gould and Susan Banks:

Susan Louisa, b. 1819; m. Joseph Gardiner Carman, q.v.
Alfred Coke, b. 1820; d. Oct. 1864, Roanoke Island, VA
'yellow fever'; Served: Civil War (bur. National
Cemetery, New Bern, NC); m. #1 1843,Sarah A. Stuart, d.
1851, daughter of Sardius Stuart, q.v.; m.1853.
Caroline Elizabeth Harrison

- - - - -

Gould, Stephen J.	b. (March 15, 1801) d. (January 14, 1883)
wife, Joanna (Beach)	b. (December 22, 1805) d. May 10, 1884
daughter, **ELIZABETH** (gmnj) (njhs) (lgl)	b. (May 25, 1823) d. November 3, 1829

*Elizabeth.
daughter of Stephen J.
& Joanna Gould
died Novr. 3d 1829
aged 6 years. 5 mos. & 9 d's*

son, **WILLIAM W.** (gmnj)	b. (January 22, 1828) d. March 29, 1838

*William W.
son of
Stephen J.
and Joanna Gould
died march 29, 1838*

aged 10.2.7

Notes:

--Stephen J. Gould and Joanna both died <u>after 1881</u> when burials at the churchyard had been disallowed.

--Stephen J. Gould, son of Josiah Gould, q.v.;"Stephen Gould m. July 6, 1822, Joann Beach" Caldwell Presbyterian Church (lgl)

Children of Stephen J. Gould and Joanna Beach

Elizabeth, b. 1823; d. 1829
Jonathan Beach, b. 1823; m. Martha Simms;
  m. Elizabeth Simms (d. Parkersburg, WVA?)
Daniel, b. 1825; m. Mary J. Ogden (d. Parkersburg, WVA?)
William Wiggins, b. 1828; d. 1838
Josiah, b. 1830; m. Ann Armstrong (d. Parkersburg, WVA?)
Rachel, b. 1835; d. 1923; m. Richard A. Speer (bur. Fairfield
  Ref. Church Cemetery)
Caleb H., b. 1838; m. #1, 1859, Sarah Elizabeth Jacobus
  m. #2 aft. 1900,Catherine VanNess
Charles B., b. 1841; m. Sarah Eveline Speer
Stephen Lot, b. 1843; m. Amanda Worley (d. Parkersburg,
  WVA?)
Sarah Elizabeth, b. 1845; d. 1915; m. Nicholas S. VanDuyne
Abigail, b. 1849; m. George Wheelock Gould

- - - - -

Gould, **STEPHEN RANDOLPH**
(gmnj) (photo)   b. (May 7, 1834)
(NJ Will 15755G. 1863)   d. October 19, 1863

Stephen Randolph
Born May 7, 1834
Died October 19, 1863
In his 29th year

wife Harriet Rhoda (Beach) b. (December 20, 1835)
                                          d. (April 14, 1873)

daughter **HARRIET/Hattie** b. (January 1861?)
                                            d. (February 1862?)

Hattie Randolph
Infant daughter
Born January 1861
Died February 22, 1862

Notes:
--Stephen Randolph Gould, son of Thomas Denman Gould,
q.v.; m. Harriet Rhoda Beach
--1850 Census: p.82 Caldwell Twp: Thomas D. Gould age
65 farmer; Caroline age 48; Adaline C. age 10; Stephen R.
age 16 farmer; Ann Mott age 72; Daniel H. Burnett age 35
merchant; Daniel G. Burnett age 5; Martha Burnett age 2; 2
laborers
--1860 Census; p.95 Caldwell Twp: Stephen R. Gould age 24
farmer; Harriet age 20; John age 4; Ada D. age 7 months; 1
laborer
--1870 Census; p.124 Caldwell: Harriet R. Gould age 31;
John 16 clerk; Addie D. age 13; Bell dau. age 9; Marilla age
7; all b. NJ; 1 servant

Children of Stephen Randolph Gould and Harriet R. Beach:

John, b. abt. 1854
Addie Denman, b. 1856
Isabel Harrison, b. 1859
Harriet/Hattie Randolph, b. 1861
Marilla Petrie, b. 1862

- - - - -

Gould, **STEPHEN S.**   b. (abt. 1786)
(gmnj) (njhs) (lgl) (photo)   d. January 6, 1842
(NJ Will 13201G. 1842)

In
Memory of
Stephen S. Gould
who died
Jan. 6th 1842
in the 56th year
of his age

Notes:
--(?)son of Samuel B. Gould and Jenneke Van Sant; m.
April. 1808, Caldwell, Sarah Van Houten

Children of Stephen S. Gould and Sarah VanHouten:
Stephen, b. PA
Eleanor, b. Oct. 1813, Caldwell; m. Lemuel W. Jacobus
Edgar Taylor, b. Nov. 1823 NJ; m. Hannah Maria Pearce
Sarah C., b. abt. 1831, NJ

- - - - -

Gould, Thomas III   b.
                           d.

wife, **ELIZABETH**   b. (abt. March 15, 1787)
(gmnj) (njhs) (lgl)   d. October 7, 1808

In
Memory of
Elizabeth
wife of
Thomas Gould 3rd
died Oct. 7th 1808
aged 21 years 6 months & 22 days

Notes:
--(?)see Thomas D. Gould
--(?)"Thomas Gould of Caldwell to Betsey Ayres of Basking
Ridge, May 31, 1806" (Sentinel of Freedom, June 1806)

- - - - -

Gould, **THOMAS**   b. (November 2, 1716)
(gmnj) (njhs) (lgl) (photo)   d. February 17, 1815

In
Memory of
Thomas Gould
who died
Feb. 17th, 1815
age 98 years
3 months and

15 days

first wife, Sarah (Johnson)
> b. (June 16, 1712)
> d. (May 2, 1767)

second wife, **MAHETABLE** (Cobb Baldwin)
(gmnj) (njhs) (photo)   b. (abt. 1733)
> d. December 26, 1813

> *In*
> *Memory of*
> *Mahetable Gould*
> *wife of Thomas Gould*
> *who died Dec. 26th, 1813*
> *in the 81st year*
> *of her age*
> (gmnj: "in 84th yr.")

Notes:
--Thomas Gould, Trustee of the Church
--Thomas, son of John Gould and Martha Osborne;
m. #1. bef. 1740, Sarah Johnson; born June 16 1712; dau. of
Albert Johnson; m. #2 Mehetable Cobb Baldwin
--"Thomas was the progenitor of 207 persons , of whom
168 were living at the time of his death."

Children of Thomas Gould and Sarah Johnson:
John, b. 1740; d. Ohio?; m. Catherine Manee
Martha, b. 1742; m. bef. 1758, Samuel Smith
     m. abt 1758, John Thomas Speer
Joseph, q.v., b. 1746; abt 1768, Sarah Ward

Mary J., b. 1749; m. at 1765, Elias Smith Courter
Timothy, q.v., b. 1751
Robert, q.v., b 1754; m. Mary Denman Bond;
    m. Rhoda Force
William, q.v., b. 1757; m. Mehitable Crane

- - - - -

Gould, **THOMAS D.**   b. (June 3, 1786)
(gmnj)   d. March 3, 1854
(NJ Will 14530G.1854)

Thomas D. Gould
died March 3, 1854
aged 68.9.0

first wife, **NANCY** (Crane)   b. (June 6, 1796)
(gmnj) (njhs) (lgl)   d. April 19, 1837

Nancy
wife of
Thomas D. Gould
died April 19th 1837
aged 40 years. 10 mos.
& 13 days

second wife, **CAROLINE**   b. (abt. 1802)
(gmnj)   d. September 18, 1862

Caroline
wife of Thomas D. Gould
died September 18, 1862

aged 60 years

daughter, **ELIZA REEVES** b. (abt. September 10, 1827)
(gmnj) (njhs) (lgl) d. October 11, 1829

Eliza Reeves.
daughter of Thomas D. & Nancy Gould
died Oct. 11th, 1829
aged 2 yrs. 1 mo. & 1 day

daughter, **HANNAH M.** b. (abt. March 4, 1821)
(gmnj) (njhs) (lgl) d. December 31, 1846

Hannah M. daughter of
Thomas D. & Nancy Gould
died December 31st 1846
aged 25 years. 9 months
& 27 days

son, **JOHN LOUIS** b. (abt. June 22, 1818))
(gmnj) (njhs) (lgl) (photo) d. November 29, 1819

In
memory of
John Louis
son of Thomas D.
and Nancy Gould
who died
Novr. 29th 1819
aged 1 year. 5 months
& 7 days

Notes:

--Thomas Denman Gould,son of Robert Gould, q.v. and Mary Denman;

--Thomas m. Nancy .....; m. Caroline Mott

--?Thomas m. Elizabeth... b. 1787; d. 1808 (see above)

--1850 Census: p.82 Caldwell Twp: Thomas D. Gould age 65 farmer; Caroline age 48; Adaline C. age 10; Stephen R. age 16 farmer; Ann Mott age 72; Daniel H. Burnett age 35 merchant; Daniel G. Burnett age 5; Martha Burnett age 2; 2 laborers

Children of Thomas D. Gould and Nancy Crane:
John Louis, b. 1818; d. 1819
Hannah Maria, b. 1821; d. 1846
Elizabeth Reeves, b. 1827; d. 1829

Children of Thomas D. Gould and Caroline .....
Adaline C., b. abt 1840
Stephen R., q.v., b. abt. 1834; m. Harriet Rhoda Beach

- - - - -

Gould, **TIMOTHY**, Esq.   b. (abt. December 9, 1751)
(njhs) (lgl) (gmnj)   d. February 19, 1841
(NJ Will 13127G. 1841)

> *Timothy Gould*
> *died*
> *Feb. 19th 1841*
> *in his 89th year*

first wife, **SUSANNA**   b. (February 8, 1761)

(gmnj) (njhs) (lgl) (photo)   d. March 16, 1788

In Memory of
Susanna Wife of
Timothy Gould
She Died March
16, 1788 Aged
27 Years 1 month
and 8 days

second wife, **ELIZABETH A.** (Reeves)
(gmnj) (njhs) (lgl)   b. (July 12, 1750)
      d. July 24, 1824

Elizabeth
wife of
Timothy Gould, Esq.
died July 24th, 1824
aged 77 yrs. 12 d.

third wife, Jemima Vreeland (Colyer)
      b.
      d.

daughter, **BETSY**   b. (abt. July, 1790)
(gmnj) (njhs) (lgl)(photo)   d. November 25, 1790

In Memory of
Betsy, Dau'r. of
Timothy and
Elizabeth Gould
She died Novr,

25th 1790 Aged
4 Months

Notes:
Served: Revolutionary War; New Jersey Militia, Sgt.
--1818: Justice, Essex County, NJ
--Timothy, son of Thomas Gould and Sarah Johnson
--Timothy m. #1, 1777, Susannah (Crane?)
--Timothy m. #2, Dec. 15, 1788, Elizabeth A. Reeves
--?Timothy m. #3, January 27, 1839, Jemima Colyer, dau. of
Isaac Colyer
--?Timothy m. Phebe (Jones): b. 1780 d. 1834, age 54 (lgl)
"Gould, Timothy; w. Phebe, ("Late widow of Nehemiah
Crane,q.v.)d. Oct. 29, 1834. Aged 54 yrs." (gmnj) (lgl) (njhs)

Children of Timothy Gould and Susannah .....
Sarah G., b. 1778; m. 1799, David Bates
Nancy Crane, b. 1781; m. Marcus Douglass,. q.v.
Ezekiel, q.v., b. 1783; m. Phebe Kitchell
Elias Baldwin, b. 1786; m. 1808, Lydia C. Farrand

Children of Timothy Gould and Elizabeth A. Reeves:
Betsey, b. 1790; d. 1790

- - - - -

Gould, **WILLIAM, Gen.**　　b. 1757 (September 27, 1757)
(gmnj) (njhs) (lgl) (photo)　　d. February 12, 1847
(NJ Will 113618G.1847)

Founding Elder

In
Memory of
General William Gould
born
in Caldwell
in the year 1757
died Feb. 12th, 1847
aged 90 years
At the age of 18, he
enlisted in the cause of the
Revolution, and was en-
gaged in the Battles of
Springfield and Monmouth.
he served for many years as
Member of the Legislature,
and Justice of the Peace
and in other offices of
Honor and Trust.
In the year 1794 he ac-
tively assisted in build-
ing the House of God,
standing near, and being
elected one of the first
Elders in the church he
filled the office faithfully
and devotedly nearly 70
years. In his manners
he was dignified and cour-
teous; amiable and tender
in his Disposition, and
industrious in his Habits.
His character was irre-

proachable, and as re-
markable for Devotion to
his Country, as for Integ-
rity in the Trust rep...
in him, a genuine Patriot
a useful Citizen, a true
Christian
His end was Peace

In Memory of his Vir-
tues, will long be a precious
Inheritance to his numer-
ous descendants

wife, **MEHETABLE** (Crane)b. (June 17, 1761)
(gmnj) (lgl) (photo)   d. December 4, 1843

Mahitable. wife of
General William Gould
died Dec. 4th, 1843
in her 80th year
She was a kind and affectionate Wife.
A mother, patient, watchful and tender.
She exemplified in a long and useful life.
All the Virtues of the Christian.
The Memory of the Just
is Blessed

grand(?)daughter **HARRIET HENRIETTA**
(gmnj) (njhs) (photo)   b. (June 9, 1805)
     d. April 8, 1813

daughter, **CHARLOTTE**   b. (April 15, 1794)
(njhs) (gmnj)   d. June 30, 1814

Harriet Henrietta
died
Apr. 8th 1813
aged 8 years
and
Charlotte
Wife of Joseph Harrison (q.v.)
died June 30th 1814
aged 21 years

Daughters of
Gen. Wm. and Mahitable
Gould

son, **STEPHEN GROVER** b. (abt. June 1789)
(gmnj) (njhs) (lgl) (photo)   d. August 12, 1789

In Memory of Stephen
Grover Son of William and
Mehetable Gould
Who Died Aug. 12
1789 Aged 2 Months
and 22 Days

Happy the babe, who privileged by fate,
To shorter labours & lighter weight,
Recev'd but yesterday ye gift of breath,
Ordered tomorrow to return to death

Notes:
Served: Revolutionary War: Pvt. NJ Militia; Served: with
Gen. Lee in the 1794 whiskey insurrection
--William, son of Thomas Gould, q.v.; m. 1779, Mehitable
Crane

Children of Gen. William Gould and Mehitable Crane:
Mary Denman, b. 1780; m. 1800, Robert Baldwin
Phebe Baldwin, b. 1782; m. Jacob Vreeland?; m. Lucius
     Douglass,q.v., m. 1817 at age 34 , Edward Fauctot
Johnson Nehemiah, b. 1784; m. 1809, Elizabeth Reeves
Elizabeth Crane, b. 1786; m. 1811, Abner Reeves
Stephen Grover, b. 1788; d. 1789
Emily, b. 1790; d. 1871
Charlotte, b. 1794; m. Joseph Harrison
Abigail Grover, b. 1796; m. 1819, Henry Kittredge
Nathaniel Marcus, q.v., b. 1799; m. #1 Margaret Francisco
     m. #2 1842, Nancy D. Ward
William C., b. 1802; m. 1828, Charlotte Ward
Harriet Henrietta, b. 1805; d. 1813
Stephen Grover, b. 1806; m. 1831, Sarah Ann Crawford

- - - - -

GROVER

Monument
(Shaft)
Rev. Stephen Grover
Died June 22d, 1836
in his 78th Year
(North Side)

Born in Tolland, Conn.
A graduate of Dartmouth College
A soldier of the Revolution
And first Pastor of this
Presbyterian Church of Caldwell.
He laid the foundation stone of the
house of God near this spot in 1794.
And there preached the Gospel
of Christ, for nearly half a century.
(East Side)
As a pastor he was devoted and
faithful, as a preacher ardent
and pathetic; and in all his social
relations kindly and affectionate.
Having finished his work he
fell asleep.
(West Side)
Mary,
wife of
Rev. Stephen Grover
Died
July 13, A.D.1847
Aged 87 years.
10 mo.
& 4 days
Blessed are the dead which die in the Lord
from henceforth yea saith the Spirit for
they rest from their labours, and their
works do follow them.

Grover, **STEPHEN, REV.**   b. (July 15, 1758)
(gmnj) (njhs) (lgl)   d. June 22, 1836

(NJ Will 12694G.1836)

wife, **MARY** (.....)   b. (August 30, 1759)
(gmnj) (njhs) (lgl) (photo)   d. July 13, 1847

Mary
wife of
Rev. Stephen Grover
died July 13, 1847
aged 87 years.10 mo.
7 days

son, **JAMES WHEELOCK**   b. (abt. June 1790)
(gmnj) (njhs) (lgl) (photo)   (bapt. June 27, 1790)
                                 Presb. Ch. Caldwell
                                 d. July 6, 1798

James Wheelock
Son of Rev. Stephen & Mary
Grover
died July 6, 1798
aged 3 (9) years. 2 mo.
& 2 days

son, **JOHN**   b. (1799)
(gmnj) (njhs) (lgl) (photo)   d. June 1799

John
son of
Rev. Stephen and Mary
Grover
died June 1799.

Aged 3 months

Notes:

Served: Revolutionary War: 21st Reg't, Continental Army; also Whiskey Rebellion and War of 1812
--Stephen, son of Ebenezer Grover and Zurviah Larabee of Tolland, Connecticut; brother of Rev. Joseph Grover, pastor at Parsippany NJ and later, Bristol, Ontario Co., NY

"Stephen Grover M.A.: He was a native of Tolland Ct. and the son (brother) of (Rev.)Joseph Grover who was also born in the same town. He was engaged as a soldier in the Revolutionary War where he received a wound. He entered college considerably advanced in life (grad. Dartmouth 1786) having attended to his preparatory studies under the tuition of the Rev. Nathan Williams D.D. He was a very pious worthy man though not a distinguished scholar. His theological course of instruction he pursued under Dr. Williams of his native place. Mr. Grover married and settled in the ministry in Caldwell a town adjoining Newark in New Jersey and there died suddenly in his bed at 3 o'clock in the morning of June 22 1836 in the 78th year of his age and the 50th year of his ministry. His brother Joseph graduated at Dartmouth in the Class of 1773 settled in the ministry and is supposed to be yet living.(died July 11, 1826)" *(The American Quarterly Register Vol. XI p.384 Boston 1839)*

Obituary: Mrs. Mary Grover: (nee Byram?) (nee Morris?)
Died in Newark at the residence of her son, S. R. Grover, Esq., July 13, 1847, in the 88th year of her age, Mrs. Mary Grover. She was born at Morristown, Sept. 9th, 1759. At the age of 17 she made a profession of religion; so that for 70 years she was enrolled a member of the church. In 1787 she was married to the Rev. Stephen Grover, who was the first pastor of the church in Caldwell, and whose relation to that church continued about half a century. She is known to have been the efficient helper of her husband in laying the foundations of the church in Caldwell. By prudent, steady and intelligent cooperation she added much to the usefulness of his ministry. Many still living can testify to the delightful influence of her character and conversation, both at home and abroad.

Her home, was distinguished for Christian hospitality. The piety of Mrs. Grover was eminently of the Scriptural type. During 40 years of her life she read the Bible through once a year. Her old age was cheerful. Retaining to the last her interest in friends, in the objects and scenes around her, she made others happy. Thus a mother who was a beautiful specimen of the sound piety of other days has passed away to her rest. Who can tell the value of such wives and mothers to the church and the world. *(New York Observer. 20 July 1847: Newark Daily Advertiser)*

Children of Rev. Stephen Grover and Mary .....:
James Wheelock, bapt. Caldwell, June 27, 1790; d. 1798
　　(named for Wheelock,founder of Dartmouth
　　College?)
Stephen R., q.v., b. 1791; d. 1853
Maria Darby, b. March 1794; d. Oct. 1825. Age 31; m. 1817
　　at Caldwell,Joseph Smith Dodd (1791-1847), son of
　　Gen. John Dodd. Joseph, graduated Princeton;
　　doctor; state senator; (both bur. Bloomfield Cemetery,
　　Bloomfield NJ) (Dr. John Darby was pastor and doctor
　　at Parsippany)
Rosalinda, b. 1795; d. 1873;m. Joseph Freeman Crowell, q.v.
John, b. 1799; d. 1799
Harriet Pierson, b. 1801; d. 1835; m. 1822 at Caldwell,
　　William Brown Baldwin (1789-1865) son of Ichabod
　　Baldwin and Joanna Dodd (died Bloomfield)

- - - - -

Grover, **STEPHEN R.**　　b. June 30, 1791
(gmnj) (njhs) (lgl)　　　　d. October 21, 1853

Stephen R. Grover
born June 30th, 1791

died Oct. 21st, 1853
Aged 62 Years. 3 Mo's
& 21 days
If a man die shall he live again

wife, **ELIZABETH** (Byram) b. October 12, 1789
(gmnj) (njhs) (lgl)   d. August 13, 1848

Elizabeth.
wife of Stephen R. Grover
born Oct. 12 1789
died Aug. 13th 1848
aged 58 Years
& 10 months

son, **GEORGE H.**   b. (abt. September 1813)
(gmnj) (njhs)   d. September 28, 1844

George H. Grover.
eldest son of
Stephen R. & Elizabeth
Grover
died Sept. 28th, 1844
aged 31 years & 9 days

son, **STEPHEN A.**   b. (June 30, 1824)
(photo)   d. (January 1869)
          d. (Norfolk, Virginia)

Stephen A. Grover
Born

June 30, 1824
Died
January ... 1869

daughter, **ESTHER** b. (abt. May 1826)
(gmnj) (njhs) (lgl) (photo) d. July 3, 1826

In memory of
Esther.
daughter of
S. R. & E. Grover
died July 3rd 1826
aged 9 weeks

son, **CHARLES** b. (abt. May 20, 1827)
(gmnj) (njhs) (lgl) d. August 18, 1827

Charles. son of
Stephen R. & Elizabeth Grover
died Aug. 18th, 1827
aged 2 mos. & 29 days

Notes:
Served: War of 1812
Served: Representative of Essex Co. to the NJ State Senate
1846-1848; lawyer; Justice of the Peace
--Stephen R. Grover, Esq., son of Rev. Stephen Grover, q.v.
--Stephen m. Elizabeth Byram, dau. of Joseph Byram, q.v.,
and Esther Douglass
--1850 Census; p.115 East Ward,Newark: Lewis C. Grover,
age 35 atty at law; Caroline 35; Anne E. 9; L. C. 8; Caroline

6; Julia 4; Rosalinda 1; Agnes 1/12; Stephen R. age 59 atty at law; all b. NJ; 2 servants

Children of Stephen R. Grover and Elizabeth Byram:
George H., b. 1813; d.1844
Lewis Conger, b. October 20, 1815; d. 1896; (1862:President
    Mutual Benefit Life Insurance Co.); m. Caroline Cochran,
    dau. of Thomas Cochran, q.v.
Mary Louisa. b. abt. 1820;d. August 17, 1863; m. William
    Solomon Leavitt (1822-1910) son of Rev. Joshua
    Leavitt, D.D. (both bur. Green-Wood Cem. Brooklyn NY)
Stephen Augustus, b. June 18,1824; d. January1869, VA
    m. Dec. 1, 1847, Jane Eliza Andruss of Newark
    Lawyer. Voyage to California via Cape Horn where
    he was engaged as the master and owner of a vesssel and traded
    between California and the Sandwich Islands. Later he was an
    officer on the U. S. Naval ship New Hampshirelaunched April
    1864. He died of pneumonia at Norfolk Va in January 1869.
Esther, b. 1826; d. 1826
Charles, b. 1827; d. 1827

- - - - -

Hammell, John, Dr.   b. (?abt. 1751)
                            d. (?March 1, 1831)
                            (?bur. Sparta Cem. Sussex Co.)

wife, HANNAH (Roome)   b. (September 12, 1758)
(gmnj) (njhs) (photo)   d. June 24, 1833

Sacred
to the memory of
Hannah Hammell

wife of
Dr. John Hammell
and daughter of
Henry and Ann Roome
late of New York
died June 24th 1833
aged 74 years. 9 months
& 12 days

Notes:

Dr. John Hammell: Patriot and Loyalist

--November 28, 1779: "John Hammell, surgeon, 4th Battalion NJ Volunteers and Hannah Roome, spinster" married at Trinity Church, New York City, daughter of Henry Roome and Anne Griggs. (After the war, Henry Roome had land confiscated at Hackensack.)

"At the beginning of the war we find Dr. Hammell on the patriot side and July 24th 1776 he was commissioned surgeon's mate of Col. Van Cortland's Battalion of Heard's Brigade New Jersey detached militia. He went to General Heard's command to re-inform the army at New York and in his professional capacity took part in the battle of Long Island. Soon after that he professed his allegiance to Great Britain and accepted service in the British Army. He was commissioned surgeon of the Fourth Battalion New Jersey Volunteers November 25th, 1776. In the fall of 1777 was captured on Staten Island by a party of troops under Major General Philemon Dickinson who commanded the New Jersey Militia in the field ..and by order of the Council of Safety November 31st 1777 he was committed to the jail for high treason. He was surgeon of the Third Battalion at the

close of the war. " (The New Jersey Volunteers. Loyalists. In the
Revolutionary War. William S. Stryker. Trenton. 1887)
    Hammell, along with Lt. Jacob VanBuskirk and Lt.
Edward Earle, (m. were scheduled for trial; however General
George Washington wrote to New Jersey Governor
Livingston:

> *"In my opinion, trying the Officers, taken by General Dickinson
> on Staten Island, for high treason, may prove a dangerous expedient. It
> is true they left the state after such an offence was declared Treason; but
> as they had not taken the Oaths, nor had entered into our Service, it will
> be said they had a right to choose their side."*

    *"Dr. John Hammell, surgeon in the 4th Battalion of
the New Jersey Volunteers, commanded by Lt. Col. Abraham
Van Buskirk. He was one of the earlier practioners at Parr
Town. He no doubt came to St. John with his regiment in the
fall of 1783. "* (Collections of the New Brunswick (Canada) Historical
Society, Vol. 1, No. 8) ("John Hammell, settled in New Brunswick
Canada, receiving British half-pay to 1801") (Dr., Lt. Col. Van Buskiek
became mayor of Shelburne, Nova Scotia)

Children of Dr. John Hammell and Hannah Roome:
William Henry, b. 1783 d. 1815; m. 1805, Phebe Scull
Anne Eliza, b. 1785; m. John Edgecomb
Sarah Roome, b. 1787, d. 1870
Henry Roome, b. 1789, d. 1815
John, b. 1791 m. Helen Freneau
Joseph Cummings, b. 1793, d. 1793

- - - - -

HARRISON

Harrison, Cyrus Freeman   b. (November 2, 1822)
                                     d. (October 30, 1893

first wife, Sarah (Crane)   b. (September 19, 1820)
                                     d. (December 21, 1868)

second wife, Abby M. Baldwin
                                     b. (January 8, 1836)
                                     d. (1908)

son, **JOSEPH W.**   b. (September 12, 1854)
(gmnj)   d. February 8, 1856

Joseph
Son of
Cyrus F. Harrison
died February 8, 1856
Aged 1.4.24

Notes:
--Cyrus Freeman Harrison, son of Samuel Harrison, q.v.,
and Mary Crane; m. #1, July 6, 1853, Sarah Crane, dau. of
Cyrus Crane and Hannah Crane; m. #2, February 1870,
Abigail M. Baldwin; (? dau. of Theron Baldwin and Caroline
Wilder)
--1850 Census:p.107&108, Livingston Twp., Essex Co., NJ:
Polly Harrison, age 64; Joanna, age 38; Mary age 37; Cyrus
F., age 27, farmer; Zenas G., age 24, farmer; Marinda, age
22; all b. NJ
--?1850 Census: p.182&183, Chatham Twp., Morris Co. NJ:
Abby M. Baldwin, age 13, b. NY; at res. of John and Mary
Davison

--1860 Census: p. 92, Caldwell Twp: Cyrus F. Harrison, age 37, farmer; Sarah, age 39; Emma C.,age 3; Laura F., age 8 months; 2 laborers

--?1860 Census: p.92, Caldwell Twp: Saml. O. Harrison,a ge 43, farmer; Sarah A., age 39; Mary A., age 2; Lizza B. age 6 mos.; Emily C. Baldwin, age 32, b. NY, seamstress; Abby M. Baldwin, age 23, seamstress, b. NY; (adj. to Cyrus F. Harrison and wife, Sarah.)

--1870 Census: p.112, Caldwell Twp: Cyrus F. Harrison,age 47, farmer; Abby M., age 33; Emma E., age 13; Laura F., age 10; Minnie C., age 7

--1880 Census, p.431.1, Caldwell Twp: Cyrus F. Harrison, age 57, b. NJ, farmer; Abbey M., age 44, b. 'NY'; Laura F., age 20; Minnie C., age 17; Everett C., age 8; Norman G., age 5; 1 farm laborer

Children of Cyrus Freeman Harrison and Sarah Crane:
Joseph Wilbur, b. 1854; d. 1856
Emma Crane, b. 1857; d.1877
Laura Frances, b. 1859
Minnie Caroline, b. 1863; m. Frederick W. Pierson
George Monroe, b. 1867; d.1869

Children of Cyrus Freeman Harrison and Abigail M. Baldwin:
Everett Clark Harrison, b. 1871, d. 1895
Norman Baldwin, b. 1874; m. 1899 Emma Burgess Smith
    --Grad. Princeton 1895; B.D., D. D.; Presbyterian pastor at Pittsburgh and Seattle; missionary at Skagway, Alaska

- - - -

Harrison, **DAVID**   b.
(gmnj) (photo)   d. 1838
(NJ Will 12881G. 1838)

> *David Harrison*
> *and his wife*
> *Lois Williams Dodd*
> *departed this life*
> *A.D. 1838*

> *As shocks of corn fully ripe*
> *they were gather'd into*
> *the garden of the Lord*

wife, **LOIS WILLIAMS** (Dodd)
(gmnj) (njhs) (photo)   b.
                   d. 1838

Notes:
--(?)David Harrison m. July 9, 1810, Lois Dodd; dau. of Ebenezer Dodd and Deborah Crane
--(?)Lois Williams m. Elijah Dodd, son of Caleb Dodd and Hannah Harrison

- - - - -

Harrison, **HARVEY**   b. (abt. April 1, 1798)
(gmnj) (photo)   d. September 30, 1869
(NJ Will 16842G.1869)

> *Harvey Harrison*

died September 30, 1869
aged 71 years 5 months
and 29 days

wife, **MARY** (Bond)   b. (abt. February 25, 1802)
(gmnj)   d. December 25, 1864

Mary Bond
wife of Harvey Harrison
died December 25, 1864
aged 62.9.29

Notes:
Served: War of 1812, pvt., Columbian Volunteers
--Harvey, son of Joseph Harrison and Phebe Tompkins
--Harvey m. May 12, 1824, Mary 'Polly' Bond (dau. of
Samuel Bond and Electa Force)
--1850 Census: p.227, Orange Twp.; Harvey Harrison, age
50, farmer; Mary, age 48; Rachel Ann Bond, age 12; all b.
New Jersey
--1860 Census, p.102, Caldwell Twp: Harvey Harrison, age
62, farmer; Mary, age 58; Ann (Bond), age 22; Samuel Bond,
age 81; all b. NJ

- - - - -

Harrison, Henry W.   b. (August 4, 1798)
                                             d. (January 27, 1879)
                                             (Prospect Hill Cemetery.photo)

wife, **ANN** (Cook)   b. (abt. 1802)

(gmnj) (njhs)   d. June 1, 1846

Ann
wife of
Henry W. Harrison
died June 1st 1846
aged 44 years

Notes:
--Henry Wells Harrison, son of Uzal Harrison and Hamutal Wade
--Henry m. September 1, 1825, Ann Cook, dau. of Francis B. Cook and Mary .....
--1850 Census, p.80, Caldwell Twp: Henry W. Harrison, age 52, farmer; Ann Eliza age 21; Ashbel G. age 18; Henry F., age 8; Abby Louisa, age 18; 1 laborer
--1860 Census, p.92, Caldwell Twp: Henry W. Harrison, age 62, farmer; Ashbel G., age 27; Sarah A., age 30; Charles H., age 3; Sarah F., age 6 mos.; Henry F., age 18, labor
--1870 Census, p.105, Caldwell Twp: Henry W. Harrison, age 76, farmer; Ashbel G., age 38, farm laborer; Henry F., age 28, farm laborer; Sarah A., age 40; Charles H., age 13; Sarah F., age 11; Elmer E., age 9; William B., age 3

Children of Henry W. Harrison and Ann Cook:
Ann Eliza, b. abt. 1829
?Abby Louisa. b, abt. 1832
Ashbel Green, b. abt. 1832; m. 1856, Sarah A. Bowman
Henry Francis, b. abt. 1842; unm. in 1880

- - - - -

Harrison, **JABEZ** b. (abt. 1771)
(gmnj) (njhs) (lgl) d. May 29, 1849
(NJ Will 12233G.1831)

Jabez Harrison
died
May 29th, 1849
in his 78th year

wife, **ABIGAIL** (Dodd) b. (May 20, 1773)
(gmnj) (njhs) (photo) d. August 26, 1803

Sacred
to the memory of
Abigail,
wife of
Jabez Harrison
she died Aug. 26th 1803
in her 31st year

daughter, **MIRANDA HARRISON**
(gmnj) (njhs) (photo) b. (abt. 1798)
 d. December 2, 1831

Sacred
to the memory of
Miranda Harrison
Daughter of Jabez and
Abigail Harrison
she died Dec. 2nd 1831
in the 33rd year
of her age

son, **DAVID B.**　　　　b. (abt. 1793)
(gmnj)　　　　　　　　　d. July 7, 1832

also of
David B. Harrison
son of Jabez and
Abigail Harrison
he died at Detroit
July 7th, 1832
of the cholera
in his 39th year

Notes:
Served: "connected with Gen. Harrison's Army of the West, Detroit."
--Jabez, son of David Harrison; m. May 20, 1793, Abby, daughter of Caleb Dodd, q.v., and Mary Harrison

Children of Jabez Harrison and Abigail Dodd:
David Burnet, b. abt. 1793; d. 1832
Caleb Dodd, b. abt. 1797; m. Phebe Steele
Miranda Harriet, b. 1798; d. 1831

- - - - -

Harrison, Jared Freeman　　b. (October 28, 1790)
　　　　　　　　　　　　　d. (July 2, 1862)

wife, Eliza (Barkalow Duryea)
　　　　　　　　　　b. (March 25, 1789)
　　　　　　　　　　d. (June 8, 1882)

son, **FRANCIS ALEXANDER**
(njhs)   b. (abt. February 22, 1827)
                              d. April 29, 1844

Francis Alexander
son of Jared F.
and Eliza Harrison
died April 29th 1844
aged 17 years. 2 months
& 7 days
Remember now thy Creator,
in the days of thy youth

Notes:
Served: War of 1812; lieutenant, Columbian Volunteers
--*"Death of My Dear Companion: Jared F. Harrison*
departed this Life: July 2nd 1862 in his 72nd yr." (Duryee
Family Bible)
--Jared Freeman Harrison, son of Joseph H. Harrison, q.v.,
and Rhoda Freeman; m. bef. 1822 Elizabeth Barkalow
Duryea, dau. of John Duryea, q.v., and Mary Lee Brinkerhoff
--1850 Census, p.108, Livingston Twp: Jared F. Harrison,
age 59, farmer; Eliza, age 61; Philip H., age 18, farmer;
Phebe Ann Williams, age 14; John Duryea, age 69,
gentleman
--1860 Census, p.196&197, Livingston Twp: Jared F.
Harrison, age 69, farmer; Eliza, age 71; Philip H., age 28,
farmer; Hester A., age 29; Harriet L., age 5; Eliza D., age 2;
1 farm laborer
--1870 Census, p.122, 7Wd, Newark: Joseph D., age 48,
flour dealer; Mary A., age 45; Alexander L., age 21, store

clerk; Lizzie A., age 18, school teacher; Henry L., age 16; Harriet H., age 12; Amy D., age 10; Helen M. age 4; Elizabeth, age 77; Phoebe, age 52; --1880 Census, p.239.2, Newark: John G. Harrison, age 55, flour dealer; Frances A., age 51; Eliza, age 91, mother, widow; 1 seamstress; 1 'adopted' female

Children of Jared Freeman Harrison and Elizabeth Barkalow Duryea:
Joseph Duryea, b. 1822; m. Mary Adeline Harrison (Rosedale)
John George, b. 1824; m. Frances Freeman
Frances Alexander, b. 1826; d. 1844
Philip Henry, q.v., b. 1831; m. Hester Ann Crane

- - - - -

Harrison, **JOANNA**   b. (abt. March 28, 1787)
(gmnj)   d. November 22, 1852

Joanna Harrison
died November 22, 1852
aged. 65.7.25

Notes:
--Joanna, dau. of Joseph Harrison, q.v., and Rhoda Freeman

- - - - -

Harrison, **JOSEPH,** Esq.   b. December 19, 1747)
(gmnj) (njhs)   d. March 1, 1837
(NJ Will 12802G.1837)

Founding Elder

Joseph Harrison
died
March 1st, 1837
aged 89 years

first wife, **RHODA**(Freeman) b. (abt. 1751)
(gmnj)   d. July 21, 1791

Rhoda
wife of
Joseph Harrison, Esq.
died July 21st 1791
in her 40th year

second wife, Phebe Tompkins b. March 31, 1759
(widow of Ezra Durand)   d. February 21, 1827
                              ("bur. in Old Burying Ground,
                              Caldwell")

third wife, **MARY** (Kirk)   b. (abt. October 27, 1762)
(gmnj)   d. August 25, 1840

Mary
wife of Joseph Harrison
died August 25, 1840
aged 77.0.29

Notes:
Served Revolutionary War
--Joseph, son of Joseph Harrison and Mary Tompkins(?)

--Joseph, m. #1, Rhoda Freeman, dau. of Abel Freeman and Abigail Smith; m. #2, 1792, Phebe Tompkins, b. 1759; d. 1807; daughter of Jonathan Tomkins and Polly Vandenburg; wid. of Ezra Durand; m. #3, Mary Kirk, 1762-1840, daughter of Zachariah Kirk.

Children of Joseph Harrison and Rhoda Freeman:
Demas, b. 1773; bapt. Jan. 5, 1783, First Presb. Ch. Hanover;
    m. #1, 1794, Jemima Wade
    m. #2, aft. 1810, Rhoda Horton Burnet
Tamar, b. 1775; bapt. Feb. 16, 1783, First Presb. Ch.
    Hanover; m. 1795, Aaron Dodd, q.v.
Rufus Freeman,q.v., 1778; bapt. Feb. 16, 1783, First
    Presb. Church, Hanover; m. 1799, Phebe Ogden
    Williams
Jared, b. 1780; d. 1780
Samuel, q.v., b. 1782;bapt. January 5, 1783, First Presb.
    Church, Hanover; m. Mary Crane
Abigail, b. 1784; d. 1854; m. Bethuel Crane
Joanna, q.v., b. 1787; d. 1852
Jared Freeman, q.v., b. abt. 1791; m. Elizabeth Barkalow
    Duryea

Children of Joseph Harrison and Phebe Tompkins:
Joseph, q.v., b. 1793; m. Charlotte Gould
Rhoda, b. 1795; m. Henry Beach
Harvey, q.v., b. 1798; m. Mary Bond
Phebe, b. 1802; d. 1847 Michigan

- - - - -

Harrison, Joseph   b. (February 8, 1793)

(photo)   d. (August 24, 1878)
                               (bur. Fargo Meth. Cemetery
                               Marengo, Morrow Co., Ohio)

first wife, **CHARLOTTE** (Gould)
(gmnj) (njhs) (photo)   b. (April 15, 1794)
                               d. June 30, 1814

In
Memory of
Charlotte
wife of
Joseph Harrison
who died
June 30, 1814
aged 21 years

Notes:
Served: War of 1812; pvt, Columbian Volunteers (militia)
--Charlotte, dau. of Gen. William Gould, q.v.

Child of Joseph Harrison and Charlotte Gould:
Charlotte, b. 1813, d. 1910; Elk Twp., Buena Vista Co.,
Iowa; m. #1, Rev. Samuel Marvin; m. #2, Chester Alden

- - - - -

Harrison, Philip Henry   b. (August 23, 1831))
                                d. (1915)

wife, Hester Ann Crane   b. (April 14, 1831)
                                d. (bef. 1910)

daughter, **ELIZA DURYEA** b. (abt. September 4, 1857)
(gmnj) (photo)   d. February 24, 1862

Eliza Duryea
daughter of
Philip and Hester
Harrison
Died February 24, 1862
aged 4 years. 5 months
and 20 days

Notes:

--Philip Henry Harrison, son of Jared Freeman Harrison, q.v.

--Philip m.,1853, Hester Ann Rogers Crane, dau. of Josiah W. Crane and Fanny Cockefair

--1850 Census, p.108, Livingston Twp: Jared F. Harrison, age 59, farmer; Eliza age 61; Philip H., age 18, farmer; Phebe Ann Williams, age 14; John Duryea, age 69, gentleman

--1860 Census, p.196&197, Livingston: Jared F. Harrison, age 69, farmer; Eliza, age 71; Philip H., age 28, farmer; Hester A., age 29; Harriet L.,age 5; Eliza D. age 2

--1880 Census, p.399.1, Caldwell: Philip H. Harrison,a ge 48, milk dealer; Hester A., age 48; Fannie C., age 19; Kittie S., age 15; Harry L., age 13; Louis P., age 10; Edith L. age 9

--1900 Census, p.8B, 11Wd, Newark: Philip H. Harrison, b. August 1831, m.46 yrs., contractor; Hester A., b. April 1831, 7 born 6 living; Edith L, b. Oct. 1870

--1910 Census, p.7A, 11Wd, Newark: Philip Harrison,age 78, widower, contractor; Edith Harrison, dau., age 35, single;

Catherine 'Saper' age 41, dau., widow?; Catherine S. 'Serine' age 10, granddaughter

Children of Philip Henry Harrison and Hester Ann Crane:
Caroline Landau, 1854, m. Benj. Parkhurst
Elizabeth Duryea, b. 1857; d. 1862
Fannie Crane, b. 1860
Catherine Schuyler, b. 1864
Harry Lincoln, b. 1867, m. Mary Verges Cresse
Louis Baldwin, b. 1869
Edith Lee, b. October 1870; unm. in 1910

- - - - -

Harrison, **RICHARD**	b. (abt. 1813)
(gmnj)	d. September 17, 1839

Richard Harrison
died Sept. 17th 1839
aged 27 years

wife, **MARIA C.** (Moore)	b. June 22, 1813
(gmnj)	d. August 15, 1866

Maria C. Moore
wife of Richard C. Harrison
born June 22, 1813
died August 15, 1866

Notes:
--Richard Harrison m. Maria C. Moore

--1850 Census, p.84, Caldwell: Jonathan Provost, age 51, tanner/currier; Paulina age 49; Mary Ann., age 24; Ellen, age 22; Phebe, age 15; Caroline, age 11; Martha, age 7; Thomas, age 1; Mariah Harrison, age 37; all b. NJ; 1 servant;1 laborer
--1860 Census, p.100, Caldwell: John W. Taylor,age 30, b. MA, lawyer; Anna (Provost?) Taylor, age 30 b. NJ; Henry Taylor, age 6; Amzi D. Taylor age 1; Phebe Burnett, age 51, b. NJ; Maria C. Harrison, age 47, b. NJ; 1 servant

- - - - -

Harrison, **RUFUS**   b.(August 28, 1778)
(gmnj) (njhs)   d. July 25, 1848
(NJ Will 13716G.1848)

Rufus Harrison
died July 25th 1848
in his 70th year

wife, **PHEBE** (Ogden Williams)
(gmnj) (njhs)   b. (November 14, 1779)
                               d. June 28, 1847

Phebe
wife of
Rufus Harrison
died June 28th 1847
aged 67 years. 7 months
& 14 days

Notes:
Served: War of 1812; Capt., Columbian Volunteers

--Rufus, son of Joseph Harrison and Rhoda Freeman
--Rufus m. December 21, 1799, Phebe Ogden Williams, dau.
of Enos Williams, q.v., and Susannah Ogden
--1840 Census: #233, Livingston Twp.,Essex Co., NJ: Rufus
Harrison

Children of Rufus Harrison and Phebe Williams:
Tamar, b. 1800
Demas, b. 1805; d. 1881; m. Dorcas Crane
Mary, b. 1813; d. 1889; m. October 16, 1833, Zenas C.
    Crane
Rufus Freeman, Jr., b. 1818; m. February 17, 1841,Harriet
    Matilda Williams, dau.of Amos Williams and
    Elizabeth Steele; granddau. of Josiah Steele, q.v.

- - - - -

Harrison, **SAMUEL**   b. September 15, 1782
(njhs)   d. March 5, 1849
(NJ Will 13840G.1849)

Samuel Harrison
born
Sept. 15th 1782
died
March 5th 1849

wife, Mary (Crane)   b. (September 15, 1784)
                                d. (March 19, 1858)

daughter, **DORCAS ELIZABETH**
(njhs)   b. July 27, 1820

d. February 21, 1830

D. Elizabeth Harrison
born July 27th 1820
died Feb. 21st, 1839

Notes:
--Samuel, son of Joseph Harrison, q.v., and Rhoda Freeman
--Samuel m. February 21, 1810, Mary Baldwin Crane, dau.
of Samuel Crane, q.v.

Children of Samuel Harrison and Mary Baldwin Crane:
Joanna, b. 1811; m. Asher Baldwin Crane
Rhoda C. b. 1815; m. Daniel S. Baldwin
Samuel Orton, q.v., b. 1816; m.#1, Sarah Elizabeth Baldwin;
    m.#2, 1853, Sarah A. Baldwin;
    m.#3, Gertrude Isabella Budd
Mary b. abt. 1819
Dorcas Elizabeth, b. 1820; d. 1830
Marilla, b. abt. 1821
Cyrus F., q.v., b. 1822; m. Sarah Crane
Zenas Gibson, b. 1826; m. Frances Amelia Reeve
Tamar Marinda, b. abt. 1892

- - - - -

Harrison, Samuel O.   b. (December 17, 1816)
(gmnj)   d. (January 30, 1897)
                              (bur. Prospect Hill Cemetery)

first wife, **SARAH ELIZABETH**
(gmnj) (njhs) (lgl) (photo)   b. (abt. January 4, 1813)

d. March 3, 1850

In
Memory of
Sarah Elizabeth
wife of
Samuel O. Harrison
died March 3d, 1850
aged 37 years. 1 mo.
& 27 days

second wife, Sarah A.   b. (September 23, 1820)
                               d. (May 12, 1864)
                               (bur. Prospect Hill Cemetery)

third wife, Gertrude (Budd)   b. (February 20. 1843)
                               d. (January 27. 1899)
                               (bur. Prospect Hill Cemetery)

daughter, **AMELIA NAOMI** b. (abt. January 18, 1847)
(gmnj) (njhs) (lgl) (photo)   d. November 3, 1850

In
Memory of
Amelia Naomi.
daughter of
Samuel O. & S.E.
Harrison
who died
Nov. 3d, 1850
aged 3 years. 9 mos.
& 16 days

daughter, **ELIZA BALDWIN**
(gmnj) (njhs) (photo)   b. (abt. September 20, 1849)
                                      d. December 1, 1850

In
Memory of
Eliza Baldwin
daughter of
Samuel O. and
S.E. Harrison
who died
Dec. 1st 1850
aged 1 year 2 months
& 11 days

son **SAMUEL EDGAR**   b. (abt. October 4, 1853)
(gmnj) (photo)   d. March 16, 1855

Samuel Edgar
son of Samuel O. Harrison
died March 16, 1855
aged 1 year. 5 months
and 12 days 12

son, EDWARD CLARK   b. (abt. March 8, 1856)
(gmnj)   d. May 23, 1857

Edward Clark
son of Samuel O. Harrison
died May 23 1857
aged 1.2.15

daughter, **LIZZIE BALDWIN**

(gmnj)   b. (abt. December 6, 1859)
                           d. December 12, 1863

Lizzie Baldwin
Daughter of Samuel O. Harrison
died December 12, 1863
aged 4.0.6

Notes:
--1850 Census, p.80, Caldwell Twp: Samuel O. Harrison,a ge
33, farmer; Naomi A., age 3; Elizabeth B. age 8 mos.; 6 other
persons
--1860 Census, p.92, Caldwell Twp: Samuel O. Harrison, age
43, farmer; Sarah A., age 39; Mary A., age 2; Lizza B., age 6
months; Emily C. Baldwin, age 32, seamstress; Abby M.
baldwin, age 23, seamstress; 1 laborer; 1 servant; (adj. to
Cyrus F. Harrison, age 37)
--1870 Census, p.105, Caldwell Samuel O. Harrison, age 52,
farmer; Mary H. age 12; Edgar S., age 8; 1 housekeeper
--1880 Census, p.423.2, Caldwell: Saml. O. Harrison,a ge 63,
farmer; Gertrude I., age 37, wife; Mary A., age 22, dau.;
Saml. Ezra, age 17, son, works on farm; Annie O., age 3,
dau.; all b. NJ

Children of Samuel O. Harrison and Sarah Elizabeth .....:
Amelia Naomi, b. 1847; d. 1850
Elizabeth Baldwin, b. 1849; d. 1850

Children of Samuel O. Harrison and 2nd. wife, Sarah A. .....:
Samuel Edgar, b. 1853; d. 1855

Edward Clark, b. 1856; d. 1857
Mary Amelia, b. abt. 1858; m. George M. Canfield
Elizabeth Baldwin, b. 1859; d. 1863
Samuel Ezra, b. abt. 1862; m. Hannah Tolland

Child of Samuel O. Harrison and 3rd wife, Gertrude Budd:
Helen Budd, b. 1873; d. 1877
Anna Clarissa, b. 1877; d. 1948

- - - - -

Harrison, **ZENAS**   b. (abt. August 25, 1768)
(gmnj) (njhs) (photo)   d. July 14, 1831

In
Memory of
Zenas Harrison
who departed this life
July 14th 1831
aged 62 years.
10 months
and 19 days

wife, **PHEBE** (Williams)   b. (abt. 1772)
(gmnj) (photo)   d. March 1, 1861

In
Memory of
Phebe
wife of
Zenas Harrison
Died March 1, 1861

aged 89 years

daughter, **ABBY**   b. (abt. May 25, 1816)
(gmnj) (njhs)   d. September 25 1818

Abby.
\daughter of
Zenas & Phebe
Harrison
died
Sept. 25th 1818
aged 2 years & 4 months

Notes:
Served: Revolutionary War
--Zenas m. Phebe Williams, daughter of Jonathan Williams
--1850 Census p.107 Livingston.. Essex Co. NJ: Joseph
Cook, age 44 farmer; Phebe age 42; Hannah M. age 13;
Zenas F. age 11; Abby L. age 8; Cyrus A. age 5; Joseph H.
age 1; Phebe Harrison age 77; all b. NJ
--1860 Census p.200 Livingston: Joseph Cook, age 53
farmer; Phebe age 52; Hannah M. age 23; Abby L. age 18
school teacher; Cyrus A. age 15; Joseph H.M. age 10; Phebe
Harrison age 88; 2 farm hands

Children of Zenas Harrison and Phebe Williams:
Cyrus , b. abt. 1794; m. #1, bef. 1823 ?Maria Martin
     m. #2, bef. 1840?, Jane .....
Henry Squier, b. 1801;d. 1880, Michigan; m. Phebe
     Harrison, daughter of Joseph Harrison, q.v.
Phebe, b. 1807; m. Joseph Cook, q.v.
Abigail, b. 1816; d. 1818

- - - - -

HARTLEY

Hartley, John   b. (abt. 1798)
(NJ Will 16843G. 1869)   d. (September 1869)

wife, **CHARLOTTE** (Martin) b. (abt. 1785)
(gmnj)   d. August 8, 1851
(NJ Will #14083G - 1851)

*Charlotte
wife of John Hartley
died August 8, 1851
In her 66th year*

Notes:
--John Hartley m. Caldwell, November 13, 1828, Charlotte
Martin, widow of Matthew Dodd; dau. of Enos Martin, Esq.,
q.v., and Jane Personett
--John Hartley married Bloomfield, July 1852, Catherine
Rutan Wilson, widow
--1840 Census: Bloomfield: John Hartley
--1850 Census, p.156B, Bloomfield, Essex Co., NJ: John
Hartley, age 52, b. England, tailor; Charlotte, age 64, b. NJ
--1860 p. 148A, Bloomfield: John Hartley, age 60, b.
England, tailor
--1869-70: Mortality Schedule: John Hartley, age 72, b.
England, tailor (chronic 'diarreha')
--Will of Charlotte Martin Hartley: # 14083G. Proved September
1851."to John Hartley use of furniture while he lives; cash to:

sisters and nieces; Board of the Foreign Missionary Society; Board of the Home Missionary Society; use of my house in Newark to sisters and nieces; $50 for the purchase of a decent head stone for myself."

- - - - -

HAYWOOD

Haywood, **NANCY**   b. (abt. 1784)
(gmnj) (njhs) (photo)   d. August 28, 1848

Nancy Haywood
died
Aug. 28th 1848
in her 64th year

Notes:
--See: Jeniah Williams whose son, Stephen, m. Phebe Ann Haywood

- - - - -

HEATH

Heath, **AARON B.**   b. (abt. 1800)
(gmnj)   d. March 8, 1851

Aaron B. Heath
died March 8, 1851
in his 51st year

first wife, **ANN MARIA** (Conover)

(gmnj) (njhs) (photo)   b. (abt. April 23, 1810)

                              d. November 16, 1830

Ann Maria
wife of
Aaron B. Heath
and daughter of
Stephen & Mary Conover
died Nov. 16th 1830
aged 20 years. 6 months
& 24 days

Note:

--Aaron Banta Heath,, son of John Heath and Rachel Banta

--Aaron m. #1, Anna Maria Conover, dau. of Stephen
Conover, q.v.; Aaron m. #2, February 16, 1832, Malvina
Conover, dau. of Stephen Conover, q.v., and Mary Jones

--Aaron B. Heath, member Broadway Tabernacle Church,
Brooklyn, 1842-1851

--1850 Census, p.129&130, 6Wd, New York City: Aaron
Heath age 48, b. NY, mason; Rachel, age 67 b. NY; Malvina,
age 35, b. NY; David, age 36 b. NY; James age 23 b. NY;
Ellen, age 22 b. NY; Edward age 15 b. NY; Malvina, age 12
b. NY; Adeline age 10 b. NY; Emma age 7 b. NY; Mary age
5, b. NY; Frederick age 2 b. NY; Agnes age 8 months b. NY;
4 other persons

- - - - -

HOAGE
HOGGE

Hoage, **PATRICK** b. 1799
(gmnj) (njhs) d. 1850

Patrick Hoage
1799 - 1850

wife, **MATILDA** (Lane) b. 1799
(gmnj) d. 1878

Matilda
wife of Patrick Hoage
1799-1878

daughter, **HANNAH ELIZA** b. 1841
(gmnj) d. 1862

Hannah Eliza
daughter of Patrick Hoage
1841-1862

son, **EDWARD** b. (abt. March 9, 1833)
(gmnj) (njhs) d. October 4, 1834

Edward Hogge
died
Oct. 4th, 1834
aged 1 year. 6 months
& 25 days

Notes:

--Patrick, b. Ireland; m. February 1828, Matilda Lane, dau. of Henry Lane and Hannah Beckhorn

--1850 Census, p.78, Caldwell Twp: Patrick Hogge age 50, b. Ireland, tobacconist; Matilda age 50 b. NJ; Mary, age 18, b. NJ; Thomas age 11 b. NJ; Eliza, age 9 b. NJ

--1860 Census, p.100, Caldwell: Matilda 'Hoag' age 62 b. NJ; Thomas age 31 segar maker; Eliza age 19 b. NJ; Wallace age 23, tobacco packer; Hannah Lane, age '50'; all b. NJ

--1870 Census, p.117, Caldwell: Thomas Hogge, age 31, cigar maker; Martha, age 24; Maggie, age 2; Matilda, age 70; all b. NJ

Children of Patrick Hoage and Matilda Lane:
Moses Austin, b. 1828; m. Mary M. Kent (bur. Prospect Hill)
Mary, b. abt. 1832
Edward, b. 1833; d. 1834
Wallace, b. abt. 1837
Thomas A.,1839; m. 1867, Martha DeCamp (bur Prospect Hill)
Hannah Eliza, b.1841; d. 1862

- - - - -

HOPKINS

Hopkins, **HYACINTH MARIA**
(gmnj) (njhs) b. (abt. April 25, 1847)
d. September 25,1849
(dysentery)

Hyacinth Maria Hopkins
died Sept. 25th 1849
aged 2 years & 5 months

Hopkins, **WILLIAM HARRIS**

(gmnj) (njhs)   b. (abt. December 27, 1842)
                                 d. September 23, 1849
                                 (dysentery)

William Harris Hopkins
died Sept. 23rd 1849
aged 6 years. 8 months
& 27 days

Notes:

--?Hyacinth and William, children of Robert Hopkins and
Mary Carberry

--?Robert Hopkins, son of .... Hopkins and Ann Tuckniss

--?Robert Hopkins m. Mary Carberry, b. abt. 1809,
Demerara, British Guyana, dau. of William Carberry and
Sarah Richards

--1850 Census, p.70, Caldwell Twp: Robert Hopkins, age 52,
farmer b. PA; Mary, age 41, b. Demerara, West Indies; Mary
E., age 16, b. PA; Charlotte W., age 14, b. NY; Catherine
Ann, age 12, b. NY; Isabella C., age 9, b. NJ

--1860 Census, p.120, Caldwell: Robert Hopkins, age 60
b.PA, clerk; Mary, age 51, b. 'England'; Charlotte age 23 b.
NY; Catherine age 22 b. NJ; Isabella, age 19, b. NJ; Robert,
age 9 b. NJ

--1870 Census, p.457, West Orange: Robert Hopkins, age 74
b. PA, farmer; Mary, age 60, b. British Guyana; Charlotte,
age 34 b. NY; Catherine age 31 b. NY; Isabella, age 28 b.
NJ; Robert, age 19, b. NJ

--1880 Census, p.250A, West Orange: Robert Hopkins, age
83 b. PA, father NJ, mother MD; Mary wife, age 70 b.

British Guiana, parents b. 'NJ'; Charlotte dau age 44 b. NY; Catherine, dau age 42 b. NY; Isabella, dau., age 39 b. NY; Robert R., son, age 29, b. NJ, carpenter

- - - - -

HOPPING

Hopping, **JOSEPH T.**   b. February 10, 1801
(gmnj)   d. September 18, 1872

*Joseph T. Hopping
died September 18, 1872
Aged 71.7.8*

wife, **ESTHER E.** (Cochran) b. March 7, 1813
    d. November 28, 1863

*Esther E.
wife of Joseph T. Hopping
born March 7, 1813
died November 28. 1863*

Notes:
--Joseph T. Hopping, son of Elijah and Mary Hopping
--Esther Cochran, dau. of Thomas Cochran, q.v.
--1860 Census; Caldwell Twp.; Joseph T. Hopping, age 59, farmer; Hester/Esther, age 47; Electa C. Miller, age 51

- - - - -

HUDSON

HUDSON, **JOHN L.**   b. (February 24, 1782)
(gmnj)   d. June 3, 1853
                      (also on monument.Prospect Hill)

John L. Hudson
died June 3, 1853
aged 71.3.9

first wife, **MARTHA** (Gould)
(gmnj)   b. (November 1, 1781)
                   d. June 23, 1818

Martha
wife of John L. Hudson
daughter of Robert Gould
died June 23, 1818
in her 37th year

Notes:
--John L. Hudson, b. Mendham, son of William Hudson and Mary Howell
--John L. Hudson m. #1, December 4, 1802, Martha 'Patty' Gould, dau. of Robert Gould, Esq., q.v.
--John L. Hudson m. #2, February 20, 1821, Phebe Personett, dau. of Moses Personett, q.v., and Betsy Crane
--John Hudson and Phebe Personett, divorced by Legislative Act, January 21, 1834. She m. #2, John G. Vanderhoof
See: Moses Personett for more about Phebe
--1810: "In 1810 John L. Hudson established a pottery on the Gould property. The pottery manufactured stone-ware jugs

and crocks, but was never very successful as a business enterprise." (lgl, p.63)

--1812: First postmaster of Caldwell.

--1832 Newark: John L. Hudson. "personal property sold at public auction; household furniture and his interest in the Dover Mail Stage."

--1834: John divorced by Phebe

--1850 Census: p. 87, Caldwell Twp: Benjamin C. Pierce, age 26, farmer; Rachel Pierce, age 25; John L. Hudson, age 70, merchant; all b. NJ

--1860 Census, p.92, Caldwell Twp: John G. Vanderhoof, age 50, laborer b. NJ; Phebe, age 59

--1870 Census, p.106B, Caldwell Twp: John Vanderhoof, age 60, no occup; Phebe, age 70

--1880 Census, p.424D, Caldwell Twp: Phebe Vanderhoof, age 79, widow; adj. to Zenas Crane

Children of John L. Hudson and Martha Gould:
Robert,
Thomas Denman, b. abt. 1814; m. Jane Wallis
Harriet Louise; b. 1816, m. Jonas C. Reeve
Mary; m. (Joseph Calvin?) Lyon

Children of John L. Hudson and Phebe Personett:
Elizabeth, b. 1820-1825; dy
Daughter, b. 1825-1830; dy
William Elias, b. 1829; m. Jane Robinson
(bur. Mount Pleasant Cemetery, Newark)

- - - - -

HULBERT

Hulbert, **O. W.** b. (April 16, 1817)
(gmnj) d. February 16, 1854

O. W. Hulbert
died February 16, 1854
aged 36.10.0

wife, **MARY S.** (Bowden) b. (abt. January 5, 1822)
(gmnj) (photo) d. April 2, 1861

In
Memory of
Mary S. Hulburt
wife of O. W. Hulburt
daughter of
John and Mary Bowden
who died
April 2, 1861
aged 39 years. 2 months.
aand 28 days

son, **JOHN OSSIAN** b. (abt. Setpember 15, 1847)
(gmnj) d. August 18, 1851

John Ossian
son of O. W. Hulbert
died August 18. 1851
aged 3.11.3

Notes:

--Obadiah Warriner Hulbert,V; son of Obadiah Hulbert, IV
and Elizabeth Warriner

--Obadiah W. Hurlburt m. January 1844, St. Mark's Church,
Orange, Mary Sophia Bowden, dau. of John Bowden and
Mary Sidebotham

--1850 Census, p.74, Caldwell Twp: Obadiah W. "Hubbard",
age 28 b. Mass., school teacher; Mary S., age 27 b. NJ; John
Ossian,age 2, b. NJ; Henry S. Courter, age 23, b. NJ, mason

Children of Oliver W. Hurlbert and Mary S. Bowden:
John Ossian, b. 1847; d. August 20, 1851
Olive W., b. abt. 1852, Caldwell

- - - - -

HUSK

Husk, **JOHN**   b. (abt. 1818)
(gmnj) (njhs) (lgl) (photo)   d. May 16, 1846
(NJ Will 13543G. 1846)

John Husk
died
May 16th 1846
in his 28th year

wife, Abigail (Courter)   b. (abt. 1815)
                                d. (abt. 1900)

daughter, **ELLEN**   b. (abt. 1839)
(gmnj) (njhs)   d. March 16, 1842

Ellen. daughter of
John & Abigail Husk
died March 16th 1842
in her 3rd year

Notes:
--John, son of John Husk and Affey .....
--John m. Abigail Courter, dau. of Thomas C. Courter and
Elizabeth Gould
--Abigail m. #2, October 23, 1850, Henry Courter, son of
John E. Courter and Sophia Jacobus
--1850 Census, p.86 Caldwell Twp: Elizabeth Cook, age 62;
Abigail Husk age 35; Mary E. Husk, age 7; all b. NJ

Children of John Husk and Abigail Courter:
Ellen, b. 1839; d. 1842
Mary Elizabeth, b. abt. 1843

- - - - -

JACOBUS

Jacobus, **AARON I.**   b. (abt. 1776)
(gmnj) (njhs) (lgl)   d. June 9, 1838
(NJ Will 12884G. 1838)

Aaron Jacobus
died June 9th 1838
in his 62d year

wife, Abby/Ache (VanRiper) b.
d.

son, **AARON I.**   b. (abt. December 30,1813)
(gmnj) (njhs) (lgl)   d. December 22, 1836

Aaron I.
son of Aaron & Abby Jacobus
died Dec. 22nd 1836
aged 22 years. 11 months
& 22 days

Notes:
--Aaron m. June 9, 1799, Abby VanRiper: "Van Riper, Ache and Aaron Jacobus, June 9, 1799" (Essex Co. Clerk's Marriage Records)

Children of Aaron I. Jacobus and Abby/Ache VanRiper
Aaron I., b. 1813; d. 1836

- - - - - -

Jacobus, Archibald   b. (1807)
        d. (July 28, 1879)
        (bur. Mount Pleasant Cem.Newark)

wife, Mariah   b. (1806)
        d. (February 11, 1892)
        (bur. Mount Pleasant Cem. Newark)

son, **EZRA**   b. (abt. 1830)
(gmnj) (photo)   d. August 25, 1836

Ezra

son of Archibald
and Maria Jacobus
died August 25, 1836
aged 6 years & 5 months

The sweetest flower that earth can yield
Must leave its beauteous blooms
The lovely youth with all its charms
Lies silent in the tomb.
There neither pain, nor sin is found
Nor death nor want nor fears
There lie his Saviour's face behold
Through everlasting years.

Notes:
--Archibald "kept the toll gate near the canal bridge'
(Woodside, The North End of Newark)

Children of Archibald Jacobus and Maria:
Ezra, b. abt. 1830; d. 1836
Horace G., d. October 1869; m. Mary C. Parsons
(bur. Mount Pleasant Cemetery, Newark)

- - - - -

Jacobus, **CORNELIUS H.**   b. (August 13, 1758)
(lgl)   d. February 8, 1835
(NJ Will 12603G. 1835)

In Memory of
my Father
February 8, 1835

aged 65 years

wife, **ABIGAIL GOULD**   b. (October 5, 1763)
(gmnj) (njhs) (lgl)   d. October 23, 1836

Abigail Gould
wife of
Cornelius Jacobus
died Oct. 23rd 1836
aged 73 years

Notes:
--Cornelius, son of Hendrick I. Jacobus and Sarah Stynmets
--Cornelius H. Jacobus m. 1778, Caldwell,Abigail Gould,
dau. of Joseph Gould, q.v.

Children of Cornelius H. Jacobus and Abigail Gould:
Elizabeth,b. abt. 1782
Stephen Gould, b. abt 1874
John C., b. abt 1785; m. 1809, Sarah Gould
Sarah, b. abt. 1786
Mercy, b. abat. 1788; m. Squire Wheaton
John S., b. 1787; d. July 1862; m. Marion Davis
Joseph S., b. 1790; d. 1862, Condit, OH; m. Mariah .....
Moses, b. abt. 1795, m. Eleanor/Ellen Gould
Maria, b. abt. 1796, m. Jotham Condit

- - - - -

Jacobus, Cornelius R.   b. (abt. April 7, 1807)
                               d. (May 11, 1869)

(bur. Fairfield Ref. Ch. Cem.)

wife, Ann (Hopper)

b. (August 8, 1811)
d. (d. January 28,1902)
(bur. Fairfield Ref. Church Cem.)

son, **GEORGE**
(njhs) (lgl)

b. (abt. 1835)
d. July 2, 1845

George.
son of
Cornelius & Ann
Jacobus
died July 2nd 1845
aged 10 years

Notes:
--Cornelius R. Jacobus, son of Richard Jacobus; m. February 21, 1835, Anna Hopper, dau. of Hessel Hopper and Ann Dey
--1850 Census, p.147, Wayne Twp., Passaic Co. NJ:
Cornelius R. Jacobus, age 42, farmer; Ann, age 36; Ann S., age 14; Jane, age 11; Peter R. Jacobus, age 50, farmer; Charles H. Brown, age 12; all b. NJ
--1860 Census, p.620, Meads Basin PO, Wayne Twp:
Cornelius R. Jacobus, age 52, farmer; Ann, age 45; Jane, age 20; Jeremiah Berdan, age 30, farmer; Ann Berdan, age 23; Lizzy Berdan,a ge 5; Cornelius Berdan, age 8 months; adj. to Thomas Jacobus, age 36, farmer
--1900 Census, p.17B, Wayne Twp: Richard Berdan b. September 1875, m. 2 yrs, farmer; Lily b. Dec. 1877; Ada b. Nov. 1899; Anna S., b. Nov. 1836, widow, mother; Anna Jacobus, age 86, grandmother b. August 1813; all b. NJ

Children of Cornelius R. Jacobus and Anna Hopper:
George, b. 1835; d. 1845
Anna Sophia, b. 1836; m. 1854, Jeremiah Ryerson Berdan
Jane, b. abt. 1841; m. 1861, George R. Berdan

- - - - -

Jacobus, Ephraim   b. (abt. 1812)
                                            d. (January 1, 1894)

wife, **CATHALINA**(Sindle) b. (abt. November 25, 1812)
(gmnj)   d. February 21, 1848

Cathalina
wife of Ephraim Jacobus
died February 21, 1848
aged 35.2.27

son, **JESSE**   b. (abt. June 16, 1841)
(gmnj)   d. May 2, 1863

Jesse
son of Ephraim Jacobus
died may 2, 1863
aged 21.10.16

Notes:
--1850 Census, p.72, Caldwell Twp: Ephraim Jacobus, age
38, mason; Leah Vangieson,age 37; Timothy Jacobus, age
18, farmer; Israel Jacobus, age 14; Jesse Jacobus, age 9; adj.

to Richard P. Jacobus, age 53, mason; near John Jacobus, age 62, mason

--1860 Census, p.117, Caldwell: Ephraim Jacobus, age 48, farmer; Leah Vangieson, age 48; adj. to Stephen Jacobus, age 38; and Margaret Jacobus, age 67

--1870 Census, p.134, Caldwell: Ephraim Jacobus, age 57, farmer; Leah "Van Gurm" age 61, housekeeper

--1880 Census, p.416D, Caldwell: Ephraim Jacobus, age 68, widower, b. NJ, farmer; Catharine Vreeland, widow age 36 b. NJ, father b. Nova Scotia, mother b. NJ; Anna L. Vreeland, age 6, b. NJ, parents b. NJ

Children of Ephraim Jacobus and Catherine Sindle:
Timothy, b. abt. 1832; m. abt, 1858, Sarah Vanderhoof
Israel, b. abt. March 1837; m. 1857, Ellen Jane Glass
Jesse, b. abt. 1841; d. 1863

- - - - -

Jacobus, **HENRY A.**　　　b. (abt. 1809)
(gmnj) (njhs)　　　　　　　d. May 10, 1838
(NJ Will 12886G. 1838)

> *Henry A. Jacobus*
> *died*
> *May 10th 1838*
> *in his 29th year*
> *also*
> *an infant daughter of*
> *Henry A. and Maria Jacobus*
> *died May 17, 1838*
> *aged 2 months & 13 days*

wife, Maria   b.
                 d.

son **MARCUS E.**   b. (abt. April 3, 1833)
(gmnj) (njhs)   d. June 5, 1848

Marcus E.
son of
Henry A.
and Maria Jacobus
died June 5th 1848
aged 15 years. 2 months
& 2 days

Jacobus, **DAUGHTER**   b. (abt. March 4, 1838)
(gmnj)   d. May 17, 1838

also
an infant daughter of
Henry A. and Maria Jacobus
died May 17, 1838
aged 2 months & 13 days

Notes:
Children of Henry A. Jacobus and Maria...:
Marcus E., b. 1833; d. 1848
Daughter, b. 1838; d. 1838

- - - - -

Jacobus, James Oliver   b. (April 28, 1835)

d. (June 10 1868)
(bur. Fairfield Ref. Ch. Cemetery)

wife, Hester/Hettie Ann Van Ness
        b. (abt. 1836)
        d. (March 28, 1905)
        (d. Caroline Co., Virginia)

son, **MARCUS I.**   b. (abt. April 13, 1858)
(gmnj)   d. January 22, 1861

Marcus I.
sond of James O. Jacobus
died January 22, 1861
aged 2.9.9

Notes:
--James, son of Peter Jacobus and Eliza Ann Oliver
--James m. March 20., 1858, Hetty Ann VanNess, dau. of
Peter VanNess and Sally Ann VanHouten; Hester/Hettie m.
#2, Peter F. Ryerson and moved to Virginia
--1850 Census, p.94&95, Caldwell Twp: Peter Jacobus, age
40, farmer; Eliza Ann, age 43; James O., age 15, farmer; 7
other Jacobus children; Daniel Vanderhoof, age 21, farmer
--1850 Census, p.95, Caldwell Twp: Peter Vanness, age 28,
shoemaker; Sally Ann, age 37; Hetty Ann, age 14; 6 other
Vanness children; Henry T. Vanness, age 76, farmer
--1860 Census, p.120 Caldwell: Jas. O. Jacobus, age 25,
clerk; Hetty A., age 24; Marcus J., age 1
--1870 Census, p.109, Caldwell: Hetty A. Jacobus, age 33;
Lewis P., age 8; Sarah A., age 6; Jacob Vanness, age 21,

cigar maker; Albert Campbell, age 16, works at tobacco factory

Children of James O. Jacobus and Hetty Ann VanNess:
Marcus I., b. 1858; d. 1861
Lewis P., b. 1862; d. 1929 (bur. Bothell Pioneer Cem. Bothell, WA)
Sarah A., b. abt 1864

- - - - -

Jacobus, **JOHN R.**   b. (abt. 1783)
(gmnj) (photo)   d. September 8, 1835
(NJ Will 12604G.1835)

John R. Jacobus
died September 8, 1835
in his 52nd year

wife, **SALLY** (Stiles)   b. (abt. July 21, 1789)
(gmnj)   d. October 26, 1856

Sally
wite of John R. Jacobus
died October 26, 1856
aged 67.3.5

daughter, **MARY JANE**   b. (abt. February 14, 1812)
(gmnj)   d. July 19, 1815

Mary Jane
daughter of John R. Jacobus
died July 19, 1815

aged 5.5.5

daughter, **MARY JANE**   b. (abt. November 12, 1815)
(gmnj)   d. October 1, 1817

Mary Jane
daughter of John R. Jacobus
died October 1, 1817
aged 1.10.19

son, **RALPH**   b. (abt. March 2, 1813)
(gmnj)   d. July 20, 1815

Ralph
son of John R. Jacobus
deid July 20, 1815
aged 2.4.18

Notes:
--John R. Jacobus, son of Roelof Jacobus and Elizabeth
'Lernes'
--John m. Sarah 'Sally' Stiles
--1850 Census, p.88, Caldwell Twp: Sarah Jacobus, age 60;
Emma Jacobus, age 16

Children of John R. Jacobus and Sarah Stiles:
Mary Jane, b. 1812; d. 1815
Ralph, b. 1813; d. 1815
Mary Jane, b. 1815; d. 1817
Sarah C., m. Henry Vanderhoof

- - - - -

Jacobus, **PETER**   b. (abt. August 5, 1760)
(gmnj) (njhs) (photo)   d. October 8, 1830

Peter Jacobus
died
Oct. 8th 1830
aged 70 years.
1 month
& 23 days

wife, **SARAH** (Gould)   b. (abt. July 30. 1765)
(gmnj) (njhs) (photo)   d. March 1, 1846

Sarah
wife of
Peter Jacobus
died
March 1st 1846
aged 80 years. 7 months
& 11 days

Notes:
--Peter, son of Peter Jacobus and Leah VanRiper
--Peter m. Sarah Gould, dau. of Joseph Gould, q.v., and
Rebecca Paxton

Children of Peter Jacobus and Sarah Gould:
Jane, b. October 18, 1792; bapt. November 11, 1792, Old
    Dutch Church, Totowa.

- - - - -

Jacobus, Peter D.   b. (June 3, 1770)
                                     d. (bef. 1830)

wife, **RACHEL** (Egberts)   b. (abt. 1775)
(gmnj) (njhs)   d. January 15, 1832

Rachel
wife of
Peter D. Jacobus
died Jan. 15th 1832
in her 57th year

son, **RICHARD**   b. (abt. 1792
(gmnj) (njhs) (photo)   d. November 22, 1797

Richard
Son of Peter
and Rachel Jacobus
he died November 22d, 1797
aged 5 years

There remembered therefore a rest
to the people of God
(Heb. 4:9)

Notes:
--Peter D. Jacobus, son of Derrick Jacobus and Sarah Stager
--Peter m. December 1, 1791, Rachel Egberts

Children of Peter D. Jacobus and Rachel Egberts:
Richard, b. 1797;d. February 1, 1886 Newark. Age 88.4.7

- - - - -

Jacobus, **WILLIAM G.**　　b. (abt. August 8, 1795)
(gmnj) (njhs) (photo)　　　　d. April 8, 1840
　　　　　　　　　　　　　　(also at Canfield/Cedar Grove Cem)

William G. Jacobus
died
April 8th 1840
aged 44 years & 8 months
and 20 days

wife, Margaret (Speer)　　b. (abt. 1802)
　　　　　　　　　　　　　d. (May 15, 1864)
　　　　　　　　　　　　　(bur.Canfield/Cedar Grove Cem)

son, **JOHN G.**　　　　　b. (abt. 1839)
(gmnj) (njhs) (photo)　　　d. January 13, 1843
　　　　　　　　　　　　　(also at Canfield/Cedar Grove Cem)

John G
son of William G.
and Margaret Jacobus
died Jan. 13th 1843
aged 4 years

son, Cyrus F.　　　　　　b. (abt. 1824)
　　　　　　　　　　　　　d. (January 22, 1863)
　　　　　　　　　　　　　(bur. Canfield/Cedar Grove Cem.)

Notes:

--family also recorded at Cedar Grove Cemetery; stone standing in 1993

--1850 Census, p.74, Caldwell Twp: Margaret Jacobus, age 48; Cyrus F., age 25, wood turner; Cornelius H. age 21, wood turner; Sarah C., age 19; Peter N., age 17, wood turner; Rebecca, age 14; Cornlia Brockaway, age 7; all b. NJ

--1860 Census, p.114, Caldwell Twp: Cyrus F. Jacobus, age 34, turner; Margaret, age 58; Rebecca, age 23; William G., age 19, laborer

Children of William G. Jacobus and Margaret .....:
Cyrus F., b. 1824; d. 1863; m. Mary .....
Cornelius H., b. abt. 1827; d. 1862
Sarah C., b. abt. 1831
Peter N., b. abt. 1833; m. Ottilie E. .....
Rebecca, b. abt 1836
John G., b. 1839; d. 1843
William G., b. abt. 1841

- - - - -

KENT

Kent, **CALVIN**   b. (abt. May 10, 1791)
(gmnj) (photo)   d. May 2, 1859
(NJ Will 15237G. 1859)

Calvin Kent
Died May 2, 1859
aged 58 years. 11 months
and 22 days

wife, Melinda (Williams)   b. (February 28, 1805)
(photo)   d. (April 6, 1874)
                             (bur. Prospect Hill Cemetery)

Notes:
Served: War of 1812, pvt., Columbian Volunteers (militia)
--Calvin, son of Jacob Kent, q.v., and Keziah Dodd
--Calvin m. July 1, 1821, Melinda Williams, dau. of Joseph
Williams and Mary Kent
--1850 Census, p.85, Caldwell Twp: Belinda Kent, age 45;
Calvin Kent, age 49, farmer; Marcus C., age 20, shoemaker;
Ira M., age 29, shoemaker; Sarah age 25; all b. NJ
--1860 Census, p.114, Caldwell: Belinda Kent, age 55;
Marcus C., age 29, shoemaker; Mary L.,a ge 28; Emma J.,
age 7; George A., age 4; Calvin W., age 1; all b. NJ
--1870 Census, p.130, Caldwell: Belinda Kent, age 65

Children of Calvin Kent and Belinda Williams:
Ira Miles, q.v., b. 1824; d. 1888; m. Sarah Ann Corby
Arza Nelson, b. 1826; m. 1846, Esther Day
        m. 1858, Sarah Jane Anderson
Marcus Calvin, b. 1830; m. 1851, Mary Louisa Condit

- - - - -

Kent, David   b.
                             d.

wife, **MARY** (Freeman?)   b. (abt. 1759)
(gmnj)   d. July 7, 1817

Mary

wife of David Kent
died July 7th 1817
in the 58th year
of her age

daughter, **ELIZABETH**   b. (abt. 1783)
(gmnj) (njhs)   d. April 15, 1812

In Memory
of Elizabeth
daughter of David &
Mary Kent who departed
this life April 15th, 1812
in the 29th Year of
her age

My tender parents kind and dear
I bid farewell to you:
Tho'nature feels, and I can find
'Tis hard to say adieu
But no not weep, or grieve for me;
You know I must go home;
I was upon a visit here
And now I must return.

Notes:

Children of David Kent and Mary (Freeman?)
Elizabeth, b. 1783; d. 1812
Ann, m. June 1821, Ira D. Corby

- - - - -

Kent, Ira Miles

b. (1824)
d. (January 31, 1888)
in his 67th yr.
(bur. Prospect Hill Cemetery)

wife, **SARAH ANN** (Corby)
(gmnj) (photo)

b. (abt. 1825
d. September 1, 1861

Sarah M.
Wife of
Ira M. Kent
Died
September 1, 1861
aged 37 years

Notes:
--Ira, son of Calvin Kent, q.v.
--Sarah Ann, dau. of Peter Corby and Catherine .....
--1850 Census, p.85, Caldwell Twp: Belinda Kent, age 45;
Calvin Kent, age 49, farmer; Marcus C., age 20, shoemaker;
Ira M., age 29, shoemaker; Sarah age 25; all b. NJ
--1860 Census, p.96, Caldwell: Ira M. Kent, age 38,
shoemaker; Sarah A., age 34
--1870 Census, p.115, Caldwell: John Williams, age 65, farm
labor; Ira Kent, age 49, farm labor; Ann Kent, age 45; Calvin
Kent, age 5; David H. Woodruff, age 21, cigar maker;
Wilbur E. Wodruff, age 13, works on r.r.
--1880 Census, p.405.2, Caldwell: Emmons B. Kent, age 33,
teamster; Sarah J., age 34; Arza N. age 4; Sarah J., 48,
mother, widow; Lizzie, age 16, sister, single; Ira M., age 58,
father's brother, widower, farm laborer

Children of Ira Miles Kent and Sarah Ann Corby:
Calvin, b. abt. 1865

- - - - -

Kent, **JACOB**   b. (October 1, 1753)
(gmnj) (njhs) (lgl)   d. June 3, 1841

*Sacred
To the memory of
Jacob Kent
a soldier of the revolution
a man of strict integrity
an affectionate Husband and
the Father of a numerous family.
He died in the hope of Heaven
greatly regretted. June 3rd
A.D. 1841. 85 years
A soldier true and brace
Firm in the truth and right
Dishonor touches not his grave
He wears a crown of light*

first wife, **EFFIE EDWARDS** b. (abt. 1751)
(gmnj) (njhs)   d. 1797

*Effie Edwards
wife of
Jacob Kent
died A.D. 1797
aged 45 years*

second wife, **KEZIAH DODD**
(gmnj) (njhs)   b. (abt. May 17, 1776)
d. May 20, 1842

Keziah Dodd
his second wife
died May 20th 1842
aged 66 years & 3 days

Notes:
Served: Revolutionary War
--Jacob Kent, son of Simeon Kent and Maritje Speer
--Jacob m. #1, Effie Edwards, dau. of Jacob Edwards and
Effie Speer; m. #2, Keziah Dodd, dau. of Jesse Dodd and
Abigail Perry.
--Jacob and Effie "had thirteen children. After Effie's death
Jacob married Keziah Dodd and had eight more. "

Children of Jacob Kent and Effie Edwards:
Rachel J., b. abt. 1776, m. William Perry
Sarah, b. 1777; d.1829; m. Rynier VanGiesen, q.v.
Elias, b. 1778; m. Ruth Williams
Mary, b. 1780; m. Joseph Williams, q.v.
Jacob, b. 1783; m. 1803, Polly VanGiesen
Effie, b. 1783; d. 1800; m. John Turner
Phebe, b. abt 1784; m. Uriah Garrabrant
Elizabeth, b. 1785; m. David Silas Baldwin
Levi, b. 1787; m. Rachel Egberts
Lydia, b. abt 1788
Aaron, b. 1789; m. Elizabeth Egberts
Joseph

Children of Jacob Kent and Keziah Dodd:
Abigail, b. 1798; m. John Ricker
Jane, b. 1799; m. Frederick Hopler
Calvin, b. 1800; m. Belinda Williams
Nancy, b. abt 1809; d. abt. 1816
Margaret, b. abt. 1810; m. Israel Brundage Corby, q.v.; she
    m. #2, his brother, Ezekiel Leonard Corby
Simon, b. 1813; m. Delilah Day
Keziah, m. John Fountain
Lucinda, m. Joseph Wyman

- - - - -

KIRKER

Kirker, **CHARLES P.**   b. (abt. 1830)
(gmnj)   d. February 7, 1852

Charles P. Kirker
died February 7, 1852
in his 22nd year

Notes:
--Charles, son of William? H. Kirker and Eliza .....
--?1850 Census, p.81, Caldwell Twp: William H. Kirker, age
45, b. NY, shoemaker; Eliza, age 45 b. NJ; Benjamin, age
19, farmer, b. NJ

- - - - -

LOCKWARD

LOCKWARD

Lockward, **JOHN T. Dr.**   b. (October 3, 1808)
(gmnj) (njhs) (lgl)   d. January 24, 1843
(NJ Inv. #13279G, 1843)

Doc. John T. Lockward
died
Jan. 24th 1843
in his 35th year

wife, Charlotte Williams (Personett)
(see Calvin G. Backus)   b. (January 15, 1817)
                              d. (October 3, 1905)
                              (bur. Prospect Hill Cemetery)

Notes:
--John T. Lockward, grad. Maryland State Medical College
--John Townley Lockward, son of James Lockward and
Abigail Fairchild
--John m. December 5, 1835, Charlotte Williams Personett,
dau. of Abram D. Personett and Joanna Williams
--Charlotte m. #2, Calvin G. Backus, q.v.
--1840 Census, p.8, Caldwell Twp: John T. Lockward
--1841: John purchased the village property of Zenas C.
Crane

Children of John Townley Lockward and Charlotte Williams
Personett:
Lewis Grover, b. 1839 d. 1913;m.Anna Maria Gibson Crane
        father of Lynn Grover Lockward. (bur. Prospect Hill Cemetery)
Harriet Louise, b. 1841 d. 1914; m.Melancthon H. Courter

(bur. Prospect Hill Cemetery)

- - - - -

LOW

Low, **CORNELIUS** b. (abt. October 15, 1788)
(gmnj)   d. May 2, 1860
(NJ Will 15368G.1860)

Cornelius Low
died May 2, 1860
aged 71.6.17

wife, **ELLEN** b. July 11, 1791
(gmnj) (photo)   d. December 23, 1861

Ellen
wife of
Cornelius Low
born July 11, 1791
died December 23, 1861

daughter, **MARY JANE** b. (abt. October 27, 1811)
(gmnj) (njhs)   d. November 29, 1833

Mary Jane
died Nov. 29th 1833
aged 22 yrs. 1 mos.
& 2 d's
Daughters of

Cornelius & Ellen Low

son, **JOHN**   b. (abt. September 20, 1817)
(gmnj) (njhs)   d. July 17, 1833

John. son of
Cornelius & Ellen Low
died July 17th 1833
aged 15 years. 9 months & 27 days

daughter, **ELLEN**   b. (abt. August 3, 1830)
(gmnj) (njhs) (photo)   d. February 17, 1850

In
Memory of
Ellen
who died Feb. 17th 1850
aged 19 years. 6 months
& 14 days

Daughters of
Cornelius & Ellen Low

Notes:
--1850 Census, p.81, Caldwell Twp: Cornelius Lowe, age 60,
farmer, b. NJ; Ellen, age 59, b. NJ; adj. to Abraham Lowe,
age 37 b. NJ, shoemaker; Sarah, Ann, age 38, b. NY and 4
children

Children of Cornelius Low and Ellen .....:
Mary Jane, b. 1811; d. 1833
Abraham, b. abt. 1813; m. Sarah Ann .....

John, b. 1818; d. 1833
Eliza, b. 1819; d. 1898; m. Cornelius H. Jacobus
Ann, b. abt 1823
Cornelius 'Nelson', b. abt 1825
Ellen, b. 1830; d. 1850

- - - - -

MAHON

Mahon, John   b. (1804)
                                d. (1885)
                                (bur. Prospect Hill Cemetery)

first wife, **ELIZA**   b. (abt. 1804)
(gmnj) (njhs)   d. June 30, 1839

Eliza
wife of
John Mahon
died June 30th 1839
in her 35th year

Notes:
--John m. #1, Eliza .....; m. #2, Nancy Agnes Menish (bur. Prospect Hill Cemetery)
--1850 Census, p.131, Belleville Twp., Essex Co., NJ: John Mahon, age 46 b. NY, gardener; Nancy, age 27, b. NJ; no children listed
--1860 Census, p.99, Caldwell: John 'Mahan', age 55, b. NY, segar maker; Nancy, age 38, b. NJ; Elizabeth, age 17; Hannah, age 15; Elmira, age 12; John, age 10; Sarah, age 7;

Clara, age 5; Horatio, age 2; all children b. NJ (adj. to Calvin
G. Backus)
--1870 Census, p.124, Caldwell: John Mahon, age 65,
gardener; Agnes, age 50; Anna P., age 24, seamstress; john
Jr. age 20, house painter; Sarah, age 17, works at tobacco
factory; Clara, age 14; Horatio, age 12; Josephine, age 12; all
b. NJ
--1880 Census, p.420.2, Caldwell Twp: John Mahon, age 75,
gardener; Nancy, age 60; Elizabeth, age 35; Sarah, age 22,
seamstress; Clara, age 20, seamstress; John, age 29, painter;
Horatio, age 21, segar maker; James Fraser Mahon, age 16,
adopted son; all b. NJ

Children of John Mahon and Nancy Agnes Menish:
Elizabeth, b. abt. 1843
Hannah, b. abt. 1845
Elmira, b. abt. 1848
John, b. 1849; m. abt. 1880, Mary Elizabeth Mead
Sarah, b. 1852 d. 1940. (bur. Prospect Hill Cemetery)
Clara, b. abt. 1855
Horatio, b. 1858 d 1911 (bur. Prospect Hill Cemetery); m. Annie
Josephine, b. 1861 d 1949 (bur. Prospect Hill Cemetery)
James Fraser, adopted, b. abt. 1864

- - - - -

MANN

Mann, John J.   b. (abt. 1830)
(photo)   d. (June 24, 1868)
Civil War. Co.D. 26 NJ Inf.   (bur. Prospect Hill Cemetery)

first wife, **LUCETTA G.** (Mead)
(gmnj)   b. (abt. December 25, 1828)
                                d. August 5, 1862

Lucetta G.
wife of John J. Mann
died August 5, 1862
aged 33.7.11

son, **WALTER S.**   b. (abt. June 4, 1853)
(gmnj)   d. December 18, 1856

Walter S.
son of John J. Mann
died December 18, 1856
aged 3.6.14

son, **WILLIE M.**   b. (abt. August 3, 1858)
(gmnj) (photo)   d. January 3, 1862

Willie M.
son of John J. Mann
died January 3, 1862
aged 3.5.0

Notes:
--John J. Mann, son of Charles Mann and Julia
--Lucetta, daughter of John Mead, q.v., and Maria
Courter
--John J. Mann m. #2, Dec. 23, 1863, Martha N. Lyon
He was age 30, widowed, son of Charles Mann and Julia

--1850 Census, p.84, Caldwell Twp: John J. Mann, age 20, b. NJ, carpenter; at res. of Jared Beach, q.v.

--1860 Census, p.101, Caldwell: John Mann, age 29, b. NJ, carpenter; Lucetta, age 30; Willie B., age 1; John Jacobus, age 17, apprentice; all b. NJ

Children of John J. Mann and Lucetta G. Mead:
Walter S., b. 1853; d. 1856
Willie M., b. 1858; d. 1862

Child of John J. Mann and Martha:
George H. b. 1867

- - - - -

MARTIN

Martin, **ENOS Esq.** b. (May 13, 1763)
(gmnj) (njhs) (lgl) (photo) d. September 1, 1810
(NJ Will #10635G)

*In Memory of
Enos Martin, Esq.
who departed this
life Sept. 1st, 1810
aged 47 years.
3 months & 20 days*

wife, **JANE** (Personett) b. (March 23, 1761)
(gmnj) (njhs) (lgl) d. May 4, 1816

*Jane. Consort of
Enos Martin, Esq.*

died May 4th 1816
aged 56 years. 1 month
and 11 days

daughter, **ELIZABETH**   b. (abt. 1793)
(gmnj)   d. March 8, 1859

Elizabeth
daughter of
Enos Martin, Esq
died March 8, 1859
in her 67th year

Notes:
Served: Revolutionary War; Essex Co. Militia
Served: Justice of the Peace
--Enos, son of Jeremiah Martin and Elizabeth Pierson
--Jane, dau. of George Personett, Esq., q.v., and Mary Condit

Children of Enos Martin, Esq. and Jane Personett:
Charlotte 'Martha', b. abt. 1785; d. 1851; m. #1, Matthew
    Dodd, son of Nathaniel Dodd and Ruth Condit; m.
    #2, John Hartley, q.v.
George Personett, Esq., q.v., b. 1787; d. 1876;m. #1, Rhoda
    Riker; m. #2, Euphemia Bowman; m. #3, Susan
    Henrietta Dodd
Nancy, b. bef. 1790; d. bef. 1840; m. Ephraim Leonard
    (1771-1843) d. Newark, NJ
Calvin, b. 1790; d. 1879; m. Phebe Crane (bur. Rosedale
    Cemetery, Orange NJ)
Elizabeth, b. abt. 1793; d. 1859

Maria, b. abt. 1796; d. bef. 1840; m. Cyrus Harrison
    (1797-1873)
Dorinda, b. 1801; d. 1855; m. Benjamin Condit (1796-1855)
Lydia, b. abt. 1803; d. 1878; m. Elihu Baldwin (?see Fairmont
    Cemetery, Newark)

- - - - -

Martin, George Personett, Esq.b. (December 3, 1787)
(NJ Will #18864G,1876)   d. (June 13, 1876)
                              (bur. Prospect Hill Cemetery)

first wife, **RHODA** (Riker)   b. (January 12, 1788)
(gmnj) (njhs) (lgl) (photo)   d. June 22, 1833

> *Rhoda*
> *wife of*
> *G. P. Martin*
> *died June 22nd 1833*
> *in her 45th year*

second wife, **EUPHEMIA** (Bowman)
(gmnj) (njhs) (lgl) (photo)   b. (abt. 1800)
                                   d. September 24, 1837

> *Euphemia*
> *wife of*
> *G. P. Martin*
> *died Sept. 24, 1837*
> *in her 37th year*

third wife, Susan Henrietta (Dodd)

b. (March 10, 1803)
d. (November 22, 1891)
(bur. Hillside Cemetery,
Hillside, Union Co., NJ)

son, **HALSEY M.**
(gmnj) (photo)

b. (abt. 1822)
d. August 29. 1861

Halsey M.
son of George P. Martin
died August 29, 1861
agd 40 years

Notes:
--Elder, First Presbyterian Church, Caldwell
--George, son of Enos Martin Esq., q.v., and Jane Personett.
--George m. #1, 1809, Rhoda Riker, dau. of Peter I. Riker
and Martha Corby; m. #2, 1834, Euphemia Bowman; m. #3,
1840, Susan Henrietta Dodd, dau. of Abner Dodd and
Hannah Gould
--1850 Census, p.73A, Caldwell Twp: George P. Martin,age
61, farmer; Susan H., age 47; Henrietta Bowman, age 21; all
b. NJ
--1860 Census, p.117B, Caldwell: George P. Martin, age 75,
farmer; Susan H., age 56; Henrietta, age 30; Charlotte
'Hanlon'. age 13
--1870 Census, p.134A, Caldwell Twp: George P. Martin,
age 82; Susan H., age 67; Henrietta Bowman, age 42, no
occup; (dau. of George W. Bowman)

Children of George Personett Martin, Esq. and Rhoda Riker:

Mary A., b. abt. 1810; d. 1881; m. Zenas Comstock
(1801-1877), Springfield, NJ
Jane, b.1812; d. 1840; m. Timothy Ward Crane (1811-1878)
(bur. Vail Memorial Cem. Morris Co. NJ)
Enos Wilson, b. 1816; d. 1887; m. Eleanor Stiles Crane (bur.
Prospect Hill Cemetery)
Marcus Ward, b. 1818; d. 1896; m. #1, 1841, Adeline M.
Crane, dau. of William C. Crane, q.v.;
m. #2, Mary Eveline Condit Perine (d. Arizona)
Halsey Munson, b. 1822; d. 1831
Enos Wilson, b. 1826; d. 1887; m. Ellenor S. Crane; (bur.
Prospect Hill Cemetery)

- - - - -

MASEKER
Masker, Massacher

Maseker, Peter	b. (abt. 1785) d. (abt. 1847)
first wife, Lydia Jacobus	b. (abt. 1785) d.
second wife, Hester Spier	b. d.
third wife, Mary (Kent)	b. (abt. 1795) d. (1875)
daughter, **HARRIET**	b. (abt. July 10, 1834)

(gmnj) (njhs) (photo)   d. December 1, 1844

Harriet
daughter of
Peter & Mary Maseker
died Dec. 1st 1844
aged 10 years. 4 months
& 21 days

Notes:
--Peter, son of John Maseker and Anna; three marriages (?)
m. #1, 1805, Lydia Jacobus; m. #2, Hester Spier; m. #3, abt.
1818, Mary Kent
--Will of Peter Masker: Probate 1847: names wife Mary;
children: Henry; Sarah,wife of Andrew Wanamaker; David
(Daniel?); Letty, wife of Abraham Vanderhoof; James;
Margaret Ann,wife of Hamilton Ellis; Mary; Executors:
Stephen Personett and wife, Mary.
--1835 Caldwell Presb. Church catalogue: Peter and Mary
Massaker had baptized: Sarah; Daniel (David?); Lettee;
James and Margaret Ann; no ages listed
--1850 Census, p.88, Caldwell Twp: Mary Masker, age 55;
Mary, age 10
--1860 Census, p.103&104, Caldwell: Peter E. Jacobus,age
30, mason; Mary, age 23; Mary E., age 5; Roswell E., age 3;
George L., age 9 mos.; Mary Masker, age 65
--1870 Census, p.126, Caldwell: Peter E. Jacobus, age 40,
brick mason; Mary age 33; Roswell E., age 13; George L.
age 10; Hattie F., age 5; Ariella age 2; Mary Masker, age 76

Children of Peter Maseker:
Henry P. b. abt. 1810

Sarah, b. 1819; d. 1880; m. Andrew Wanamaker
Daniel K., b. abt. 1818
Letty, b. abt 1820; m. abt. 1840, Abraham Corn. Vanderhoof
James b. abt. 1830
Margaret Ann, b. abt. 1830; m. 1845, Hampton Lyle Ellis
Harriet, b. 1834; d. 1844
Mary, b. 1837; m. Peter Edward Jacobus

- - - - -

MC CHESNEY

McChesney, John

b. (July 15, 1814)
d. (March 16, 1883)
(bur. Prospect Hill Cemetery)

first wife, **SARAH FORDHAM** (Crane)
(gmnj) (Prospect Hill photo)

b. (September 16, 1814)
d. May 13, 1862
(& bur. Prospect Hill Cemetery)

Sarah Fordham
wife of John McChesney
daughter of Timothy and Margaret Crane
died May 13, 1862
in her 48th year

son, **CHARLES PITTMAN**
(gmnj) (no date)

b. (abt. 1848)
d. (Aug. 7, 1857)

son, **SAMUEL**   b. (December 27, 1849)

(gmnj) (no date)   d. (bef. 1870)

daughter, **SARAH N.** b. (November 1852)
(gmnj) (no date)   d. (November 1852))

(children: one stone, no dates)

Notes:
--John, son of Robert B. McChesney of Monmouth Co. NJ
--John m. #1, Sarah Fordham Crane, dau. of Timothy Crane
and Margaret Francisco; m. #2, 1867, Eliza A. Williams.
daughter of Daniel Williams, granddaughter of Jeniah
Williams, q.v.
--1850 Census, p.83, Caldwell Twp: John McChesney age
36, harness maker; Sarah F., age 35; Lydia Ann, age 11;
Emily D., age 9; Hannah M., age 6; Jacob B., age 5; John J.,
age 4; Charles P., age 2; Samuel, age 5 months
--1860 Census, p.102, Caldwell: Jno. McChesney, age 45,
county clerk; Sarah, age 45; Lydia A., age 21; Emily D., age
19; Hannah M., age 17; Jacob, age 16; John J., age 14;
Samuel, age 10; Sarah J., age 6; Justus A., age 4
--1870 Census, p.113, Caldwell: John "McCluney" age 55,
no occupation; Eliza A., age 39; Jacob B., age 25; Sarah J.,
age 15; Justus B., age 13; Lydia A. Courter, age 32,
dressmaker
--1880 Census, p.399B, Caldwell: John McChesney, age 65,
b. NJ, justice of the peace; Eliza A., age 52 b. NJ; Lydia A.,
dau., widow, age 41, b. NJ, dressmaker; Nettie, age 26;
Justus B., son, age 23, b. NJ

Children of John McChesney and Sarah Fordham Crane:
Lydia Ann, b. 1838 d 1889; m. Richard Henry Courter

Emily D., b. abt 1841
Hannah M., b. abt 1843
Jacob Beach, b. abt 1845; aft. 1880; m. Eugenia C. .....
John J., b.1846, d. 1912; m. #1, Eliza A. Williams;
    m.#2, Catherine J. Bush (1848-1873); m. #3, Caroline
    Bush (1851-1933) (see Prospect Hill Cemetery)
Charles Pittman, b. abt 1848; d. August 7, 1857, age 10
Samuel, b. abt. 1850; d. bef. 1870
Sarah N., b. Nov. 1852; d. Nov. 1852; age 0
Sarah J., b. abt. 1854
Justus B., b. abt. 1856; m. Marie Bond (bur. Prospect Hill)
William H., b. 1869; d. 1950 (bur. Prospect Hill Cemetery)
Nettie,

- - - - -

MEAD

Mead, John   b. (abt. 1802)
                          d. (October 13, 1882)

first wife, Maria   b. (September 30, 1805)
                          d. (August 5, 1862)

daughter, **ARMINDA C.**   b (abt. June 3, 1843)
(gmnj)   d. February 4, 1861

Arminda C.
daughter of John Mead
died February 3, 1861
aged 17.8.0

son, **WILLIAM J.**   b. (abt. July 30, 1837)
(gmnj)   d. July 14, 1858

William J.
son of John Mead
died July 14, 1858
aged 20.11.14

Notes:

--John, son of John Mead and Sarah Dodd;
   m. Maria, dau. of John E. Courter and Sophia
   Jacobus; m. #2, Ann .....
--1850 Census, p.85&86, Caldwell Twp: John Mead, age 48,
farmer; Mariah, age 45; Lucetta, age 21; William J., age 12;
'Amanda' age 7; Henry Courter, age 33, shoemaker;
Nicholas McClue, age 50, shoemaker
--1860 Census, p.104&104, Caldwell: John Mead, age 56;
Maria, age 53; Amanda C., age 17;
--1870 Census, p.124, Caldwell: John Mead age 67,
shoemaker; Maria, age 63; Martin Riker, age 23, cigar
maker; Maggie A., Riker, age 19
--1880 Census, p.430.4, Caldwell: John Mead, age 77; Ann,
age 72, b. England

Children of John Mead and Maria .....:
Lucetta G., b. 1828; m. John J. Mann, q.v.
?Levi, b. abt. 1829; d. 1871, Paterson
William J., b. 1837; d. 1858
Arminda C., b. 1843; d. 1861

- - - - -

MESLER

Mesler, Abraham   b. (abt. 1822)
                             d. (April 28, 1882)

wife, **SARAH WILLIAMS** b. (August 11, 1824)
(gmnj)   d. May 14, 1860

Sarah Williams
wife of Abraham Mesler
died May 14, 1860
aged 34.9.3

Notes:
--Abraham m. November 28, 1840, Sarah Williams; dau. of
Joseph Williams, q.v,
--1850 Census, p.105, Livingston Twp: Abraham Mesler age
29, farmer; Sarah, age 24; Mary, age 9; Joseph, age 6;
Parmelia, age 4; John G., age 1
--1860 Census, p.194, Livingston Twp. Abraham Mesler, age
38, farmer; Mary, age 19; Joseph A., age 16; Amelia, age 4;
John, age 11
--1870 Census, p.239, Livingston Twp: Abraham Messler,
age 49, farmer; Joseph, age 26, horse dealer; John, age 21,
farm labor; Simeon T. Sayre, age 26; Mary Sayre, age 29;
Gracie Sayre, age 8 months

Children of Abraham Mesler and Sarah Williams:
Mary, b. 1841; d. 1909; m. Simeon Thompson Sayre, b.
    1844; d. 1912
Joseph Abraham, b. 1844; d. 1926; m. Lavinia Phebe
    Williams (bur. Prospect Hill Cemetery)

Parmelia, b. 1845
John G., b. 1849; d. 1925 (bur. Prospect Hill Cemetery)

- - - - -

MILLER

Miller, Benjamin C.   b. (December 10, 1802)
                              d. (March 8, 1900)
                              (bur. Mount Pleasant Cem. Newark)

wife, Sally (Doremus)   b. (August 24, 1806)
                              d. (November 28, 1892)
                              (bur. Mount Pleasant Cem. Newark)

son, **WILLIAM HENRY**   b. (abt. April 14, 1825)
(njhs)   d. April 26, 1828

William Henry
son of
Benjamin C.
& Sally Miller
died April 26th 1828
aged 3 yrs & 12 d's

Notes:
--Benjamin m. September 25, 1824, Sarah Doremus, dau. of
Simeon Doremus and Jane Dey
--Benjamin C. Miller was Secretary of the Mutual Benefit
Life Ins. Co.; later he was Treasurer
--1847: Mrs. Sarah Miller, of Benj. C. Miller was an
incorporator of the Newark Orphans Asylum Assoc.

--1850 Census, p.132, East Ward, Newark: B. C. Miller, age 47, secretary,insurance co.; Sarah,age 43; Phebe J., age 20; 1 servant

--1860 Census, p.457, 4Wd, Newark: Benjn C. Miller, age 54, secy. life ins. co.; Sarah, age "5"; Phebe J. Vansickle, age 39; Peter D. Vansicle, age 30, patent roofer; Benjn, Vansickle, age 2; Benjn. C. Miller, Jr., age 10; Hannah E. Miller, age 35; 1 servant

--1870 Census, p.360 4Wd, Newark: Benj. C. Miller, age 60, treas. life ins. co.; Sarah age 60; ". W. Van Stickle", age 40, clerk; Phoba Van Stickle age 35; B. M. Van Stickle, age 12; Thos. D. VanStickle, age 6; Lloyd VanStickle, age 3; Benj. C. Miller, age 20, student; 2 servants

--1880 Census, p.261.1 Newark: Benjamin C. Miller, age 77, treas. life insurance co.; Sarah, age 73; Peter D. Vansickle age 50, insurance clerk; Phebe J. Vansickle, age 49; Benjamin M. Vansickle, age 22; Thomas D. Vansickle, age 16

Children of Benjamin C. Miller and Sarah .....:
William Henry, b. 1825; d. 1828
Phebe J., b. abt. 1830; m. Peter D. VanSickle
Benjamin C. Jr., b. abt 1850

- - - - -

Miller, **ISAAC SLOVER**   b. November 18, 1783
(gmnj) (njhs) (photo)   d. July 20, 1832
(NJ Will 12341G.Inv.1832)

Isaac Slover Miller
born Nov. 18th 1783

died July 20th 1832
aged 48 years. 8 mos. & 2 days

wife, **ELEANOR** (Voorhees) b. April 2, 1784
(gmnj) (njhs) (photo)   d. August 18, 1858

Eleanor Voorhees Miller
born Apr.2d. 1784
died Aug. 18th 1858
aged 74 years. 4 mos. & 16 days

daughter, **ELEANOR P.C.**   b. (abt. April 25, 1830)
(gmnj) (njhs)   d. February 5 1831

Eleanor P. C.
daughter of Isaac S. & E. Miller
died Feb. 5th 1831
aged 9 mos. & 11 days

Notes:
--Isaac, son of William Miller and Maria Slover
--Isaac m. January 19, 1809, Eleanor Voorhees, dau. of Peter
G. Voorhees and Maria Boice

Children of Isaac Slover Miller and Eleanor Voorhees:
Peter V., q.v., b. 1809; m. Electa Catherine Cochran
Grace Slover, b. 1812; m. 1832, James Richard Talmadge
Catherine Maria, b. 1814; m. Henry A. Raymond
Ezekiel, b. 1816; d. bef. April 1818
Ezekiel, b. 1818; m. Elizabeth Van Patten
Amelia, b. 1820; d. 1851
John Anderson, b. 1823; m. Sarah Jane Davis

Anna Voorhees, b. 1825; d. 1842
William Henry Stoothoff, b. 1827; m. Margaret S. Clark
Elenor Phebe Caroline, b. 1830; d. 1831
Isaac Slover, b. 1833; d. 1902

- - - - -

Miller, **PETER V.**   b. December 7, 1809
(gmnj)   d. October 28, 1854
(NJ Will 14579G. 1854)

Peter V. Miller
born December 7, 1809
died October 28. 1854
in his 45th year

wife, **ELECTA C.** (Cochran) b. March 18, 1809
(gmnj)   d. December 11, 1863

Electa C.
wife of Peter V. Miller
born March 18, 1809
died December 11, 1863

Notes:
--Peter V. Miller, son of Isaac Slover Miller, q.v., and
Eleanor Voorhees; m. Electa Catherine Cochran
--1860 Census, p.102, Caldwell: Electa C. Miller, age 51, b.
NJ; at res. of Joseph T. and Hester (her sister) Hopping

- - - - -

312

Miller, Philetas   b. (abt. 1767)
                           d.

wife, **JOANNAH** (Kitchell) b. (abt. 1771)
(gmnj) (njhs)   d. February 17, 1847

Joannah
wife of
Philetas Miller
died
Feb. 17th 1847
aged 76 years
& 1 month

Notes:
--Philetas (Philetus) P. Miller m. September 20, 1791,
Joanna Kitchell, dau. of Aaron Kitchell and Phebe Farrand
--(her father,Aaron Kitchell (1744-1820) served as New
Jersey Senator and Representative to the United States
Congress)

Children of Philetas P. Miller and Joanna Kitchell:
Phebe, b. abt. 1797
Elias, b. abt. 1799
Jemima, b. abt. 1801; m. Abraham Pierson, son of Caleb
        Pierson, q.v.)

- - - - -

MOORE

Moore, Daniel   b. (February 24, 1804)

d. (January 18, 1843)
(bur. Bloomfield Cemetery)

first wife, Jane Eliza (Stockholm)
(photo)   b.
d. (May 22, 1835)
(bur. Mount Hebron Cem. Montclair)
Plaque: "Remains of
Persons/removed from the
Churchyard Cemetery of the First
Methodist Episcopal Church of
Bloomfield. April 1926")

daughter, **ELLEN**   b. (abt. August 6, 1826)
(gmnj) (njhs) (lgl)   d. January 8, 1828

Ellen.
daughter of Daniel
& Jane Eliza Moore
died Jan. 8th 1828
aged 1 year. 5 months
& 2 days

Notes:
--Daniel, son of Samuel Martin Moore, q.v., and Hannah
Crane; m. November 19, 1825, Jane Elizabeth Stockholm
--Daniel m.#2, April 13, 1836, Adeline Harriet Cooley
--1850 Census, p.267, South Ward, Newark: Adaline H.
Moore, age 37; Sarah M., age 12; Emma E., age 8; Francis
D., age 21, carpenter; Edwin J., age 20, trimmer; all b. NJ
(Harriet not listed)

--1860 Census, p.778, 9Wd, Newark: Mrs. 'Adalade' Moore, age 45, widow; Emma Moor, age 18; at res. of James H. Woodhull and his wife, Adalade.

--1880 Census, p.577B, Livingston Twp: Wm. H. Harrison, age 38, farmer; Harriet A., age 40; Gertrude, age 2; Clair Bell, age 0; Adeline Moore, mother-in-law, widow, age 65, b. NJ

Children of Daniel Moore and Jane Elizabeth Stockholm:
Ellen, b. 1826; d. 1828
Francis D., b. abt. 1829
Edwin J., b. abt. 1830; d. bef. 1891

Children of Daniel Moore and Adeline Harriet Cooley:
Sarah Maria, b. abt. 1838; m. S. M. Walsh
Emma Elizabeth, b. abt. 1842; d. aft. 1891
Harriet Augusta, b. abt. 1843; d. 1912; m. William Henry
    Harrison (184-1935) (bur. Prospect Hill Cemetery)

- - - - -

Moore, **JOSEPH C., Rev.**   b. February 10, 1800
(gmnj) (njhs) (lgl)   d. June 25, 1844
(NJ Will 13368G. 1844)

Rev. Joseph Moore. whose remains rest beneath this stone was born in Caldwell Feb. 10th 1800. United with the Church in 1823. was licensed to preach the Gospel in 1832. was settled as Pastor in Clyde, New York one year; in Succasunna Plains, NJ three years in West Milford, NJ 8 years and died June 25th 1844. aged 44 years

Historical Memorial, Presbyterian Church, Succasunna, N.J.1765-1895. Dover, N.J.

"Rev. Joseph Moore began labor with this church April 17, 1836. He was born in Caldwell, N.J. February 10, 1800 and died there of consumption June 25, 1844. He married October 4, 1823, Miss Matilda Steele, and removed to Western New York and began business keeping a store. During several years he was impressed that he ought to preach the Gospel. His early advantages for education were limited, but he began the study of theology and was licensed and ordained by the New Jersey Presbytery. In April 1836 he began the supply of this Church and preached with great zeal and fervor. He labored here about two years (2 yrs. 6 mos.) and removed to West Milford, N.J. Failing health weakened him, and when he was not able to walk he was carried to the pulpit in order to speak truly, 'as a dying man to dying men'."

wife, Matilda Steele   b. (October 5, 1801)
                              d. (May 16, 1875)
                              (bur. Rosedale Cemetery
                              two monuments; one with
                              Harriet L. Moore 1819-1894)
                              (sister of Joseph Moore?)

Notes:

--Joseph Crane Moore, son of Samuel Martin Moore, q.v., and Hannah Crane; m. October 4, 1823, Matilda Steele, dau. of Josiah Steele, q.v., and Phebe Smith

--Matilda m. #2, Feb. 5, 1851, Sauk Co., Wisconsin, Daniel Pound (Daniel b. 1792, Middlesex Co. NJ; d. 1867 Boulder, Colorado; he m. #1, Sarah Webster; Daniel, "a successful merchant in Boulder"

--1850 Census, p.35, Prairie Du Sac, Sauk Co., Wisconsin: Daniel Pound, age 58, b. NJ, farmer; Elias Pound, age 22, b. PA; Mary A. Pound, age 15, b. PA; Moses Smith, age 38, b. NH, farmer; Lara Smith, age 39, b. NH

--1860 Census, p.92 Caldwell Twp: <u>Matilda Pound</u>, age 58, b. NJ; at res. of Zenas C. Crane and his wife, Mary H.
--1860 Census, p.170, Westmoreland Twp., Oneida Co., NY: Wm. A. Steele, age 53 b. NJ, shoemaker; Rachel, age 51, b. CT; "Wilstein I.", age 23, b. NY, shoemaker; Charles H., age 19 b. NY, shoemaker; George M., age 17, b. NY; Mary J., age 15 b. NY; Martha A., age 9; b. NY; <u>Matilda S. Moore</u>, age 59, b. NJ, relative
--1870 Census, p.147, 7Wd Newark: George D. Moore, age 47, b. NJ, surrogate; Justina M. Moore, age 40 b. OH; <u>Matilda</u>, age 68, b. NJ

- - - - -

Moore, **JOSHUA**   b. (abt. 1772)
(gmnj) (njhs) (lgl)   d. February 22, 1844

Joshua Moore
died
Feb. 22nd 1844
aged 72 years

wife, **PARNELLA** (Halsted) b. (abt. 1774)
(gmnj)   d. May 20, 1851

Parnella
wife of Joshua Moore
died May 20, 1851
In her 77th year

Notes:
--Joshua Moore m. February 22, 1801, 'Parney' Halsted

--1850 Census, p.84, Caldwell Twp: Justus A. 'Bennett' age 52, shoemaker; Phebe H., age 45; Anne M., age 22; Permilia Moore, age 75; Edward Reynolds age 10; John W. Taylor, age 21, school teacher

Children of Joshua Moore and Parnella Halsted:
Paulina, b. 1801; m.Sept. 9. 1822, Jonathan Provost, q.v.
Phebe H., b. m. 1805, Justus Allen Burnet

- - - - -

Moore, **SAMUEL** b. (July 3, 1762)
(gmnj) (njhs) (lgl) d. February 25th 1835
(NJ Will 12614G. Inv. 1835)

Samuel Moore
died Feb. 25th 1835
in the 73rd year
of his age

wife, **HANNAH** (Crane) b. (April 1, 1781)
(gmnj) (njhs) (lgl) d. May 18, 1844

Hannah
widow of
Samuel Moore dec'd
died May 18th 1844
in the 64th year
of her age

son, **FRANCIS** b. (March 16, 1802)
(gmnj) (njhs) (lgl) d. December 9, 1826

Francis Moore
died Dec. 9th 1826
in his 25th year

Notes:
--Samuel m. March 28, 1799, Hannah Crane, dau. of Joseph
Crane and Eunice Dodd
--Samuel was sexton of the church for many years.

Children of Samuel Moore and Hannah Crane:
Joseph Crane, q.v., b. 1800; m. Matilda Steele
Francis D., b. 1802; d. 1826
Daniel, q.v., b. 1804; m.#1, 1825, Jane Elizabeth Stockholm
    m. #2, 1836, Adeline Harriet Cooley
Stephen Conover, q.v., b. 1806, m. Rachel Crane
Archibald, b. 1808; m. 1832, Mary Carl..............
Nancy Crane, b. 1811; m. 1832, Henry L. Parsells
Martin S., b. 1813; m. 1834, Caroline O. Crane
Sarah Maria, b. 1816; m. 1833, Aaron Reuck;
    daughter? Harriet E. m. Henry Darcy Gould, son of
    Nathaniel M. Gould, q.v.
George DeGraw, b. 1822; d. 1891; m. #1,Justina Melrose
    Whitehead, d. 1887; daughter of Amanda Steele and
    Jonathan Whitehead; granddaughter of Josiah
    Steele, q.v.; m. #2, abt. 1891, Mary S. Fitch
    "received law degree, Union College, NC; frontier
    lawyer in Prairie du Sac, Wisconsin; than, Urbana,
    Ohio; returned to Newark; 1869-1879, Surrogate for
    Essex County, NJ; served on first Board of Directors
    of Prudential Life Insuance Co."

There were no children. His lengthy 1891 Will mentions many persons: e.g. sister, Harriet; nephews; nieces, etc.; $400 to Rosedale Cemetery at Orange "to keep my burial lot in order"; several Presbyterian charities; and for founding a Home for Aged Respectable People of both sexes, after death of sister, Harriet, $1,000. If he dies away from home, wishes his body brought back if possible at any expense and placed beside his wife, and if his body is not recovered that the vault be opened and the box I have had made containing our likenesses be placed in the grave as directed on the wrapper of the box."

- - - - -

Moore, **STEPHEN C.**   b. (October 5, 1806)
(gmnj) (njhs) (lgl) (photo)   d. November 10, 1835
(NJ Will 12716G. Inv.1836)

The Tomb
of
Stephen C. Moore
who departed this life
Nov. 10th 1835
in the 30th year
of his age

wife, Rachel (Crane)   b.
d.

son, **FRANCIS A.**   b. (July 6, 1828)
(gmnj) (njhs) (lgl)   d. February 15, 1829

Francis A. son of Stephen & Rachel Moore
died Feb. 15th 1829

aged 7 months & 9 days

Notes:

--Stephen Conover Moore, son of Samuel Moore, q.v., and Hannah Crane; m. October 10, 1827, Rachel Crane, dau. of Bethuel Crane and Abigail Harrison

Children of Stephen Conover Moore and Hannah Crane:
Aaron Nelson, d. bef. 1891
Francis A., b. 1828; d. 1829

- - - - -

MORRIS

Morris, Stephen A.   b.
                                d.

wife, **JANE** (Chitterling)   b. (abt. May 7, 1809)
(gmnj) (njhs) (lgl) (photo)   d. March 7, 1836

Jane
wife of
Stephen A. Morris
and daughter of John
& Rachel Chiterling
died March 7, 1836
aged 26 yrs.
and 10 months

Notes:

--Jane, daughter of John Chitterling and Rachel Bond (see William and Keturah Bond)

- - - - -

MOTT

Mott, **ANN**   b. (abt. August 20, 1778)
(gmnj)   d. October 9. 1853

Ann Mott
died October 9. 1853
aged 75.1.19
Beloved Mother

Notes:
--Ann Mott, mother of Caroline, wife of Thomas D. Gould, q.v.
--1850 Census, p.82, Caldwell Twp: Thomas D. Gould, age 65, farmer; Caroline, age 48; Adaline C., age 20; Stephen R., age 16, farmer; <u>Ann Mott, age 72</u>

- - - - -

MOWERSON

Mowerson, Aaron   b.
                             d.

wife, **PHEBE**   b. (abt. 1770)
(gmnj) (lgl)   d. December 24, 1857

Phebe
wife of Aaron Mowerson
died December 24, 1857
In her 87th year

Notes:
--Aaron, son of Jacob Mowerson and Margaret Kierstead
--Aaron m. March 14, 1790, Phebe 'Mowerson'
--?1850 Census, South Ward, Newark: Caroline "Morrison" age 40, b. NJ; Phebe "Morrison" age 78, b. NJ; Anna Reeves, age 25, b. NY

Children of Aaron Mowerson and Phebe:
Henry, bp. November 18, 1793, Montville Ref. Church
Anny, b. May 15, 1795, Montville Ref. Church Records

- - - - -

NESBIT
Nisbet

Nesbit, Hugh	b.
	d.
wife, Margaret	b.
	d.
daughter, **AMANDA**	b. (1809)
(gmnj) (njhs) (lgl)	d. January 30, 1810

Amanda
daughter of Hugh

and Margaret Nesbit
died Jan. 30th 1810
aged 6 months

Notes:

Children of Hugh Nesbit and Margaret.....:
Amanda, b. 1809; d. 1810

- - - - -

NICHOLS

Nichols, Pearson   b.
     d. (February 20, 1831)
     (d. his residence, Montreal)

wife, **CAROLINE** (Holmes) b. (abt. 1808)
(gmnj)   b. March 19, 1855

Caroline Nichols
died March 19 , 1855
aed 47 years

son, **HOLMES P.**   b. (abt. 1828)
(gmnj)   d. June 8, 1857

Holmes P. Nichols
son of Caroline Nichols
died June 8, 1857
aged 29 years

Notes:

--Caroline, daughter of Samuel Rathburn Holmes and Susan Banks, dau. of David Banks, q.v.; step-dau. of Stephen Gould Esq., q.v.

--Pearson Nichols, son of Hon. Moses Nichols, Esq.;Brig. General, (b.1740 MA; d. 1790; bur. Amherst, N.H) and Hannah Eaton; brother of Perkins Nichols, Esq.; grandson of Timothy Nichols and Hannah <u>Perkins</u>.

--"Married: at New York on the 15th instant, by the Rev. Dr. McAulay, Mr. Pearson Nichols, Merchant of this city to Miss Caroline Holmes, step-daughter of Stephen Gould, Esq. of New York" (Montreal Gazette. November 26, 1827)

--"Death: March 3, 1831. Montreal, Quebec, Canada: "at his residence, February 20, last Pierson Nichols, a merchant"

--Pearson Nichols "was a remarkably shrewd active man.... his operation in smuggling goods from the United States into Montreal...Nichols continued his smuggling to the last...." (History of the County of Huntingdon and of the Seigniories of Chateaugay and Beauharnois. Robert Sellar. Quebec. 1888)

Child of Pearson Nichols and Caroline Banks Holmes:
Holmes Pearson, b. abt. 1828, Canada d. June 9, 1857 NYC
     1850: Holmes P. Nichols, gentleman, b. Canada, age 20; William M. Gould, age 32, gentleman; arv. NY; via SS Haire

- - - - -

NORTHRUP

Northrup, John   b.

d.

wife, Margaret   b.
                      d.

son, **ELIAS**   b. (abt. November 5, 1824)
(gmnj) (njhs)   d. January 5, 1826

Elias
son of John
and Margaret Northrop
died Jan. 5th, 1826
aged
1 year. 2 months
&5 days

Notes:
--(?)Northrup family of Sussex Co., N.J.

- - - - -

OGDEN

Ogden, **DAVID**   b. (January 2, 1754)
(gmnj) (njhs) (lgl) (photo)   d. August 13, 1790
(NJ Will 7042-7047G.1790)

In Memory of
David Ogden He
died Augt. 13th, 1790
aged 36 years. 7
months & 11 days

Hear from the tomb the doleful sound
My ears attend the Cry
Ye living men come view the ground
Where you must shortly lie

Notes:
Served: Revolutionary War
--David, son of Samuel Ogden and Phebe Baldwin
WILL: Signed August 1790; Proved Oct. 1790: "Ogden, David, of Newark Twp., Will of: To brothers and sisters: Thomas Ogden (m. Jemima Wheeler), Swain Ogden (m.Mary...), Molly Dod (m. Adonijah Dod), Sarah Edison (m. John Edison), Susannah Williams (m. Enos Williams,q.v.), Hannah Bebout (m. William Bebout), Phebe Brundage (m. James Brundage), all real and personal estate. Brother John (m. Elizabeth Magie) is to have no share.
Executors: Joseph Harrison and Thomas Ogden
Witnesses: Joel Condit, Josiah Steele, Enos Williams
Note: brother Simeon, q.v., died April 1790, before David's will was written; brother Samuel died 1777;

- - - - -

Ogden, **JOHN**   b. (abt. January 17, 1736/37)
(gmnj) (njhs) (lgl) (photo)   d. April 27, 1797
(NJ Will 8948-8963G.1797)

In Memory of
John Ogden who
died April 27, 1797
Aged 60 Years
3 Months & 10 days

Cease fond Companion to deplore
Nor say your friend he is no more
For all their dust shall ye abide
And you shall meet him in the skies.

wife, **ELIZABETH** (Magie) b. (abt. September 11, 1745)
(gmnj) (njhs)   d. August 24, 1802

Widow Elizabeth Ogden
died Aug. 24th
1802
aged 55 years. 8 months
& 13 days

Notes:
Served: Revolutionary War

Children of John Ogden and Elizabeth Magie:
Mary Elizabeth, b.1773; m. Stephen Condit
Samuel, b. 1777; m. Rachel Lyon
Abigail, b. 1781; m. John Harrison
Aaron, b. 1783; m. Rebecca Farrand
Hannah, b. .....

- - - - -

Ogden, **SIMEON**   b. (June 27, 1763)
(gmnj) (njhs) (lgl)   d. April 2, 1790
(NJ Will 7056-7059G.1790)

In memory of

Simeon Ogden
died April 2d, 1790
aged 26 years. 11 months
& 5 days

wife, Catherine (Cory)   b. (August 24, 1765)
                                d. (aft. 1816, Ohio?)

Notes:
Served: Revolutionary War
--Simeon, son of Samuel Ogden and Phebe Baldwin; brother
of David Ogden, q.v. and John Ogden, q.v.; first cousin of
Mary Condit, wife of George Personett, Esq.
m. Catherine Cory. Catherine m. #2, Moses C. Edwards, son
of Jacob Edwards, of Livingston as his second wife.
--Will of Simeon Ogden: signed March 22, 1790; proved
Nov. 10, 1790: "He gave his wife a negro woman named Sal
for service during life, then to become a part of his personal
estate. He also made provision for son, Swaine and a child
unborn." Executors: Capt. Wm. Gould and Enos Williams;
Witnesses Samuel Tompkins, John Davison, Josiah Smith;
Adm. George Personett, Esq.

Child of Simeon Ogden and Catherine Cory:
Swaine, b. March 18, 1787; d. October 18, 1832; Ohio: age
        45; m. Dec. 1809, Catharine Dean; (bur. Early Settlers
        Burying Ground, Bethel, Clermont Co., Ohio)
Simeon, b. May 29, 1790; d. Nov. 17, 1854, Aurora,
        Dearborn Co., Indiana; m. Mary Ann Swing; b. 1801
        Bethel, Clairmont Co., Ohio

- - - - -

O'NEAL

| O'Neal, Hiram | b. (abt. 1815) |
| | d. (bef. 1870) |

| wife, Harriet (Lane) | b. (abt. 1820) |
| | d. (aft. 1870) |

| daughter, **HARRIET S.** | b. (abt. June 19, 1851) |
| (gmnj) (photo) | d. April 6, 1856 |

In
Memory of
Harriet S.
daughter of Hiram O'Neal
who died April 6, 1856
aged 4.9.18

Notes:
--Hiram D. O'Neal m. August 1, 1840, Harriet H. Lane
--1850 Census, p.83, Caldwell Twp: Hiram D. Oneal age 35, blacksmith; Harriet, age 30; Edward J., age 9; Thomas, age 5; George H., age 3; all b. NJ
--1860 Census, p.95, Caldwell: Hiram Oneal age 45; Harriet, age 40; George H., age 12; Clarence, age 6; William, age 4; Anna, age 4 months
--1870 Census, p.118, 1Wd., Newark: Harriet Oneal age 50; Thomas H., age 25, cigar maker; Susan E., age 8; Elfrida, age 6; Mary E. Bailey, age 24, store clerk; Ellen F. Norris, age 60; Rose Norris age 30; Raphael C. Norris, age 36, tailor; Jennie Norris, age 10

Children of Hiram D. O'Neal and Harriet H. Lane:
Edward J., b. abt 1841
Thomas H., b. abt. 1845; m. Susan E. .....
George H., b. abt 1847
Harriet S., b. 1851; d. 1856
Clarence, b. abt 1854
William, b. abt 1856
Anna, b. abt. 1860
Susan E., b. abt. 1862; m. 1880 James H. Vreeland
Elfrida, b. abt. 1864

- - - - -

OPENSHAW

Openshaw, Richard   b. (abt. 1792)
         d. (December 4, 1844)

wife, Phebe (Dodd)   b.
         d.

daughter, **RACHEL MARIA**b. (abt. June 20, 1816)
(gmnj) (njhs)   d. July 21, 1818

Here lies interred
the Body of Rachel Maria
daughter of Richard & Phebe Openshaw
who departed this life
July 21st, 1818 aged
2 years. 1 month & 1 day

Notes:

--Richard Openshaw, b. England; d. Indiana?

--(?) (bur. Richard Openshaw, no dates; Wakeman Cemetery, Waterville, Lucas Co., Ohio)

--Richard Openshaw m. Phebe Maria Dodd, dau. of Caleb Dodd, q.v., and Mary Bates

- - - - -

OSBORN

Osborn, Aaron b. (abt 1762)
d. (September 1796)
(age 34)

wife, Rachel (Condit) b. (1765)
d. (aft. June 17, 1812)

son, **JOHN** b. (abt. August 13, 1791)
(gmnj) (njhs) d. June 19, 1793

John
son of Aaron
& Rachel Osborn
died June 19th, 1793
aged 1 year. 10 months
& 6 days

Notes:

--Aaron m. July 14, 1789, Rachel Condit, dau. of Capt. Jonathan Condit and Jemima Condit

Children of Aaron Osborn and Rachel Condit:

Hannah, b. 1790; m. Josiah Steele, q.v.
John, b. 1791; d. 1793
Isaac, b. abt. 1793
Phebe, b. abt. 1795; m. #1, 1814, Isaac Hyer; m.1869,
    m. #2 Artemas Force

- - - - -

PERSONETT
PERSONETTE

Note: Personett is the true and original spelling. The
Personette variation was sometimes used at will, even within
a family.

Personett, **ABRAM**   b. (January 31, 1790)
(gmnj) (lgl) (photo)   d. May 5, 1881

Abram Personett
died May 5, 1881
in his 92nd year

wife, **JOANNA** (Williams)   b. (September 13, 1795)
(gmnj)   d. April 2, 1863

Joanna
wife of Abram Personett
died April 2, 1863
In her 67th year

son, **WILLIAM B.**   b. (August 24, 1822)
(gmnj) (njhs) (lgl) (photo)   d. August 6, 1824

William B.
son of
Abraham & Joanna
Personett
died Aug. 6th 1824
aged 1 year
11 months
& 12 days

daughter, **MARY JANE**   b. (October 7, 1834)
(gmnj) (njhs) (lgl) (photo)   d. October 16, 1836

In Memory of
Mary Jane
daughter of
Abraham & Joanna
Personett
she departed this life
Oct. 16th, 1836
aged 2 years & 8 days

Notes:
--Abram D. Personett, son of John Personett, Esq., and
Elenor Doremus; grandson of George Personett, Esq., q.v.
--Abram m. November 10, 1814, Joanna Williams, dau. of
Jeniah Williams and Charlotte Pearce
--"Abram was sexton of the church for many years and
owned a home across Bloomfield Avenue opposite the
lecture room entrance." (lgl, p.78) Abram was the last person
interred at the Old Burying Ground, Caldwell.

--1850 Census, p.84B, Caldwell Twp: Abraham Personett, age 60, tanner/currier; Joanna, age 54; Anna Maria, age 10
--1860 Census, p.106A, Caldwell: Abram D. Personett, age 70, tanner/currier; Joanna, age 64; Charlotte Williams, age 84; Mary Bone, age 40; all b. NJ
--1870 Census, p.112A, Caldwell: Abram Personett, age 80; Charlotte L. Backus age 53; Mary K. Backus, age 33; James A. Backus, age 23; Edmund P. Backus, age 19; Fannie Backus, age 16; Clara L. Backus, age 13; Lewis Grover Lockward, age 31, tobacconist
--1880 Census, p.401A, Caldwell: Abram Personette, age 90, retired tanner; Abram D. age 47, works at tobacco factory; Sarah E., dau-in-law, age 45; Emma, granddaughter, age 23; Eliza B. granddaughter, age 21; George D. grandson, age 17, works tobacco factory; Bertha, granddaughter age 14; Frederick, grandson, age 7

Children of Abraham D. Personett and Joanna Williams:
Elenor, b. 1814; m. 1836, Richard Bailey (?bur. Prospect Hill)
Charlotte Williams, b. 1817; m. #1, 1835, John Townley
    Lockward, M.D., q.v.; m. #2 Calvin G. Backus, q.v.
Moses Williams, b. 1820; d. 1907, went to California 1849

    Hon. Moses William Personette, born April 12, 1820, Caldwell Township, New Jersey; died February 26, 1907 California. He was tanner/currier; carpenter; miner; mechanic; saloon keeper; store clerk; toll bridge owner; ranch owner. In 1862 he was a State Assemblyman (Union Party) for Trinity County, California. In 1885, he was Deputy Sheriff there.
    MONUMENT: Masonic Cem., at Decoto Cemetery, Hayward, Alameda Co., California

William B., b. 1822; d. 1824
William Sears, b. 1825; d. aft 1910 Newark; m. 1849, Anna Maria Morton

Cyrus Emmons, b. 1828; m. 1850, Sophia Banta (bur.
Green-Wood Cemetery, Brooklyn, NY)
Abram Derance, b. 1831; m. 1854, Sarah Ellen Gould (bur.
Prospect Hill Cemetery)
Mary Jane, b. 1834; d. 1836
Anna Maria Crane, b. 1840; d. Oct. 14, 1921, Alameda Co.,
CA; m. 1859, John Coleman b. May 1833 England;
d. Jan. 21, 1914, Alameda Co., California

- - - - -

Personett, **GEORGE, ESQ**   b. (August 14, 1725)
(gmnj) (njhs) (photo)   d. June 9, 1816
(NJ Will 11000G. 1816)

Founding Elder

George Personett, Esq.
died June 9th, 1816
in the 92nd year
of his age

wife, **MARY** (Condit)   b. (22 January 1731)
(gmnj) (njhs) (photo)   d. June 9, 1810

Mary
wife of
George Personett, Esq.
died June 9th 1810
in her 80th year

Notes:

--George Personett, Esq., son of George Personett and
Jane/Jannetje Mangels Roll of Staten Island, New York
--George m. abt 1749, Mary Condit, dau. of Nathaniel Condit
and Elizabeth Ogden
--George, Justice of the Peace; res. Newark Twp.,(Orange),
Cedar Grove and Verona
--In 1811, George left his 80 acre Verona 'plantation' to his
grandson, Joseph Personett. In 1882 after many estate law
suits against the estate of Dr. Stephen Personette, his great
grandson, the property was sold to cover expenses. (Cases
Decided in the Court of Chancery. The Court of Errors and Appeals. NJ.
1882. Vol. VIII. pp.355-358)

Children of George Personett, Esq. and Mary Condit:
John Personett, Esq., b. abt. 1750; (Pvt. Rev.War Militia, Capt.
    Reeve's Co.) m. #1, abt. 1780, Elenor Doremus; m. #2,
    Oct. 1814, Mary Baldwin, wid. of Joseph Cone
    (John, prob. bur. Canfield/Cedar Grove Cem)
Nathaniel, b. 1753; d. 1754 (? bur.First Presb. Ch. Yard,Orange)
Mary, b. 1755; d. 1758 (? bur. First Presb. Ch. Yard, Orange)
Nathaniel, b. 1758; d. 1766(? bur. First Presb. Ch.Yard, Orange)
Jane, b. 1761; m. Enos Martin, Esq., q.v.
Mary, b. 1764; m. Encrease Gould, Esq., q.v.
Lydia, b. 1767; m. Caleb Crane, q.v.
Moses, q.v., b. 1772; m. 1797, Elizabeth 'Betsey' Crane

- - - - -

Personett, John, Jr.   b. (March 4, 1805)
                              d. (August 17, 1886)
                              (bur. St. Mark's Cemetery, Orange)

first wife, **FANNY** (Harrison)
(gmnj) (njhs) (lgl) (photo)   b. (January 15, 1806)
                                     d. February 10, 1842

In
Memory
of
Fanny
wife of
John Personett
who died Feb. 10th, 1842
aged 36 years &
26 days
No mortal woes
Can reach the sleeper here
while angels watch the soft
repose

Notes:
--John Personett, Jr., son of John Personett, Esq. and Elenor
Doremus
--John m. #1, Fanny Harrison; dau. of Robert? Harrison and
Margaret .....; m. #2, aft. 1842, Elenor/Ellen .....
--1850 Census, p.74&75, Caldwell (Cedar Grove): John
Personett, age 45, hatter; Ellen, age 38; Almira, age
17;George, age 14; Charles, age 12; Ellen, age 10; John, age
5; Stephen, age 3; Sarah, age 2; Alfred, age 5 mos.; Alonzo,
age 1 yr (son of Almira); all b. NJ
--1860 Census, p.111, Caldwell: John Personett, age 55,
hatter; Elinor, age 47 b. NJ; John, age 15; Stephen age 13;
Sarah, age 12; Alfred, age 10; Mary, age 7; Robert, age 4;
Cornelius Jerolaman, age 46, hatter; all b. NJ

--1870 Census, p.350A, 2Wd., Orange: James Lennox, age 40, carpenter, b. Ireland; Ellen, age 29, b. NJ; Wm., age 10; Harry, age 8; Elmer, age 6; Frank, age 3; Almira, age 7 mos.; Mary Personett, age 16, works at hat factory; Ada Brower, age 17; Alonzo Lennox , age 21, carpenter; Alfred Personett, age 20, carpenter;Robert Personett, age 14, b. NJ; John Personett, age 65, works at hat factory

--1880 Census, p.474A, East Orange: George Gardner, age 34, painter; Sarah M., age 27; Frederic W., age 7; John Personett, father-in-law, age 75, works at hat shop

Children of John Personett and Fannie Harrison:
Margaret Ann, b. abt 1828; m. Abram David Brower; (bur. St. Mark's Cem., Orange)
Lydia, b. 1830; m. Charles H. Hull (bur. St. Mark's Cem.Orange)
Almira, b. 1833; m. James E. Lennox (bur. St. Mark's Cem.)
George, b. 1833; m. Caroline Smalley; (bur. Canfield/Cedar Grove Cemetery)
Charles, b. abt. 1839; m. Hester A. ..... (bur. Mount Hope Cemetery, Mattapan, Suffolk Co., Massachusetts)
Ellen, b. abt 1840; m. James E. Lennox (sister of Almira) (bur. St. Mark's Cem.Orange)

Children of John Personett and Elenor.....:
John, b. 1845; d. 1864 (Civil War) (bur. National Cemetery, Chattanooga, Tennessee)
Stephen, b. 1847; d. 1876 (locomotive accident)
Sarah M., b. 1848; m. George Gardner (bur. Glendale Cem. Bloomfield)
Alfred, b. 1850; m. Sarah Jane Everson (bur. Rosedale Cem.)
Mary, b. 1853; m. Charles W. McEntee (bur. Rosedale Cem.)
Robert Fillmore, b. 1854; m. Annette C. Bernard (bur. Rosedale Cemetery, Orange.)

- - - - -

Personett, **MOSES** (gmnj) (njhs)	b. (September 21, 1772) d. March 11, 1801

Moses Personett
died
March 11th, 1801
in his 29th year

wife, Betsy Crane	b. (abt. 1777) d. (October 7, 1823) (bur. Presbyterian Church Cemetery, Elizabeth, NJ)
daughter, **PHEBE** (gmnj) (njhs)	b. (abt. March 1800) d. March 10, 1801

Phebe. daughter of Moses Personett
died March 10, 1801
age 1 year

Notes:
Served: Essex County Militia
--Moses, son of George Personett, Esq., q.v., and Mary
Condit
--Moses m. November 16, 1797, Betsey Crane, dau. of Jacob
Crane and Phebe Woodruff of Elizabeth, NJ; Betsey, m. #2,
1807, Andrew Parcell of Elizabeth. (bur. First Presbyterian
Church Yard, Elizabeth)

Children of Moses Personett and Elizabeth 'Betsey' Crane:

Phebe (I), b. abt. 1800; d. March 1801

Phebe (II),(posthumous) b. April 13, 1801; m. #1, 1821,
John L. Hudson, q.v.; divorced from John L.
Hudson, January 1834; m. #2, aft. January 1834, John
G. Vanderhoof

--Phebe (on monument in the Hudson Plot, Prospect Hill
Cemetery: "Phebe/Mother of William Elias Hudson/born April
13, 1801/died February 7, 1885/aged 83.10.6")

--Phebe (II), great-grandmother of Edward Joseph
Hudson, 1904-2003; "*Mr. Hudson, graduated Stevens
Inst. of Technology ...founded Hudson Engineering Corp. in
Houston in 1933 and Hudson Products Corp. until its 1969
merger with J. Ray McDermott & Co. ...where Mr. Hudson
was Chairman of the Board. Mr. Hudson headed at least
five corporations to construct, own and operate gas
processing plants and pipelines, all of which were merged into
Hudson Gas and Oil Corporation and sold to Continental Oil
Company in 1963. Founded scholarship fund at Baylor College
of Medicine.*"(Obit. excerpt: New York Times.January 26, 2003)

- - - - -

PIERSON

Pierson, **CALEB**   b. (abt. 1738)
(gmnj) (njhs) (lgl) (photo)   d. March 6, 1801

*In Memory of
Caleb Pierson
who Died March
6th, 1801, In the 63rd
Year of his Age*

wife, Joanna (Baldwin)   b. (abt. 1745)
                           d. (aft. 1785)

Notes:
Served: Revolutionary War
--Caleb, son of Caleb Pierson and Ruth Ogden
--Caleb m. Joanna Baldwin, dau. of Jonas Baldwin

Children of Caleb Pierson and Joanna Baldwin:
Sarah, b. abt. 1763;
John, b. 1765; d. Seneca Falls, NY; m. 1787, Susanna
          Russell (bur. Traver Cemetery, Senaca Falls, NY)
Elizabeth, b. 1767; d. 1793; m. Linus Dodd, q.v.
Jeptha, q.v., b. 1775; d. 1857; m. Sarah/Sally .....
Israel, b. abt. 1776; d. Kentucky; m. .....
Joanna, b. abt. 1777; m. David Pierson
Abraham, b. abt. 1778; m. Jemima Miller
Jane, b. 1778; d. 1784
Elijah, q.v., b. 1780; m. #1 1805, Martha Williams
          m. #2, Mary Williams
Lydia, b. abt. 1781; m. James Crockett (bur. First Presbyteiran
          Churchyard Memorial Garden, Newark)
Naomi, b. abt. 1783; m. Simeon Baldwin
Rhoda, b. abt. 1785; m. 1804, Thomas James (bur. Mount
Pleasant Cemetery, Newark)

- - - - -

Pierson, **CALEB C.**   b. (abt. June 9, 1796)
(gmnj)   d. February 9, 1864
(NJ Will 15991G. 1864)

Caleb C. Pierson
died February 9, 1864
aged 67.8.0

wife, Hannah M. (Ayres)	b. (June 6, 1812)
	d. (aft. 1860)
son, **JOSEPH A.**	b. (abt. December 9, 1847)
(gmnj)	d. October 26, 1865

Joseph A. Pierson
son of Caleb C. Pierson
died October 26, 1865
aged 17.10.17

Notes:
--Caleb C. Pierson, son of Jeptha Pierson, q.v.
--Caleb m. January 1, 1844, Hannah Maria Ayres, widow of Bethuel H. Pierson
--1850 Census, Caldwell Twp: Caleb Pierson, age 52, laborer; Hannah M., age 38; Hannah C., age 16 (stepdaughter); Daniel A., age 5; Joseph J., age 2; adj. to Jeptha Pierson
--1860 Census, Caldwell Twp: Caleb Pierson, age 64, laborer; Hannah M., age 48; Daniel A., age 15; Joseph A., age 12

Children of Caleb C. Pierson and Hannah Maria Ayres:
Daniel Ayres, b. 1845; m. Sarah Elizabeth Parks
Joseph J., b. abt 1848

- - - - -

Pierson, **ELIJAH**   b. (June 8, 1780)
(gmnj)   d. July 8, 1862

Eliljah Pierson
died July 8, 1862
in his 83rd year

first wife, **MARTHA** (Williams)
(gmnj)   b. (abt. 1784)
                              d. November 27, 1851

Martha
wife of Elijah Pierson
died November 27, 1851
in her 67th year

second wife, **MARY** (Williams)
(gmnj)   d. (abt. September 27, 1791)
                              d. October 13, 1868

Mary
wife of Elijah Pierson
died October 13, 1868
aged 77.0.16

Notes:
--Elijah, son of Caleb Pierson, q.v., and Joanna Baldwin
--Elijah m. #1, February 26, 1805, Martha Williams; m. #2,
aft. 1851, Mary Williams; (both daughters of Jonathan)

--1850 Census, p.80, Caldwell Twp: Elijah Pierson, age 70, shoemaker; Martha, age 66; Nathan W., age 29, farmer; Susan E., age 28; Frederick H., age 5; Emma L., age 3; Louisa Mann,a ge 18; all b. NJ

--1860 Census, p.318, 1Wd, Orange: Elijah Pierson, age 80, shoemaker; Mary, age 69

Children of Elijah Pierson and Martha Williams:
James Crocket, b. 1806; d. 1806
Louisa, b. abt. 1807, m. Aaron Dodd
Elijah B., b. 1810; m. Sally Mingus
Calvin D., b. 1811; m. Margaret Dodd
Maria, b. 1813; m. Samuel Crane
Caleb Nelson, b. 1815; m. Jane E. Crane
David Harrison, b. 1818; m. Caroline Peck
Nathan Williams, b. 1824; m. Susan Harrison

- - - - -

Pierson, **JEPTHA**   b. (May 10, 1769)
(gmnj)   d. August 1, 1851
(NJ Will 14113G. 1851)

Jeptha Pierson
died August 1, 1851
aged 82.2.0

wife, **SARAH**   b. (abt. 1771)
(gmnj) (njhs) (lgl)   d. May 31, 1847

Sarah
wife of

Jeptha Pierson
died May 31st, 1847
aged 76 years
& 8 months

Notes:
--Jeptha Pierson, son of Caleb Pierson, q.v., and Joanna
Baldwin
--1850 Census, p.80 Caldwell Twp: Jeptha Pierson, age 80,
'farmer' and currier; Sarah M., age 32; Mary Dixon, age 68;
adj. to Caleb and Hannah M. Pierson

Children of Jeptha Pierson and Sarah .....:
Nancy, b. abt. 1792
Joanna, b. abt. 1794
Cyrus, b. 1796; m. ?Mary .....
Stephen S., b. 1798; m. ?Mary .....
John, b. abt. 1801; m. #1, Deborah .....;m. #2, after 1839,
        Lydia L. Ives
Bethuel H., b. abt 1804;d. 1836; m. Hannah Maria Ayres
Abiathar H., b. abt 1804; m. Ann D. .....
David H., b. abt 1806; d.y.
Caleb C., q.v., b. abt 1808; m. 1844, Hannah Maria Ayres
Sally Maria/ Sarah M., b.abt.1810; m. John D. Schuyler, q.v.

- - - - -

PLUNKET

Plunket, William   b.
                          d.

wife, **ANN**   b. (abt. February 1,1792
(gmnj) (njhs)   d. November 19, 1815

Ann Plunket
wife of
William Plunket
died Nov. 19th, 1815
aged 23 years. 9 months
& 18 days

Notes:
(?)See: *Biographical Annals of Franklin County,*
Pennsylvania. Heritage Books. 2007. Vol. I. pp.149-150. Re:
Dr. William Plunket

- - - - -

PRICE

Price, **SAMUEL**   b. (abt. February 1789)
(gmnj) (njhs) (lgl)   d. June 16, 1815
(?NJ Will 11003G.Inv. 1816)

Samuel Price
died June 16th 1815
aged 26 years. 3 months
& 19 days

wife, Thankful (Crane)   b. (1789)
                            d. (1862)
                            (bur. Wellsburg Baptist Cem.
                            Chemung Co., New York)

(widow of Samuel Price)

Notes:
--Thankful, daughter of Azariah Crane, q.v.

- - - - -

PROVOST

Provost, **JOHN**   b. (abt. 1806)
(gmnj)   d. April 27, 1864

John Provost
died at Mauston, Wisconsin
April 27, 1864
in his 58th year

wife **LUCY** (DeCamp)   b. (abt. March 17, 1836)
(gmnj)   d. September 17, 1856

Lucy
wife of John Provost
died September 17, 18556
aged 20.6.0

daughter, **LUCY**   b. (abt. August 24, 1856)
(gmnj)   d. April 5, 1857

Lucy
daughter of John Provost
died April 5, 1857
aged 7 amd 1/2 months

Notes:
John, son of Jonathan Provost and Mary Vreeland
--John Provost m. October 24, 1855, Lucy A. DeCamp
--?1850 Census p.7 North Ward Newark: John Provost age
45 b. NJ teacher; boarder

Child of John Provost and Lucy A. DeCamp:
Lucy A. b. 1856; d. 1857

- - - - -

Provost, **JONATHAN,** Senr. b. (abt. 1767)
(gmnj)   d. July 21, 1854

Jonathan Provost, Senr.
died July 21, 1854
in his 87th year

Notes:
--?1850 Census p.309 Pequannock Morris Co. NJ: John P.
Cole age 33 farmer; Eliza age 33; Jonathan Provost age 82;
Mahlon Morris age 23 blacksmith

Children of Jonathan Provost and Mary Vreeland:
John, q.v., m. Lucy DeCamp
Jonathan q.v. b. 1798; m. Paulina Moore (Prospect Hill Cem.)

- - - - -

Provost, Jonathan   b. (December 2, 1798)
(photo)   d. (November 3, 1875)

(bur. Prospect Hill Cemetery)

wife, Paulina (Moore)	b. (January 12, 1801)
(photo)	d. (October 1, 1877)
	(bur. Prospect Hill Cemetery)

son, **GEORGE**	b. (abt. 1824)
(gmnj) (njhs) (lgl)	d. October 26, 1829

George Provost
son of Jonathan
& Pauline Provost
died Oct. 26th, 1829
in his 5th year

son, **JAMES**	b. (abt. 1833)
(gmnj) (njhs) (lgl)	d. July 2, 1848

James
son of Jonathan
& Paulina Provost
died July 2d, 1848
aged 15 years

daughter, **CAROLINE**	b. (abt. 1839)
(gmnj)	d. July 4, 1851
	in 12th yr.

Notes:
--Jonathan, son of Jonathan Provost and Mary Vreeland
--Jonathan m. September 9, 1822, Paulina Moore dau. of Joshua Moore, q.v.

--1850 Census p.84 Caldwell Twp: Jonathan Provost age 51 tanner/currier; Paulina age 49; Mary Ann age 24; Ellen age 22; Phebe age 15; Caroline age 11; Martha age 7; Thomas age 1; Mariah Harrison age 37; 3 laborers

--1860 Census p.95 Caldwell: Jno. Provost age 61 dealer in leather; Paulina age 60; Ellen age 30; Martha age 17; Thomas age 11; 2 labors

--1870 Census p. 113 ,Caldwell: Jonathan Provost age 71 farmer; Paulina age 69; Phebe H. Burnet age 63 (sister-in-law); Pauline Williams age 13; 3 laborers

Children of Jonathan Provost and Paulina Moore:
George, b. 1824; d. 1829
Pernella, b. abt 1825; m. December 10, 1845,
    Jotham Marshfield Williams
Mary Ann, b. 1826; m. October 9, 1852, George C. Bush
Ellen P., b.1828; m. Sept. 3, 1861, John W. Taylor
James, b. 1833; d. 1848
Phebe Burnet, b. 1835; d. 1858
Caroline, b.1839; d. 1851
Martha, b. abt 1843; d. 1860
Thomas Clinton, b. 1849

- - - - -

PRYME
Pryne, Pruyn

Pryme, David D.   b. (July 23, 1812)
(NJ Inv. #13560G)   d. (February 22, 1846)
                      (bur. Old Ref. Dutch Cemetery

Scotia, Glenville, Schenectady Co.,
New York. with his parents)

wife, Catharine D. (Personett)
- b. (January 7, 1815)
- d. April 9, 1867

son, **JOSEPH**
(gmnj)
- b. (abt. October 1838)
- d. March 22, 1839

Joseph
son of David D. Pryne
and Catharine
died March 22, 1839
aged 0.5.0

Notes:

--David D. Pryme, son of David Pryme (1771-1856) and Rebecca Toll

--David m. October 3, 1833, Catherine D. Personett, dau. of Joseph Personett and Alletta Doremus

--1840 Portraits of David 'Pryme' and Mrs. David Pryme: (Collection of the Albany Institute of History and Art. Recorded by the Smithsonian, American Art Museum's Inventories of American Painting.)

--1850 Census, p.71B, Caldwell: Joseph Personett, age 64, farmer, real estate $5000; Alletta, age 57; Jeptha C., age 28, farmer, real estate $4000; Catherine Pryne, age 35, widow; Anna L. Pryne, age 8

--1856 June 14: In her father's will, Catharine is to receive a room and furniture in the homestead and "if she should leave vigil - married to have one cow or twenty five dollars as she chooses...and also to have three hundred dollars to be paid to her in two years."

--1860 Census, p.113B, Caldwell Twp: Joseph Personett, age 74, farmer $6000; Alice/Alletta, age 66; Jeptha, age 38; Catherine Prime, age 45; Anna L. Prime, age 18

Children of David D. Pryme and Catherine D. Personett:
Joseph, b. 1838; d. 1839
Anna Louisa, b. 1841; d. aft. 1930; m. 1883, Moses Edward
    Gould, (son of Benj. Helme Gould, grandson of
    Encrease Gould, Esq., q.v.) (both died Rensselaer, NY)
    --Anna Louisa and others brought suit against the
    estate of Dr. Stephen Personette, her uncle, who died
    1880 intestate and insolvent; e.g., "Lindsley v.
    Personette" (Cases Decided in the Court of Chancery. The
    Court of Errors and Appeals. NJ. 1882. Vol. VIII. pp.355-358)

- - - - -

REEVES
(REEVE)

Reeves, **ABNER**, Dr. b. (abt. 1784)
(gmnj) (njhs) (lgl)   d. January 1, 1812
(NJ Will 10810G.Inv. 1813)

Doct. Abner Reeves
died Jan. 1st, 1812
in his 27th year
Cut down in his prime.

The lovely youth in fullest bloom of life,

Snatched from his helpless babes & wife,
But ah! my Freind mourn not for me,
I hope to meet again,
In realms of everlasting day,
In endless bliss to reign.

wife, **ELIZABETH** (Gould) b. (August 16, 1786)
(gmnj) (njhs)   d. April 25, 1814

Elizabeth
relict of
Doct. Abner Reeves
and daughter of
Gen. William & Mehetable Gould
died April 25th, 1814
in her 28th year

Notes:
--Abner, son of Isaac Reeve
--Abner m. March 8, 1811, Elizabeth Crane Gould, dau. of
Gen. William Gould, q.v.

Child of Abner Reeves and Elizabeth Crane Gould:
Abner, b. 1811; m. Mary Cochran, dau. of Thomas Cochran,
q.v., and Esther Byram.

- - - - -

REUCK
REOCK

Reuck, Aaron   b. (abt. 1807)

d. (1875)

(bur. Rosedale Cem. Orange)

wife, Sarah M. (Moore)   b. (abt. 1827)

d. (aft. 1860)

(bur. Rosedale Cem. Orange)

son, **BYRON S.**   b. (abt. March 1838)

(gmnj) (njhs)   d. September 22, 1838

Byron S.
son of Aaron
& S.M. Reuck
died Sept. 22d, 1838
aged 6 months

son, **GEORGE MOORE**   b. (abt. 1840)

(gmnj) (njhs)   d. May 5, 1844

George Moore
son of Aaron
& Sarah M. Reuck
died May 5th, 1844
aged 4 years

Notes:

--Aaron m. July 6, 1833, Sarah Maria Moore, dau. of Samuel Moore, q.v.

--1850 Census, West Wd., Newark, NJ: Aaron Reuck, age 44, tailor; Sarah 34; Joseph age 16 sash & blind maker; John, age 14; Harriet, age 7; Harriet E. Moore, age 31

--1860 Census, 4wd. Newark: Aaron Reuck, age 57, b. NJ, 'taylor'; Sarah M. age 43 b. NJ; Harriet E., age 17, b. NJ music teacher; John M., age 24, b. NJ, painter; Corrine D.S. age 19 b. Ohio; Monroe age 1, b. NJ

Children of Aaron Reuck and Sarah Moore:
Joseph, b. abt. 1834; m. ?Elizabeth D. Sanford
John M., b. abt. 1836; m., Ohio, Corrine D S Werstele
Byron S., b. 1838; d. 1838
Harriet, b. abt. 1843

- - - - -

RIKER

Riker, Asa P.   b. (abt. 1817)
                                   d. (October 23, 1848)
                                   Age 32

wife, Sarah (Paxton)   b. (abt. 1814)
                                   d. (aft. 1870)

daughter, **JOANNA FRANCES**
(gmnj) (njhs) (lgl) (photo)   b. (abt. January 9, 1840)
                                   d. February 9, 1845

*Joanna Frances
daughter of
Asa P. & Sarah Riker
died Feb. 9th, 1845
aged 5 years. 1 month
& 29 days*

daughter, **SARAH JANE**   b. (abt. August 31, 1839)
(gmnj) (njhs) (lgl) (photo)   d. September 13, 1839

Sarah Jane
daughter of Asa P.
& Sarah Riker
died Sept. 13th, 1839
aged 13 days

Notes:
--Asa P. Riker, son of William Parker Riker, q.v.
--Asa m. Sarah Paxton, dau. of Obadiah Paxton
--Sarah m. #2, Sept. 1851, Peter Cadmus (1814-1860)
"Peter Cadmus, widower, m. Sept. 1851, Fairfield, Sarah
Riker, widow, dau. of Obadiah Paxton"
--1840 Census, p.332, Caldwell Twp: Asa P. Riker
--1850 Census, p.68, Caldwell Twp: Sarah Riker, age 24;
William P. age 9; Edmund age 8; Asa J., age 3; all b. NJ
--1860 Census: 2 Wd. Orange: Peter Cadmus, 46; Sarah, age
47; Catherine, age 11; Georgianna age 6
--1870 Census, p.13, Belleville, Essex Co. NJ: Sarah
Cadmus, age 56; Asa J. Riker, age 23; Georgianna Cadmus,
age 16; all work in wool mill; Maria Paxton, age 2; 2
boarders b. Ireland

Children of Asa P. Riker and Sarah .....
Jane, b. 1839; d. 1839
Joanna Frances, b. 1840; d. 1845
William P. , abt. 1841; d. January 1851
Edmund, b. abt 1842; d. February 1851
Asa J., b. abt. 1847

- - - - -

Riker, **PETER I.**   b. (August 27, 1751)
(gmnj) (njhs) (lgl)   d. August 1, 1806
(NJ Will 10501G.Inv.1807)

Peter I. Riker
died
August 2d, 1806
aged 55 years. 11 months
& 16 days

1st wife, Mary Stager   b.
     d.

2nd wife, **MARTHA** (Corby) b. (June 8, 1766)
(gmnj) (njhs) (lgl)   d. August 28, 1828

Martha
relict of
Peter I. Riker
died Aug. 28, 1828
aged 63 years. 2 months
& 20 days

daughter, **HANNAH GROVER**
(gmnj) (njhs) (lgl) (photo)   b. (abt. September 11, 1795)
     d. October 19, 1813

In
Memory of

Hannah Grover Riker
daughter of
Peter I. & Martha Riker
who died Oct. 19th, 1813
aged 18 years. 1 month
& 8 days

daughter, **MEHETABLE GOULD**
(gmnj) (njhs) (lgl) (photo)   b. (abt. September 1, 1795)
                                     d. January 15, 1818

In
Memory of
Mehitable Gould
daughter of Peter
and Martha Riker
she departed this life
Jan. 15th, 1818
aged 22 years. 4 months
& 4 days

Notes:
--Peter Isaac Riker, son of Isaac Riker and Annetje Egberts
--Peter m. 1, Mary Stager; m. #2, abt. 1786, Martha Corby,
dau. of John Corby and Rhoda Parker

Children of Peter Isaac Riker and Martha Corby:
(Essex Co. Surrogate Docket #600)
Rhoda, b. abt. 1788; m. November 19, 1809; m. George
        Personett Martin, q.v.
Anna, b. abt. 1790, m. 1815, Daniel Munn
Mary, b. 1791, m. Stephen Dodd

William Parker, q.v., b. 1794, m. #1, Joanna Perry; m. #2,
    Abigail Kent
Hannah Gould, twin, b. 1795, d. 1813
Mehetable/Hettie Gould, twin, b.1795; d. 1818
    Her will, 1818, names mother, sisters: Mary, Phebe,
    Rhoda and Anna
Phebe, b. abt. 1798; m. 1818, Enos S. Munn
Reuben, b. abt. 1800, m. 1822, Matilda Spear
Abiah, b. 1801-1805
Noah Sayre, b. abt. 1806; d. 1882, m. Mary 'Marr?'

- - - - -

Riker, **WILLIAM P.**   b. (abt. March 3, 1795)
(gmnj)   d. October 26, 1852
(NJ Will 14413G. Inv 1853)

William P. Riker
died October 26, 1852
aged 57.7.23

1st wife, Joanna Perry   b. (abt. 1795)
     d. (1815) age 20

2nd wife, Abigail Kent   b.
     d.

Notes:
--William Parker Riker, son of Peter I. Riker, q.v., and
Martha Corby
--William m. #1, December 27, 1814, Joanna Perry, age 20;
m. #2, Abigail Kent

--1850 Census, p.71, Caldwell Twp: William P. Riker, age 56, tanner/currier; Abigail, age 53; Levi King, age 11; all b. New Jersey

--?"Abigail Riker, d. Sept. 23, 1882, age 86, Newark"

Children of William Parker Riker and Joanna Perry:
Asa P., q.v., b. abt. 1817; m.Sarah Paxton
Hetty Maria, b. abt. 1822
Catherine, b. abt. 1826
Mary Jane, b. abt. 1828; d. 1837

- - - - -

SANFORD
SANDFORD

Sanford, Gamaliel   b. (May 25, 1778)
                               d. (February 1863)
                               (bur. Mount Pleasant Cem, Newark)

first wife, **ELIZABETH** (Brown)
(gmnj) (njhs)   b. (abt. November 8, 1787)
                               d. February 1, 1832

Elizabeth
wife of
Gamaliel Sandford
died
Feb. 1st, 1832
Aged 45 years, 2 months
& 22 days
Blessed are the dead which die in the Lord

Notes:
--See: *Thomas Sanford. The Emigrant to New England.* Carlton E.
Sanford. Tutle Co. Rutland, Vermont. 1911. Volume I.
--Gamaliel, son of Capt.John Sanford who Served in the
Revolutionary War; d. Butler, NJ and Rebecca DeBow
--Gamaliel m. #1, September 8, 1805, Elizabeth Brown, dau.
of Capt. Martin Brown and Hannah Post of Newfoundland,
Morris County; m. #2, 1834 at Caldwell, Sarah 'Blanbelt'
(Blauvelt?)
--Gamaliel had ten children by first marriage all b. in
Caldwell.

--1850 Census, p.289, South Ward, Newark: Gamaliel
Sandford, age 72, b. NY?, farmer; Sarah, age 64, b. NY;
Rosana Decker, age 17, b. NJ
--1860 Census, p.352&353, 1Wd., Orange: Peter Sanford,
age 54 b. NJ, farmer; Rhoda, age 52, b. NJ; Gamaliel
Sanford, age 82 b. NJ; Sarah, age 74, b. NJ; Rodeman
Backus, age 34, b. NY, farmer; Maria Backus, age 28 b. NJ;
Peter S., age 6 b. NJ; Mary Garrison, age 24, b. NJ; Robert
Ray, age 11, b. NY; 5 laborers

Children of Gamaliel Sanford and Elizabeth Brown:
Peter, b. 1806; d. 1875; m. 1827, Rhoda Coonrod
Hannah, b. 1808; d. bef. 1822
Jane, b. 1810
Rebecca, b. 1812; d. March 1872; m. George Ross
John, b. 1814; d.1866; m. Harriet A. Wilson
Eliza Jane, b. 1817; d. 1893; m. 1839, John Joline Ross
Benjamin, b. 1820; d. 1902; m. 1844, Esther Damon
Hannah Maria, b. 1822; m. John Vinson

Martin B., b. 1825

Joseph Board, b. 1831;d. 1906; m. Margaret J. Cummings;
"the most expert dredger dock builder and harbor
improver in the United States...filled in the Potomac
flats...unloaded and placed in position the Statue
of Liberty..."

- - - - -

Sandford, **WILLIAM, Capt.** b. (abt. 1766)
(gmnj) (njhs) (lgl) (photo)   d. November 8, 1811

In Memory of
Capt.
William Sandford
who died
Nov. 8th, 1811
in the 45th year
of his life

Notes:

Served: Revolutionary War: "William Sanford,Sergeant in
the Essex Troop" (History of Essex & Hudson Counties, N.J. Chapter
12. Wm. H. Shaw, 1884)

--(??) Mary Van Ness, b. Sept. 8, 1760, dau. of Capt. Lt.
Peter Van Ness (1730-1820), m. "William Sanford"

- - - - -

SCHUYLER

Schuyler, John D.   b. (abt. 1812)

d. (aft. 1880)

1st wife, **CATHARINE PROVOST**
(gmnj) (njhs) (photo)   b. (abt. 1812)
                                 d. November 25, 1837

In
Memory of
Catharine Provost
wife of
John D. Schuyler and
(daughter of Jonathan Provost?)
died Nov. 25th, 1837
in her 24th year

2nd wife, **SARAH MARIA PIERSON**
(gmnj) (photo)   b.
                           d. September 7, 1865

In
Memory of
Sarah M. Pierson
wife of John D. Schuyler
Died Sept. 7th, 1861
aged 49 years 4 months
and 9 days

Notes:
John D. Schuyler m. Nov. 19, 1834, Catherine Provost; m.
#2, aft. 1837, Sarah Maria Pierson
--1850 Census: Caldwell Twp.; Henry F. Crane, age 323,
farmer; Sarah Ann, age 28; Gilbert D., age 6; Cornelia J., age

4; Edward W., age 8 mos.; John D. Schuyler, age 38, merchant; Cyrus E. Crane, age 21, laborer; John H. Vanderhoof, age 17, clerk; 1 servant
--1860 Census: Caldwell: John D. Schuyler, age 49, farmer; Sarah M., age 45; Jennetta, age 1; house between Caleb Pierson,age 64 and Asher Crane, age 50
--1870 Census: Little Falls, Passaic Co., NJ: John D. Schuyler, age 55, country store keeper; Elizabeth, age 34, b. NY; John Scott, age 19, b. NY

- - - - -

SIMONSON

Simonson, Anthony	b. (1809)
	d. (July 28, 1886)
wife, Rhoda (Sigler)	b. (September 1, 1815)
(Will dated July 1877)	d. (March 5, 1879)
	(bur. Brookdale Ref. Ch. Cem.)

daughter, **CAROLINE OLIVIA**
(gmnj) (njhs) (lgl)   b. (abt. December 25, 1834)
                                       d. April 20, 1849

Caroline Olivia
daughter of Anthony
& Rhoda Simonson
died April 20th, 1849
aged 15 years. 3 mos.
& 26 days

Notes:

--Anthony m. November 16, 1832, Rhoda Sigler, dau. of
Isaac Sigler and Sophie Garrabrant. (Isaac left farm to dau.,
Rhoda, wife of Anthony Simonson)

--1850 Census, p.95, Caldwell Twp: Anthony Simonson, age
42, farmer; Rhoda, age 35; Isaac, age 12; George, age 10;
Jesse, age 5; William J., age 3; Jane A., age 7 months; 1
servant

--1860 Census, p.179, Bloomfield: Anthony "Simons" age
50, farmer; Rhoda, age 50; George, age 19; Emeline age 19;
Jesse, age 15; Adaline, age 10; adj. to John Sigler, age 66
and wife Sophia

--1870 Census, p.266, Montclair: Anthony Simonson, age
60, farmer; Rhoda, age 54; Robert Sherman, age 23, b.
Rhoda Island, works on farm; Anthony Sherman, age 3;
Caroline Sherman, age 1; 1 servant

--1877 July: Will of Rhoda Sigler Simonson: leaves use of
farm,et.al., situate in Montclair, to husband, Anthony, to use
during his lifetime; all to be sold after his death; an amount
to erect a tombstone or monument over her grave to cost not
less than $100; 2 trusts for grandchildren; all the rest to four
sons: John, Isaac, George, and Jesse.

--1880 Census, p.53.1, Montclair: George Simonson, age 40,
widower, farmer; Frances, dau., age 16; Andrew, age 11;
Clara J. age 9; Anthony, age 70, father, widower; Anthony,
age 12, nephew

Children of Anthony Simonson and Rhoda Sigler:
Caroline Olivia, b. 1834; d. April 1849; age 15
Isaac, b. abt. 1838; m. Ann?; m. Sarah J.?
John H., b. 1839; d. 1890; m. 1859 Ellen Jane Kiersted

George, b. abt. 1840; (bur. Brookdale Ref. Ch. Cemetery) m. #1,
    Emeline Garrabrant; m.#2, Charlotte Andrews
Lucy Frances, b. abt. 1844; d. 1858; age 13.10.28; (bur. Old
    Meth. Cem., Bloomfield) and (bur. Brookdale Ref. Ch. Cem.)
Jesse, b. abt. 1845; d. 1882 (bur. Brookdale Ref. Ch. Cemetery
    Served: Civil War. Co.A, 39th NJ Infantry
?William J., b. abt. 1847; d. April 1876?
Jane Adaline, b. Nov. 1849; m. 1868, Robert Sherman

- - - - -

Simonson, **BARNEY**   b. (abt. 1753)
(gmnj) (njhs) (lgl)   d. February 19, 1819
(NJ Will #11225G, 1818-19)

Barney Simonson
died
Feb. 19th, 1819
in his 66th year

Farewell, ye friends whose tender care
Has long engaged my love,
Your fond embrace I now exchange
For better friends above

first wife, **JANE** (Jones)   b. (abt. April 11, 1769)
                  d. August 24, 1804

Jane
wife of
Barney Simonson
died Aug. 24th, 1804

aged 35 years. 4 months
& 13 days

Notes:

--Barney m. #1, Jane Jones, dau. of Thomas Jones

--Barney m. #2, December 16, 1804, Elizabeth VanHouten, (1764-1846) dau. of Cornelius VanHouten and Marritje VanGiesen

Children of Barnabas/Barney Simonson and Jane Jones:

Barnabas Jr., b. 1774;d.1848;(bur. Old Bapt. Cem., Hamilton Co., Ohio); m. 1795, Catherine Freeman

John S., b. 1789; d 1828;

Rachel, m. 1802, Caldwell, Stephen Personett, son of John Personett, Esq. of Cedar Grove. He died before 1811; She m. #2, Caldwell, 1811, Isaac Van Riper

- - - - -

Simonson, **JOHN S.**   b. (abt. December 12, 1789)
(gmnj)(njhs) (lgl)   d. April 9, 1828
(NJ Will #12004G)

John S. Simonson
died
April 9th, 1828
aged 38 years. 3 months
& 28 days

wife, **FANNY LINES**   b. (abt. May 24, 1789)
(gmnj)   d. December 7, 1869

Fanny Lines
wife of John Simonson
died December 7, 1860
aged 80.6.13

daughter, **ELIZA C.**   b. (abt. 1814)
(gmnj) (njhs) (lgl)   d. February 13, 1835

Eliza C. daughter of
John & Fanny Simonson
died Feb. 13th, 1835
in her 21st year

Notes:
--John S. Simonson, son of Barney Simonson, q.v., ?
--John m. Fanny Lines
--1860 Census, p.112, Caldwell Twp: Fanny Simonson, age 71; Frances DeHart, age 19; Adj. to Isaac Simonson, age 47, farmer

Children of John S. Simonson and Fanny Lines:
Barnabas, b. .....; m. 1830, Maria Ellis; moved to Lima, NY
Anthony, q.v., b. abt. 1808, m. 1832; Rhoda Sigler
Isaac, b.abt 1812; d. 1887; m.Ann Sandford (Prospect Hill Cem)
Eliza Caroline, b. abt 1814; m. 1834, Isaac VanNess
Jane, b. .....; m. Samuel DeHart

- - - - -

SINDLE

Sindle, **JACOB**   b. (abt. December 18, 1789)

(gmnj)   d. August 10, 1864
(NJ Will 16014G 1864)

Jacob Sindle
died August 10, 1864
aged 74.7.23

wife, **REBECCA DEMAREST**
(gmnj) (njhs) (lgl)   b. (abt. April 17, 1789)
                                    d. November 10, 1850

Rebecca Demarest
wife of
Jacob Sindle
died Nov. 10th, 1850
aged 61 years.
7 months & 23 days

son, **JOSEPH H.**   b. (abt. 1828)
(gmnj)   d. August 21, 1851

Joseph H.
died August 21, 1851
in his 23d year

Notes:
--Jacob m. February 7, 1812, Rebecca Demarest
--1850 Census, p.74, Caldwell Twp: Jacob Sindle, age 60,
farmer; Rebecca, age 61; Hester Jacobus, age 35; Rebecca
Jacobus, age 15; Peter W. Jacobus, age 10
--1860 Census, p.114, Caldwell Twp: Jacob Sindle, age 69,
farmer; Hester (Jacobus) age 46; Rebecca (Jacobus) age 24

Children of Jacob Sindle and Rebecca Demarest:
Hester, b. abt. 1815;, m. ..... Jacobus
Rebecca Ann, b. abt. 1819; m. 1835, Jacob E. Jacobus
Peter S., b. abt 1822; m. bef. 1850, Elizabeth Smith;
Joseph H., b. abt. 1828; d. 1851
James C., b. abt 1829;d. 1851; m. Mary Supenor; dau. of
    Abraham Supenor, q.v.

- - - - -

Sindle, **THOMAS J.**   b. (abt. July 30, 1804)
(gmnj)   d. September 17, 1851
(NJ Will 14127G. 1851)

Thomas J. Sindle
died September 17, 1851
aged 47.1.18

wife, Mary (VanNess)   b. (January 25, 1804)
    d. (October 11, 1892)

Notes:
--Thomas m. January 1, 1835, Maria VanNess, dau. of Henry
R. VanNess and Mary Wandle
--1850 Census, p.74, Caldwell Twp: Thomas J. Sindle, age
46, shoemaker; Mary, age 46
--1860 Census, p.64, Pequannock, Morris Co.: Abraham
Milledge, age 53; Hannah Milledge, age 52; Mary 'Zindle',
age 56

--1870 Census, p.201, Montville, Morris Co.; Martin J. Cook age 63, farmer; Elizabeth age 57; Sarah, age 33; Mary Sindle, age 65, domestic servant
--1880 Census, p.194.4, Montville: Abraham Milledge, age 73, farmer; Hannah, age 71; Maria Sindle, age 76, sister-in-law, widow

- - - - -

SLOVER

Slover, Isaac	b. (March 6, 1740)
	d. (September 3, 1805)
wife, **GRACE** (Corle)	b. (abt. April 28, 1740)
(gmnj)(njhs) (photo)	d. August 18, 1827
(NJ Will 11895G.1827)	

In
Memory of
Grace.
widow of
Isaac Slover
died Aug. 18th 1827
aged 87 years.
3 months & 21 days

Notes:
--Isaac, son of Isaac Selover and Syche Pittenger
--Isaac m. Grace Corle
--Grace is buried in the "Miller Plot" at Caldwell
--See: Isaac Slover Miller, above

- - - -

SQUIRE

Squire, **EZRA K., Doctor**   b. (abt. 1777)
(gmnj)   d. April 2, 1814
(NJ Will 10864G. 1814)

> *Doct. Ezra K. Squire*
> *died April 2, 1814*
> *in the 37th year*
> *of his age*

wife, Phebe (Bates)   b.
                             d.

Notes:
Served: War of 1812
--Ezra Kitchell Squire, son of Dr. Samuel Squire who m.
Nov. 1774, Mendham, NJ, Rhoda Kitchell, b. 1752, Hanover
Twp.
--Ezra m. Phebe Bates; after his death she m. #2, Abner
Dodd as his second wife.
--Will: signed April 1814; Proved Oct. 1814: Ezra K. Squier
of Caldwell Twp.; Intestate; Inventory by Nathanial Douglass
and Thomas Cochran: 'includes military pantaloons & a vest;
medical books and supplies'. Admx: Phebe Squier
--sister of Ezra: Nancy Squire 1780-1851; m. Daniel Dod;
mother of Rev. Albert Baldwin Dod

Children of Ezra K. Squire and Phebe Bates:

Emma, b. May 1805; bapt. Presb. Church, Hanover, NJ

- - - - -

STAGER

Stager, John	b. (1817)
	d. (1884)
	(bur. Prospect Hill Cemetery)
wife, Mary J. (Cadmus)	b. (1811)
(photo)	d. (1871)
	(bur. Prospect Hill Cemetery)
daughter, **SARAH E.**	b. (abt. March 15, 1847)
(gmnj) (njhs)(lgl)	d. March 26, 1848

Sarah E.
daughter of John and Mary Stager
died March 26th 1848
aged 1 year & 11 days

Notes:
--John Stager, son of John H. Stager, q.v.
--John m. #1, Mary J. Cadmus; m. #2, Margaret Devoe
--1850 Census, p.79, Caldwell Twp: John H. Stager, age 72, farmer; Sophia, age 67; John H. Jr., age '30' farmer; Mary J. age 36; Amelia F. age 11 mos.; Caroline L., age 11 mos.; Martha Thompson, age 16, b. NY; Louis Thompson, age 3 mos. b. NJ

--1860 Census, p.110, Caldwell: John J. Stager, age 42, farmer; Maria, age 47; Amelia C., age 11; Caroline L., age 11; Marcus E., age 8; John O., age 8; William E., age 4
--1870 Census, p.129, Caldwell: John Stager, 51, farmer; Mary 55; Carolina age 20; Marcus, age 18; William E., age 14; Sophia, age 88
--1880 Census, p.417B, Caldwell: John Stager, age 62, b. NJ, laborer; Margaret, wife, age 61 b. NJ, parents b. NJ

Children of John Stager and Mary J. Cadmus:
Sarah E., b. 1847; d. 1848
Amelia Tuttle, b. abt. 1849
Caroline Lavinia, b. abt. 1849
John O., b. 1852
Marcus E., b.1852; d. 1936 (bur. Prospect Hill Cemetery) m.
    Maria Albert, dau. of Charles Albert, q.v.
William E., b. abt. 1856

- - - - -

Stager, **JOHN H.**   b. (abt. 1778)
(gmnj)   d. March, 1859
(NJ Will 15288G.1859

wife, **SOPHIA** (Speer)   b. (abt. August 30, 1783)
(gmnj)(lgl)   d. December 27, 1870

Sophia
widow of John H. Stager
died December 27, 1870
aged 87.3.27

Notes:

--John m. December 18, 1801, Sophia Speer, dau. of Richard Speer and Sarah Stagg

--1850 Census, p.79, Caldwell Twp: John H. Stager, age 72, farmer; Sophia, age 67; John H. Jr., age '30' farmer; Mary J. age 36; Amelia F. age 11 mos.; Caroline L., age 11 mos.; Martha Thompson, age 16, b. NY; Louis Thompson, age 3 mos. b. NJ

--1860 Census, p.94, Caldwell: Alvah Bond, age 60, farmer; Maria, age 45; Harvey H., age 17, farmer; Emma S., age 11; Sophia S., age 77

--1870 Census, p.129, Caldwell: John Stager, 51, farmer; Mary 55; Carolina age 20; Marcus, age 18; William E., age 14; Sophia, age 88

Children of John H. Stager and Sophia Speer:
?Maria, b. abt 1815; m. Alvah Bond
John H., q.v., b. abt 1817; m. #1, Mary Cadmus
      m. #2, Margaret Devoe
Cornelius, b. abt 1824; m. #1, Caroline VanRiper, dau. of
      John Van Riper, q.v.; m.#2, Effy .....

- - - - -

Stager, Thomas	b. (1807)
	d. (1891)
wife, Rachel (Van Ness)	b. (abt. 1808)
	d.
son, **JOSEPH B.**	b. (abt. March 4, 1847)
(gmnj) (njhs) (lgl)	d. September 4, 1849

Joseph B.
son of Thomas
& Rachel Stager
died Sept. 4th, 1849
aged 2 years & 6 months

daughter, **SARAH J.**   b. (abt. December 6, 1843)
(gmnj) (njhs) (lgl)   d. February 6, 1849

Sarah J.
daughter of
Thomas & R. Stager
died Feb. 6th, 1849
aged 5 years & 2 months

daughter, **SOPHIA**   b. (abt. March 13, 1842)
(gmnj) (njhs) (lgl)   d. June 13, 1847

Sophia
daughter of
Thomas & R. Stager
died June 13th, 1847
aged 5 years & 3 months

Notes:
--1850 Census, p.88, Caldwell Twp: Thomas Stager, age 44, farmer; Rachel, age 42; John H., age 19, farmer; Martha, age 15; Rachel, age 14; Cornelius, age 10; 1 laborer
--1860 Census, p.103, Caldwell Twp: Thomas J. Stager, age 50, farmer; Rachel, age 49; Martha, age 20; Cornelius, age

21; Lemuel, age 8; adj. to John H. Stager, age 28 and wife, Ann

Children of Thomas J. Stager and Rachel Van Ness:
Eliza,b. 1827; d. 1914; m. 1850 Moses Van Ness (bur. Laurel
  Grove Mem. Park, Totowa, Passaic Co.)
John H., b. 1829; m. 1856, Ann Demarest
Martha, b. abt. 1835; m. Artemis Zeliff (bur. Pompton Plains)
Rachel, b. 1837; d. 1924; m. John H. Milledge; (bur. Pompton
  Plains Ref. Church Cemetery)
Cornelius, b. abt. 1840
Sophia, b. 1842; d. 1847
Sarah J., b. abt. 1843; d. 1849
Joseph B., b. abt 1847; d. 1849
Lemuel

- - - - -

STEELE

Steele, George

b. (January 13, 1804)
d. (September 12, 1881)
(bur. Ferncliff Cemetery,
Clark Co., Ohio)

wife, Lydia P. (Crane)

b. (April 26, 1809)
d. (January 16, 1899)
(bur. Ferncliff Cemetery,
Clark Co., Ohio)

son, **SAMUEL GIBSON**
(gmnj) (njhs) (lgl)(photo)

b. (abt. February 21, 1829)
d. October 21, 1830

In
Memory of
Samuel Gibson
son of
George & Lydia Steele
died Oct. 21st, 1830
aged 1 year & 8 months

Notes:

--George Colton Steele, son of Josiah Steele, q.v., and Phebe Smith

--George m. January 21, 1828, Lydia P. Crane, dau. of Caleb Crane, q.v., and Lydia Personett

--1850 Census, p.82, Caldwell Twp: George C. Steele, age 46, merchant, b. NJ; Lydia P., age 41; Mariah C., age 17; George W., age 15; Matilda Moore, age 48

--1860 Census, p.372, Springfield, Clark Co., Ohio: George C. Steele, age 56, oil&gas manufacturer; Lydia P., age 51; Maria C., age 26; George W., age 24, gas mfr.; all b. NJ

--1870 Census, p.281, Springfield, Clark Co., Ohio: George C. Steel, age 66, ret. merchant; Lydia, age 61; Maria 'Crain', age 37, (dau.)b. Ohio(?); Aaron 'Crain' (son of Caleb S. Crane), age 30 b. Ohio(?), office clerk; 1 servant

--1880 Census, p.300.2, Springfield, Clark Co., OH: George C. Steele, age 76 b. NJ, retired merchant; Lydia P., age 71 b. NJ; Nettie Hartman, age 18, servant

Children of George Colton Steele and Lydia P. Crane:
Samuel Gibson, b. 1829; d. 1830
Maria Crane, b. 1832; d. 1872; m. 1868, Aaron Dodd Crane, son of Caleb S. Crane, q.v.

George Whitfield, b. 1836; d.1863, (monument: Ferncliff
Cemetery, Springfield, Ohio) Camp Chase (Civil War)
m. 1861, Jane Lavinia Crane

- - - - -

Steele, **JOSIAH**, II   b. (August 24, 1760)
(gmnj) (njhs) (lgl)   d. October 22, 1836

Josiah Steele
a native of West Hartford, Conn.
died Oct. 22, 1836
aged 76 years. 1 mo.
& 29 days

wife, **PHEBE** (Smith)   b. (January 16, 1771) (?)
(gmnj) (njhs) (lgl)   d. December 7, 1846

Phebe
wife of
Josiah Steele
died Dec. 7th, 1847
aged 76 years. 6 months
& 9 days

Notes:
Served: Revolutionary War
--Josiah Steele, II, b. Hartford, Connecticut, son of Josiah
Steele, I, and Elizabeth Colton; grandson of Eliphalet Steele
and Catherine Marshfield.
--Josiah m. at Caldwell, August 15, 1790, Phebe Smith

--Josiah's sister, Mercy, m. Noah Webster and was the mother of Noah Webster, L.L.D., author of the *American Dictionary of the English Language*

Children of Josiah Steele, II. and Phebe Smith:

Josiah, III, b. March 16, 1791; d. November 8, 1877, Schuyler Co., Illinois; (bur. Pleasant View Cemetery, Schuyler Co., Illinois); m. at Caldwell, August 26, 1813, Hannah Osborne, dau. of Aaron Osborn and Rachel Condit; 10 children

Amanda, b. 1793; d. Feb. 1830) (bur. Ayers Cemetery, Franklin Co., Ohio"Consort of Jonathan Whitehead), Jonathan W. Whitehead, (1788-1872) son of Silas Whitehead and Ruth Condit. Jonathan m. #2 Widow Wicks "Justina Melrose Whitehead, (1832-1887) dau. of Jonathan Whitehead and his second wife was adopted and raised by her aunt, Matilda Steele Moore." q.v.; Justina m. George DeGraw Moore, son of Samuel Moore, q.v.,and Hannah Crane. Children of Amanda Steele and Jonathan Whitehead were Alfred; Josiah; Asa; Edmund; and Lucinda (1812-1876) who married Jeptha Condit Noe.

Elizabeth, b. 1795; d. 1833?; m. 1813, Amos Williams, (1794-1875) of Livingston, son of Joel Williams and Eunice Dodd; 5 children; (son, George Steele Williams grad. Yale Medical School...settled in Caldwell...had illness of several months...died there 1859 abt. 30 years old. m. Sarah Amanda Bunnell.)
(dau., Harriet Matilda Williams 1821-1884 m. Rufus Harrison, q.v.)

Marshfield Smith, b. 1797;d. 1868;(bur. Ferncliff Cem.,
    Springfield, Ohio); m. 1820, Mary Corlock; 10 children
Phebe, b. 1799; d. 1890; m. 1822, Caleb D. Harrison, son of
    Jabez Harrison, q.v. (bur. Prospect Hill Cemetery)
Matilda, b. 1801;d. 1875; (bur. Rosedale Cemetery, Orange; stone
    with Harriet L. Moore 1819-1894) m. #1, Rev. Joseph C.
    Moore, q.v.;
    m. #2, Daniel Pound, b. 1792; d. 1867;Boulder, CO.
George Colton, q.v., b. 1804; m. 1828, Lydia P. Crane
Aaron W., b. 1806; d. 1881; m. #1, Almira Rice; m. #2,
    Rachel ....; (bur. Evergreen Cem, Westmoreland, Oneida Co.,
    New York)
Lot Chester, b. 1808; m. 1834, Catherine M. Dodd; (bur.
    Fairmount Cemetery, Jackson Co., Ohio)
John Amzi, b. 1811; m. 1830, Adrianna Lyon (bur. Clayton
    Cemetery, Montgomery Co., Ohio

- - - - -

STILES

Stiles, John   b. (abt. 1819)
                                d. (aft. 1900)

wife, Lillis Matilda (Cobb)   b. (abt. 1823)
                                d. (aft. 1900)

daughter, **HARRIET MATILDA**
(gmnj) (njhs) (lgl)   b. (abt. January 27, 1846)
                                d. August 27, 1847

Harriet Matilda

> *daughter of John*
> *& Lillis M. Stiles*
> *Aug. 27th, 1847*
> *aged 1 year & 7 months*

Notes:

--John, son of Moses Stiles, q.v., and Elizabeth Goould Burnet

--John Stiles m. abt. 1841, Lillie Matilda Cobb

--1850 Census, p.68, John Stiles, age 31, drover; Lillis M., age 25; both b. NJ

--1870 Census, p.110 Caldwell: John Stiles, age 50, lumber dealer; Matilda, age 46; Anna M., age 15

--1880 Census, p.165.2, Newark: John Stiles, age 66, lumber dealer; Lille M., age 54; Anna M., age 28, dau.

--1900 Census, p.2A. Newark: John Stiles, b. Sept. 1818, m. 59 years, b. NJ, lumber dealer; Lillie M, b. March 1824 NJ, parents b. NY, 1 born 1 living

Children of John Stiles and Lillie Matilda Cobb:
Harriet Matilda, b. abt 1846; d. 1847
Anna M., b. abt. 1853

- - - - -

Stiles, Moses   b. (May 15, 1794)
                              d. (November 29, 1880)

wife, Betsy/Elizabeth Gould Burnet
                              b. (June 1795)
                              d. (June 14, 1890)

son, **WILLIAM BURNET**   b. (abt. October 23, 1816)
(gmnj) (njhs)   d. October 16, 1823

William Burnet
son of Moses
& Betsy Stiles
died Oct. 16th, 1823
aged 6 years. 11 months
& 23 days

Notes:
--Moses, son of Deacon John S. Stiles of Parsippany and
Mary Sandford
--Moses m. Elizabeth Gould Burnet, dau. of William Burnet,
q.v., and Annah Dodd.
--1850 Census, p.68, Caldwell: Moses Stiles, age 56, drover;
Elizabeth age 55; Judson, age 19, toll gatherer; Louis F., age
14; William B., age 12; all b. NJ
-1860 Census, p. 221, Newark: Moses Stiles, age 66, drives
team; Elizabeth G., age 65; Delia, age 32; Sarah, age 27;
William, age 21, store clerk; George 'Augustus' (Agens), age
28, clerk; Harriet E. (Agens), age 29; William, (Agens) age
10 months; Louisa F. age 29, huxter; Caroline, age 26; all b.
NJ
--1870 Census, p.142&143, 7Wd, Newark; Moses Stiles, age
76, drover; Elizabeth, age 75; Delia, age 39
--1880 Census, p.239.2 Newark: Moses Stiles, age 86, bark
dealer; Elizabeth age 85; Adelia R., age 50, dau., single,
fancy goods store

Children of Moses Stiles and Annah Dodd:
William Burnett, b. abt. 1816; d. 1823

John, q.v., b. abt. 1818; m. Lillis Matilda Cobb
Anna Maria, b. abt. 1820; m. 1853, Rev. Elias L. Boing
Phebe Catherine, b. abt. 1823; d. 1857; (bur. Michigan)
    m. August 1853, Rev. Elkanah Whitney,q.v.
Adelia Righter, b. abt. 1825; d. 1888 unm.
Harriet Eliza, b. abt. 1828; m. 1857, Thomas C. Cox
Judson, b. abt. 1830; m. 1858, Cornelia Bond dau. of
    Stephen Bond, q.v.
Sarah Elma, b. abt 1833
Louisa Frances b. abt. 1835
William Burnet, b. abt 1838; m. 1863, Ann E. Hutson

- - - - -

STUART

Stuart, **SARDIUS**   b. (December 4, 1797)
(njhs) (lgl)   d. December 5, 1825

Sardius Stuart
died
Dec. 5th, 1825
aged 28 years
& 1 day

wife, Rebecca (Jacobus)   b. (1803)
(Stagg)   d. (March 4, 1886)
      (bur. Prospect Hill Cem.)

Notes:
--Sardius, son of Alpheus Stuart and Pamela Rice of
Leominster, Massachusetts

--Sardius, m. Rebecca Jacobus, daughter of Cornelius H.
Peter Jacobus and Sarah Gould; she m. #2, bef 1830,
Nicholas Stagg (1792-1871)
--1850 Census: Caldwell: Nicholas Stagg, age 58, turner;
Rebecca, age 47; Eliza, age 19; Lemuel W. age 14, farmer;
William E., age 14; Farrand K., age 12; Alfred G. age 9;
David H. Dobbin, age 19, teacher. ADJ. to Sardius Stuart,
age 24, wood turner; Salena E. age 22; Charles, age 2.

Children of Sardius Stuart and Rebecca Jacobus:
Sarah A., b. abt. 1824; d. 1851; m. 1843, Alfred Coke Gould
  who m. #2, 1853, Caroline Elizabeth Harrison
Sardius, b. Feb. 1826; d. West Virginia; m. abt 1848,
  Salenna Elizabeth Davenport

- - - - -

SUPENOR

Supenor, Abraham   b. (abt. 1806)
(?NJ Will 19493G.1878)   d.

second wife, **CATHARINE** (VanNess)
(gmnj) (lgl)   b. (June 12, 1802)
                              d. September 2, 1851

Catharine
wife of Abraham Supanor
died September 2, 1851
aged 49.2.24

son, **WILLIAM H.**   b. (May 8, 1828)
(gmnj)   d. February 25, 1854

William H.
died February 25, 1854
aged 22.9.17

Notes:
--Abraham, son of Christopher, q.v.; m. #1 Mary Courter; m. #2, 1828, Catharine Van Ness
--1850 Census, p.75, Caldwell Twp: Abraham Supiner, age 44, carpenter; Catherine, age 48; William H., age 19, carpenter; John F., age 12; Sarah C., age 7; adj. to Cornelius Supenor, age 39; adj. to Cornelius Supenor, age 87
--1870 Census: Caldwell: James G. Williams, age 32; Sarach C. Williams, age 21; Jessie 8; Lizzie 4; John H. Courter, ag

Children of Abraham Supenor and Catherine Van Ness:
William H., b. 1828; d. 1851
Mary, b. Feb. 1830; m. #1, James Sindle; m. #2, 1857, John
       Henry Courter
John F., b. 1838
Sarah Catherine, b. abt. 1843

- - - - -

Supenor, **CHRISTOPHER** b. (abt. 1761)
(gmnj)   d. September 17, 1851
(NJ Will 14138G.1851)

Christopher Supenor
died September 17, 1851

aged 90 years

wife, **MARY** (Simonson)   b. (April 28, 1765)
(gmnj) (njhs) (lgl)   d. December 19, 1848

Mary
wife of Christopher Supener
died Dec. 19th, 1848
aged 83 years. 7 mos.
& 21 days

Notes:

--Christopher m. #1, Mary 'Polly' Simonson

--1850 Census, p.75, Caldwell Twp: Abraham Supiner, age '44', carpenter; Catherine, age 48; William H., age 19, carpenter; John F., age 12; Sarah C., age 7; adj. to Cornelius Supenor, age 39; adj. to Cornelius Supenor, age 87
--1850 Census, p.75, Caldwell Twp: Christopher Supenor, age 87, carpenter; Sarah Sindle, age 49; Ellen M. Jacobus, age 22; Edward I. Jacobus, age 21, hatter; James L. Jacobus, age 1 month; all b. NJ

Children of Christopher Supenor and Mary Simonson:
Isaac, b. abt. 1785; m. Catherine Vanderhoof
John, b. abt. 1793; m. Maria Vreeland
Catherine, b. Feb. 2, 1796; m. Levi Gardner
Sarah, b. 1799; m. Christopher T. Sindle
Abraham, q.v., b. abt. 1806; m. #1, Mary Courter
         m. #2, 1828, Catherine VanNess
Cornelius, b. abt. 1810; m. 1834, Mary Post(bur. Cedar Grove)
Rachel

- - - - -

TOMPKINS
TOMKINS

Tompkins, Aaron   b. (1735)
                         d. (1823)
                         (burial place not found)

Founding Elder

first wife, Hannah (Canfield) b.
                              d.

Notes:
Included here as a Founding Elder of the Church
--"Aaron Tomkins was a descendant of Michael Tomkins,
one of the original Milford settlers, and was a brother of Rev.
Ichabod Tomkins, pastor of the Baptist church at
Morristown. He lived on his farm, which was a part of what
is the Eagle Rock Reservation. He moved to Ohio in the late
1790's." (lgl. p.78)
--Aaron Tompkins, son of John Tompkins
m. Jan 1759, Morristown, Hannah Canfield; m. #2 ...Beach;
m. 3# Sarah Morehouse

Children of Aaron Tompkins and Hannah Canfield:
Stephen, b. 1760; d. 1840; m. Lucretia
Elizabeth, b. 1762; m. John Morehouse

Children of Aaron Tompkins and ..... Beach:
John, b. 1764; d. 1823; m. Elizabeth Montanye

Aaron, b. 1766; d. 1846; (bur. Roseland Methodist Churchyard)
    m. Catherine Dodd, dau. of Adonijah Dodd, q.v.
Moses, Dr.; b. 1772; d. 1816; m. Eunice Fairchild
Phebe, b. 1773 m. Jonathan Meeker

Children of Aaron Tompkins and Sarah Morehouse:
Isaac, b. 1790; d. 1857; m. Nancy Condit
Sarah, b. 1795; d. 1842; m. Ezra Beach

- - - - -

TUCKER

Tucker, **NANCY**   b. (abt. September 15, 1771)
(gmnj) (njhs) (lgl)   d. February 22, 1815

*Nancy Tucker
died Feb. 22nd, 1815
aged 43 years. 5 months
& 7 days*

*A pale consumption seized her cheek,
She felt the heavy load,
And often said, 'tis right and just;
It is the will of God*

Notes:

- - - - -

VANDERHOOF

Vanderhoof, Henry   b. (abt. 1826)
(?NJ Will 24776G. 1892)   d. (March 1892)
                                  (bur. Mount Pleasant Cem. Newark)

1st wife, **SARAH C.** (Jacobus)b. (abt. 1827)
(gmnj)   d. January 27, 1850

Sarah C.
wife of Henry Vanderhoof
daughter, of John R. and Sarah Jacobus
died January 27, 1850
in her 23rd year

2nd wife, Cornelia R. Fairchild
                       b. (abt. 1835)
                       d. (March 1904)
                       (bur. Mount Pleasant Cem. Newark)

Notes:
--Henry m. #1, 1847, Sarah C. Jacobus, dau. of John R.
Jacobus, q.v., and Sarah Stiles
--Henry m. #2, November 13, 1853, Cornelia Rebecca
Fairchild, dau. of Joseph Fairchild and Elizabeth Hoppock
--1850 Census, p.367, West Ward, Newark: William F.
Jacobus, age 22, blacksmith; John Vanderhoof, age 22,
carpenter; Henry Vanderhoof, age 24, mason; Jane
Vanderhoof, age 18; at res. of Priscilla Crawford
--1860 Census, p.305, 7Wd, Newark: Henry Vanderhoof, age
32, livery stable; Cornelia, age 24; Eugene age 5;
--1870 Census, p.41, 7 Wd, Newark: Henry Vanderhoof, age
40, mason; Cornelia R., age 35; Joseph E., age 15; all b. NJ

--1880 Census, p.16D, Newark: Henry Vanderhoof, age 54, brick mason; Cornelia R., wife, age 46, b. NJ; Joseph E. son, age 22, huckster

--1900 Census, p.9A, 7Wd, Newark: Cornelia Vanderhoof, age 65, b. NJ

Child of Henry Vanderhoof and Cornelia R. Fairchild:
Joseph Eugene, b. abt. 1855;d.1899 (bur. Mount Pleasant Cem.)

- - - - -

VAN DUYNE

Van Duyne, Cornelius J.   b. (March 21, 1803)
    d. (May 16, 1870)
    (bur. Pine Brook Cemetery)

first wife, **SALLY** (Sarah Mead Burnet)
(gmnj) (njhs) (lgl)   b. (abt. 1803)
    d. May 12, 1832

Sally
wife of
Cornelius J. Van Duyne
died May 12th, 1832
in her 29th year

daughter, **MARIA LOUISA** b. (abt. September 26, 1826)
(gmnj) (njhs) (lgl)   d. June 3, 1832

Maria Louisa

daughter of Cornelius J.
and Sally Van Duyne
died June 3rd, 1832
aged 5 years. 8 months
& 8 days

Notes:
--Cornelius m.#1, abf. 1826, Sarah/Sally Mead Burnet,
daughter of William Burnet, q.v.
--Cornelius m. #2, bef. 1850, "Percilly" (Priscilla?) b. VT
--1850 Census, p.334, Rockaway Twp., Morris Co.NJ:
Cornelius T. VanDuyne age 47, farmer; Percy, wife, age 47
--1860 Census, p.7, Pequannock Twp., Morris Co., NJ:
Cornelius VanDuyne, age 57, farmer; Percy, age 57
--1870 Census, p.215, Montville, Morris Co., NJ: Cornelius
VanDuyne, age 75, farmer, b. NJ; Percy, age 75, keeping
house, b. Vermont

Children of Cornelius VanDuyne and Sarah Mead Burnet:
Maria Louisa, b. 1826; d.1832
Harriet Marinda,

- - - - -

VAN EMBERG
VAN EMBURGH

Van Emberg, **HANNAH JANE**
(gmnj) (njhs) (lgl)   b. (abt. 1809)
                                       d. April 10, 1843

Hannah Jane Van Emberg

died
April 10, 1843
in her 34th year

Notes:

--Hannah Jane: possible sister of Thomas H. Van Emburg?
--?1850 Census: p.82, Caldwell Twp: Thomas Van Emburgh, age 49, potter; Emeline, age 42; Elizabeth, age 24; Julia Ann, age 19; Emeline, age 14
--?Thomas H. Van Emburg b. Dec. 28, 1800; d. Feb. 21, 1858, Age 57; (bur. Rosedale Cemetery, Orange); m. 1823 Emeline Merrit. Daughter, Emeline b. 1836 d. 1917 m. Minard F. Magie; (bur. Rosedale Cemetery)
--?See: Matthias Canfield

- - - - -

VAN GIESEN

Van Giesen, Rynier	b. (abt. 1775) d. (March 3, 1863) (bur. Mount Hebron Cemetery, Montclair. Mass Grave in SW Quarter)
wife, Sarah (Kent)	b. (May 9, 1777) d. (May 17, 1851) (bur. Mount Hebron Cemetery, Montclair. Mass Grave in SW Quarter)
son, **AMZY EDWARD**	b. (January 15, 1809)

(gmnj) (njhs) (lgl) (photo)   d. January 8, 1829

In Memory
of
Amzy-Edward Van Gieson
son of Rynier
and Sarah Van Gieson
who died Jan. 8th, 1829
aged 19 years. 11 months
& 24 days

Notes:

--Rynier m. Sarah Kent, daughter of Jacob Kent, q.v., and Effie Edwards.

--1850 Census, p.173, Bloomfield, Essex Co., NJ: Rynear VanGiesen, age 75, farmer; Sarah, age 74; Sarah Vreeland, age 16; Eveline VanPatten, age 33; Philip VanPatten, age 6

--1860 Census, p.180, Bloomfield: Reaniner VanGiesen, age 86, farmer; Emeline, age 45

?Children of Rynier Van Giesen and Sarah Kent:

Effie, b. July 1797 (Second River Ref. Ch. records)
Israel, b. May 1800 (Second River Ref. Ch. records)
Jared, b. April 2, 1806; m. Nancy .....
Amzi Edward, b. January 15, 1809; d. 1829
Horace, b. 1811; ?m. 1830, Getty Sigler
Eveline, b. 1814; m.1835, Philip S.VanPatten
Rynier, b. abt. 1816; m. Caroline Corby, dau. of Stephen
Anthony, b. abt 1819; m. Sarah .....
Augustus Theodore, b. 1821; ?m. 1841, Eliza Post
        ?m. 1845, Elizabeth Harvey

- - - - -

VAN HOUTEN

Van Houten, **HENRY**   b. (abt. 1747)
(gmnj) (njhs) (lgl)   d. April 17, 1815
(NJ Will 10943G.1815)

Henry Van Houten
who died of lingering consumption
April 17th 1815
in his 69th year

Notes:
--?son of Cornelius VanHouten and Rachel Post

- - - - -

VAN NESS

Van Ness, **EPHRAIM S.**   b. (abt. November 19, 1777)
(gmnj) (njhs) (lgl)   d. October 24 1837

Ephraim S. Van Ness
died Oct. 24th, 1837
aged 59 years. 11 months

wife, **SARAH** (Personett)   b. (abt. February 11, 1782)
(gmnj) (njhs) (lgl)   d. January 21, 1844

Sarah
wife of

Ephraim S. Van Ness
died Jan. 21st, 1844
in her 62nd year

son, **MOSES**   b. (abt. 1803)
(gmnj) (njhs) (lgl) (photo)   d. December 5, 1832

In
Memory of
Moses Van Ness
who died
Dec. 5th, 1831
in the 29th year
of his age

Notes:
--Ephraim, son of Simon Evert VanNess and Margaret Riker
--Ephraim m. May 25, 1799, Sarah Personett, dau. of John
Personett, Esq. and Elenor Doremus

Children of Ephraim S. VanNess and Sarah Personett:
Maria, b. abt. 1800; m.1819, Melvin Foster
Moses, b. abt. 1804; d. 1832
Simon E., b. 1804; m. #1, 1828, Elizabeth Arbuthnot
        m. #2, aft. 1829, Catherine Brown
Ezra, b. abt. 1808; m. #1, 1829, Jane Halstead
        m. #2, bef. 1850, Sarah D. .....
Artemas, b. abt. 1811; m. Ann .....
Daniel, b. abt 1813; m. #1, Letitia .....;
        m. #2, bef. 1860, Julia A. .....
George, b. 1820; m.#1, bef. 1850, Anna C. .....
        m. #2, bef. 1880, Sarah .....

Lydia, b. abt 1823

- - - - -

Van Ness, Jacob F.	b. (January 1, 1820) d. (August 21, 1897) (bur. Hillside Cemetery Fairfield, NJ)
wife, Margaret M. (Bond)	b. (March 5, 1823) d. (February 17, 1897) (bur. Hillside Cemetery)
son, **HENRY** (gmnj) (njhs) (lgl) (photo)	b. (abt. July 30, 1846) d. June 24, 1850

Henry
son of
Jacob F. & Margaret
Van Ness
died
June 24th 1850
aged 3 years.
10 months.
& 25 days

son, **JAMES M.** (lgl) (njhs) (gmnj) (photo)	b. (November 16, 1849) d. July 3, 1833 (1855)

James M.
son of
Jacob F. & Margaret

Van Ness
died July 3rd, 1833 (1855)
aged 5 year. 9 months
& 17 days

Notes:
--Jacob m. October 20, 1842, Margaret M. Bond, dau. of Alvah Bond and Jane VanNess
--1850 Census, p.87&88 Caldwell Twp: Jacob F. VanNess age 33, carpenter; Margaret, age 30; Electa, age 5; Isaac M., age 3; James M. age 6 months; all b. NJ
--1860 Census, p.91, Caldwell: Jacob F. VanNess, age 40, carpenter; Margaret, age 38; Electa age 16; Isaac M., age 14; Sarah A., age 8; Gilbert, age 5; Walter, age 3; Emma M., age 3 months
--1870 Census, p.109, Caldwell: Jacob F. VanNess, age 50, carpenter; Margaret, age 47; Sarah A., age 18; Gilbert, age 14; Walter, age 12; Emma, age 9
--1880 Census, p.431.1, Caldwell: Jacob F. VanNess, age 60, carpenter; Margaret, age 54; Emma M., age 10

Children of Jacob F. VanNess and Margaret M. Bond:
Electa J., b. abt 1843; m. 1864, Joseph H. Green
Isaac M., b. 1845; m. Margaret A. Fredericks
Henry, b. abt 1846; d. 1850
James M., b. abt. 1849; d. 1855
Sarah A., b. abt 1852
Gilbert, b. 1854; m. Mary L. ..... (bur. Hillside Cemetery)
Walter B., b. abt 1856; m. Mary E. .... (bur. Hillside Cemetery)
Emma M., b. abt 1860

- - - - -

VAN RIPER

Van Riper, John

b. (1797)
d. (1882)
(bur. Prospect Hill Cemetery)

wife, Charity

b. (1797)
d. (1883)
(bur. Prospect Hill Cemetery)

son, **GEORGE**
(njhs) (lgl)

b. (abt. July 1, 1835)
d. September 20, 1838

George
son of John &
Charity Van Riper
died Sept. 20th, 1838
aged 3 years. 2 months
& 19 days

daughter, **CAROLINE STAGER**
(gmnj) (lgl) (photo)

b. (abt. March 22, 1825)
d. July 31, 1851

In Memory of
Caroline Stager
daughter of
Charity and John Van Riper
died July 31, 1851
aged 26.4.9

Notes:
--John VanRiper m. Charity .....
(--?John VanRiper, Jr., m. May 5, 1832, Sally VanWinkle)

--1850 Census, p.87, Caldwell Twp: John VanRiper, Jr., age 51, carpenter; Charity, age 52; George, age 12; Harriet, age 9
--1860 Census, p.103, Caldwell: John VanRiper, age 62, farmer; Charity, age 62; Hester A., age 20; Harriet, age 19; 1 laborer
--1870 Census, p.127 Caldwell: John VanRiper, age 72, farmer; Charity, age 72; George H., age 30, carpenter; Joseph Courter, age 30, carpenter; Harriet, age 28; Newton,age 7;' Louis, age 6; William, age 8 mos.; 1 laborer
--1880 Census, p.404.3, Caldwell: Charity VanRiper, age 82, widow, farmer; Harriet Courter, age 39, widow; John N. Courter, age 17, grandson; Lewis Courter, age 16, grandson; 1 boarder,pauper

Children of John VanRiper and Charity.....
Caroline, b. 1825; d. 1851; m. bef. 1850, Cornelius Stager
George, b. 1835; d. 1838
George, b. 1838; ?m. 1865, Sarah Newman
Harriet, b. abt 1841; m. 1861, Joseph Courter (1837-1872), son of John Courter and Sarah Crane

- - - - -

WADE

Wade, **JOSEPH**   b. (abt. 1805)
(gmnj) (njhs) (lgl)   d. October 6, 1850

Joseph Wade
died Oct. 6th, 1850
aged 45 years

Notes:

--Joseph, son of Obadiah Wade,q.v., and Nancy Edwards
--1850 Census: Livingston: Nancy Wade, age 69, b. NJ;
Joseph Wade, age 44, b. NJ shoemaker; Abner Wade, age 44,
b. NJ farmer; Ann Eliza Norwood, age 20; Margaret 'Wade'
age 25, b. Ireland; Abraham 'Wade' age 6, b. NY; Nancy
Turner, age 2, b. NJ

- - - - -

Wade, **OBADIAH**   b. (July 6, 1773)
(gmnj) (njhs) (lgl) (photo)   d. December 28, 1837
(NJ Will 12933G.Inv.1838)

Obadiah Wade
died
Dec. 28th, 1837
aged 64 years

wife, **NANCY** (Edwards)   b. (abt. 1781)
(gmnj)   d. 1864

Nancy
wife of Obadiah Wade
died August 20, 1864
in her 83rd year

Notes:

--Obadiah, son of Jonathan Wade and Elizabeth Ward
--Obadiah m. 1794, Nancy Edwards
--1850 Census: Livingston: Nancy Wade, age 69, b. NJ;
Joseph Wade, age 44, b. NJ shoemaker; Abner Wade, age 44,
b. NJ farmer; Ann Eliza Norwood, age 20; Margaret 'Wade'
age 25, b. Ireland; Abraham 'Wade' age 6, b. NY; Nancy
Turner, age 2, b. NJ

- - - - -

WARD

Ward, **ICHABOD B.**   b. (abt. 1794)
(gmnj) (njhs) (lgl)   d. September 30, 1846
(NJ Will 13677G.Inv.1847)

Ichabod B. Ward
died
Sept. 30th, 1846
in his 52nd year

wife, ?Sarah Crane   b.
                    d.

Notes:
Served: War of 1812
--?Ichabod m. March 14, 1819, Sarah Howell Crane, dau. of
Zenas Crane, q.v., and Abigail Grover
--?Sarah Howell Crane b. abt. 1800 m. Samuel Dobbins, d.
in Illinois

- - - - -

Ward, Job D.   b.
                             d.

1st wife, **FRANCES R.**   b. (abt. 1819)
                             d. August 9, 1846

Frances R.
wife of Job D. Ward
died August 9, 1846
in her 27th year

daughter, **FRANCES R.**   b. (abt. June 10, 1846)
(gmnj)(njhs) (lgl)   d. July 31, 1847

Frances R.
daughter of Job D.
and Frances R. Ward
died July 31st 1847
aged 1 year. 1 month
& 21 days

Notes:
--Job D. Ward m. #2, March 1847, Sarah G. Coe

- - - - -

Ward, John   b. (1785)
                             d.

wife, Sarah (Williams)   b. (October 3, 1785)
                             d. (January 3, 1847)

son, **ZOPHAR W.**   b. (December 31, 1807)
(gmnj) (njhs) (lgl) (photo)   d. June 30, 1845

In
Memory of
Zophar W.
son of John M. and
Sarah Ward
who died
June 30th, 1845
aged 37 years (35?)
& 6 months

Notes:
--John, son of Jonathan Ward; m. Sarah Williams, b. 1785, Albany, New York

Children of John Ward and Sarah Williams:
Zophar W., b. 1807; d.1845; m. 1829, Maria Gould

- - - - -

Ward, Zebediah, Capt.   b. (December 1755)
                         d. (August 24, 1836)
                         (d. Clark County, Indiana)

first wife, Sarah (Zeluff)   b. (Staten Island)
                              d. 1921-1827 Indiana

daughter, **EUNICE**   b. (abt. November 1779)
(gmnj) (njhs) (lgl)   d. April 23, 1800

Eunice, daughter of
Capt. Zebediah & Sarah Ward
died April 23rd, 1800
aged 20 years. 5 mos.
& 20 days

Notes:
Served: Sgt. Col. Ogden's Reg't.; Ranger, Capt. Elijah Squire's Co.
--He m. #1, Sarah Zeluff; m. #2, July 1828, Harriet Jones
1837 Will of Zebediah Ward. Clark Co. Indiana: $1.00 to each of 6 grown child of his first wife; land to son, Sylvester; cow and bed to daughter, Mary Jane

- - - - -

WARDELL

Wardell, **ELENOR**   b. February 3, 1786
(gmnj) (njhs) (lgl) (photo)   d. October 15, 1831

The grave
of
Elenor Wardell
born
Feb. 3rd, 1786
died
Oct. 15th, 1831

Notes:

- - - - -

Wardell, Peter   b.
                           d. (bef. April 1800?)

wife, **JOANNAH**   b. (abt. 1750)
(gmnj) (njhs) (lgl) (photo)   d. August 10, 1814

Joannah
wife of
Peter Wardell
died
Aug. 10th, 1814
aged 64 years

Notes:
--(?)Will of Jacob Wardell of Shrewsbury. Dated 1790
Proved 1796: names wife, Hannah; son Joseph; <u>son Peter and
his wife, Johanna and their son, Jacob.</u>
--(?) Will 1798: Hannah Wardell, administrator, Joseph
Wardell
--(?)Ward: April 1800: William Wardell, upwards of 14
years of age, <u>of Essex County, son of Peter Wardell</u>, late of
Monmouth County
--(?)July 1776: Jacob Wardell, Joseph Wardell and Peter
Wardell: persons apprehended by a detachment of the
Monmouth militia on accountof furnishing the enemy with
provisions. Ordered: Jacob Wardell be committed to the
custody of the sheriff and pay 28 pounds expenses. Joseph
and Peter Wardell be discharged on giving bond, each with
the security of five hundred pounds. (History of Monmouth
County. Franklin Ellis. Phildelphia, 1885)

--(?)February 1780: Sales of Loyalist property in Monmouth County: Peter Wardell

Children of Peter Wardell and Joannah.....:
William
Jacob

- - - - -

WESTERFIELD

Westerfield, **PETER**   b. (abt. December 28, 1798)
(gmnj)   d. January 28, 1824

Peter Westerfield
a native of New York
died January 28, 1824
aged 25.1.0

Notes:
--Peter m. December 24, 1818, Phebe Edwards

- - - - -

WESTERVELT

Westervelt, Luke J.   b. (abt. 1829)
                        d. (aft. 1880)

first wife, **HARRIET E.** (Keene)
(gmnj)   b. (abt. 1836)
                   d. December 18, 1865

Harriet E.
wife of Luke J. Westervelt
died December 18, 1865
in her 33rd year

Notes:

--Luke m. #1, Harriet E. Keene, dau. of (Nathan?) Keene and Elizabeth .....; #2, before 1860, Elizabeth .....

--1850 Census, p.29, North Ward, Newark: Elizabeth Keen, age 48; Mary Keen, age 14; Martha Keen, age 8; Harriet Westervelt, age 17; Luke J. Westervelt, age 21, works at patent leather

--Harriet Elson Westervelt and Luke J. Westervelt, bapt. Feb, 1858, witn. the Fairfield Congregarion

--1860 Census, p.97, Caldwell: Luke J. "Westrurto" age 30, tobacco cutter; Harriet E., age 24; John W., age 7; Alonzo M. age 4; Anna E., age 1; all b. New Jersey

--1870 Census, p.115, Caldwell: Luke Westervelt, age 40, works at tobacco factory; Elizabeth, age 30; John, age 17, works at tobacco factory; Alonzo, age 13, works at tobacco factory; Lizzie, age 11; Charles age 6; Alfred Stickles, age 8

--1880 Census, p.260.3, Kearney, Hudson Co., NJ: Luke Westervelt, age 52, cigar maker; Lizzie, age 35; Charles, age 16, works roller factory; Hatty, age 9; all b. NJ

Children of Luke J. Westervelt and Harriet E. Keene:
John W., b. 1852; d. 1930 m. Emma .....(bur. Prospect Hill)
Alonzo M., b. 1855; m. Elizabeth .....
Anne Elizabeth, b. 1858; d. 1933
Charles, b. abt. 1864

Child of Luke J. Westervelt and Elizabeth ......
Harriet "Hattie", b. abt. 1871

- - - - -

WHITNEY

Whitney, Rev. Elkanah   b. (January 30, 1820)
                          d. (June 11, 1863)
                          Age 48.4.19
                          (bur. Oxford Cemetery,
                          Oakland Co., Michigan)

wife, **PHEBE C.** (Stiles)   b. (abt. February 8, 1823)
(gmnj) (lgl)   d. May 9, 1857

Phebe C. Stiles
wife of Rev. E. Whitney
died May 9. 1857
aged 34.3.1

Notes:
--Elkanah Whitney, b. Province of Upper Canada
--Rev. E. Whitney m. August 3, 1853, Phebe Catherine
Stiles, dau. of Moses Stiles, q.v., and Annah Dodd
-- Elkanah Whitney, grad. Auburn Theological Seminary,
NY. 1849?; served in St. Lawrence Co., NY; Executive
Committee of the American Missionary Society;
Illinois,Wisconsin, Michigan, Kansas (The Congregational
Quarterly. Vol. VI. Boston. 1864); In 1862, board of American
Home Missionary Society in Orion, Michigan.

Children of Elkanah Whitney and Phebe C. Stiles:
Infant
Child: ("consigned to the care of a kind Christian family")

- - - - -

WILLIAMS
Note: Most data from <u>The Williams Families</u>
<u>of New Jersey</u>. Lyle K. Williams. Iowa. 1998

- - - - -

Williams, Daniel Z.
b. (abt. November 25, 1813)
d. (February 21, 1863)
(bur. Prospect Hill Cemetery)

wife, Jane (Vreeland)
b. (abt. 1819)
d. (December 11, 1884)

son, **NICHOLAS**
(lgl)
b. (abt. 1842)
d. 1864

Nicholas
son of Daniel Z. Williams
died ....., ..., 1864
aged 21 years

daughter, **SARAH M.**
(gmnj) (photo)
b. (abt. August 8, 1854)
d. May 13, 1855

Sarah M.
daughter of

Daniel and Jane
Williams
died May 13, 1855
aged 0.9.5

Notes:
--Daniel, son of Zadok Williams, Jr. and Jane Corby; m. 1838, Jane Vreeland
--1850 Census, p.85, Caldwell Twp: Daniel Williams, age 31, butcher; Jane, age 31; Esther, age 11; Nicholas, age 8; Mary E., age 6; James R., age 4
--1860 Census, p.118, Caldwell: Daniel Williams, age 42, butcher; Jane, age 41; Esther age 21; Nicholas, age 18; Mary E., age 16; James, age 13; Joanna, age 11; David, age 9; Phebe A., age 4; Zadoc, age 81
--1870 Census, p.79, Bloomfield: David Eagles, age 21, works at saw mill; Joanna, age 20; Jane Williams, age 51, all b. NJ
--1880 Census, p.544.1, East Orange: David Eagles, age 30, work at organ mfr.; Johanna, age 28; Norman, age 9; Emma, age 6; Aaron, age 4; John, age 1; Jane Williams, age 63, mother-in-law, widow; 1 boarder

Children of Daniel Z. Williams and Jane Vreeland:
Esther, b. abt. 1839
Nicholas B., b. abt. 1842; d. 1864 (Civil War?)
Mary E., b. abt. 1844; m.1865, John Courter (bur. Prospect Hill Cemetery, Caldwell)
James R., b. abt. Dec. 1846 (? Pvt. James R. Williams, no dates, bur. Prospect Hill Cemetery, Caldwell)
Joanna, b. Sept. 1849; m. bef. 1870, David Eagles (?see Sgt. David Eagles, Millbrook Methodist Cem. Morris Co., N.J.)

David, b. January 1852
Phebe A., b. abt. 1856
Sarah M., b. 1854; d. 1855

- - - - -

Williams, **ENOS**   b. (abt. 1751)
(gmnj)   d. March 8, 1811
(NJ Will 10709G. Inv. 1811)

Enos Williams
died May 8, 1811
in his 60th year

wife, Susannah (Ogden)   b. (abt. 1749)
                                                    d. (aft. 1811)

Notes:
Served: June 1780. Capt. Thomas Williams Co. of Militia
--(Lyle K. Williams first thought him to be son of Zadoc
Williams. He published a correction.)
--Enos, son of Amos Williams, III, and Abiah .....; m. 1773,
Susannah Ogden, dau. of Samuel Ogden and Phebe Baldwin;
sister of David Ogden, q.v.; John Ogden, q.v.; and Simeon
Ogden, q.v.
--1811 Will. Intestate. Inventory: "includes cider spirits,
agreed by the heirs that the widow sell the spirits to buy
things for her immediate comfort."

Children of Enos Williams and Susannah Ogden:
Samuel Ogden, b.1775 d. 1858; m. Huldah Whitehead (bur.
    Jersey Presbyterian Church Cem. Jersey, Licking Co., Ohio)

Nancy, b. 1777; d. 1856; m. Adonijah Edison (1772-1825)
(both bur Estherville Cem.,Bayham, Elgin Co., Ontario, Canada)
Dorcas Lucy, b.abt 1778; m. Elijah Meeker, d. Licking Co.,
Ohio
Phebe Ogden, b. 1779 d. 1847; m. Rufus Freeman
Harrison, q.v.
Swaine Ogden, b. 1782; d. 1816; m. #1, Frances McFarland;
m. #2, Miss Peffer, his niece, daughter of David
Peffer and Mary/Polly Williams
Mary/Polly, b. 1782 d 1860; m. David Peffers; d. Ohio
(bur. Jackson Universalist Ch. Cem. Licking Co. Ohio)
Gershom Simeon, b. 1783 d.1861;m. Elizabeth Francis
'Fanny' Brundage, daughter of James Brundage and
Phebe Ogden
Elizabeth, b. 1790; m. Israel Williams (1781-1870), her first
cousin (Condits and Cousins Family History) (bur. Beech
Grove Cemetery, Muncie, Delaware Co., Indiana)

- - - - -

Williams, **JENIAH**   b. (abt. 1769)
(gmnj) (njhs) (lgl)   d. September 26, 1831

Jeniah Williams
died
Sept. 26th, 1831
in his 62nd year

wife, Charlotte (Pearce)   b. (February 3, 1776)
d. (April 7, 1863)

Notes:

--Jeniah, son of Zophar Williams (1741-1798) and Sarah Hedden (or Elizabeth Miller of Westfield)

--Jeniah m. October 17, 1793, Charlotte Pearce, dau. of Henry Pearce/Pierce and Elizabeth Speer

--1850 Census, p.83&84, Caldwell Twp: William Fairchild, age 67, tailor; Mary Fairchild, age 50; Charlotte Williams, age 75; Phebe Ann Williams, age 30; Warner H. Williams, age 7; David Williams, age 5; Robert Williams, age 3; Florence Williams, age 1

--1860 Census, p.106A, Caldwell: Abram D. Personett, age 70, tanner/currier; Joanna, age 64; Charlotte Williams, age 84; Mary Bone, age 40; all b. NJ

Children of Jeniah Williams and Charlotte Pearce:

Joanna, b. 1795; m. 1814, Abram D. Personett, q.v.

Elizabeth, b. 1797; m. 1819, Gabriel M. Baldwin

Mary Bates, b. 1799; m. 1819, William W. Fairchild, q.v.

Job Crane, b. 1802; m. 1827, Catherine Tichenor Stiles
(bur. Rosedale Cemetery, Orange, N.J.)

Daniel, b. 1804; m. 1826, Catherine Riggs
m. abt. 1830, Sarah Ann VanRiper

Dorcas, b. 1806; m. 1825, John Jarvis

Matilda F., b. 1809; m. 1829, Aaron James Quimby(Rosedale Cemetery, Orange NJ)

Harriet, b. 1811; m. 1834, Robert Walker (Bloomfield Cemetery)

Henry L., b. 1814; m. Mary Townsend;m. 1841, Fanny L. Howe

Stephen, b. 1816; m. 1842, Phebe Ann Haywood
(See: William Fairchild)

- - - - -

Williams, **JONATHAN H.**   b. (abt. December 1841)
(gmnj)   d. August 30, 1866

Jonathan H. Williams
died August 30, 1866
aged 24.8.10

Notes:
--Not found in Lyle K. Williams book.
--Jonathan, son of ..... Williams

- - - - -

Williams, **JOSEPH**   b. (May 6, 1780)
(gmnj)   d. April 13, 1853
(NJ Will 14455G. Inv.1853)

Joseph Williams
died April 13, 1853
in his 73rd year

wife, **MARY**   b. (abt. 1780)
(gmnj)   d. January 30, 1843

Mary
wife of Joseph Williams
died January 30, 1843
in her 63rd year

Notes:
--Joseph Williams, son of Zadock Williams,q.v., and Rachel
Kent

--(?)"Joseph Williams to Polly Ward, both of Bloomfield by Rev. Abel Jackson" (Sentinel of Freedom, January 1800)
--(?)Joseph m. #2, after 1843, Elizabeth .....
--1850 Census; p.105, Livingston, Essex Co. NJ: Joseph Williams, age 69, farmer; Elizabeth, age 57
--"his farm later owned by his grandson, Joseph A. Mesler" (prob. son of Abraham Mesler, q.v., and his wife, Sarah Williams)

Children of Joseph Williams and Mary :
Aaron,
Jacob, b.. 1804; m. 1823, Effy Kent
(?)Amelia,
Caroline, m. 1838, William Mosier (1814-1890)
Lydia, d. unm.
Abner, b. abt. 1803; m. #1, 1827, Hannah Elizabeth Conklin
        m.#2, Rachel Kent; m.#3, Ellen Babcock
Melinda, b. 1805; m. 1821, Calvin Kent, q.v.
Elizabeth, b. abt. 1808; d. Luzerne Co., PA; m. Matthew
        Bowden Corby, son of Ezekiel Corby
Levi, b. 1814; d. 1864; m. Phebe Ann Kent (see Roseland
        Methodist Churchyard Cemetery)
Sarah, b. 1824; d. 1860; m. Abraham Mesler, q.v.

- - - - -

Williams, Jotham M.   b. (January 28, 1819)
                             d. (May 28, 1871)
                             Age 53

wife, **PERNELLA** (Provost) b. (abt. 1824)
(lgl)   d. March 5, 1862

Pernella Provost
wife of Jotham M. Williams
died March 5, 1862
in the 38th year of her age

daughter, **LAURA PROVOST**
(gmnj) (lgl)   b. (abt. 1847)
                                        d. February 1, 1864 (1861?)

Laura Provost
daughter of Jotham M. Williams
died February 1, 1864
in her 17th year

son, **JOSEPH M.**   b. (abt. 1849)
(gmnj) (lgl)   d. July 19, 1868

Joseph M.
son of Jotham M.Williams
died July 19, 1868
aged 19 years

Notes:
--Jotham Marshfield Williams, son of Amos Williams and
Elizabeth Steele
--Jotham m. December 10, 1845, Pernella Provost, dau. of
Jonathan Provost, q.v., and Paulina Moore
--Jotham, widower, m. April 1865, Margaret Cole, wid., dau.
of John Cole
--1850 Census, p.109, Livingston, Essex Co., NJ: Jotham M.
Williams, age 31, shoemaker; Pernella, age 25; Laura P., age

3; Joseph M., age 11 months; Sarah Mann, age 16; adj. to Amos Williams age 56

--1860 Census, p.106, Caldwell: Jotham Williams, age 41, merchant; 'Paulina' age 35; Laura, age 13; Joseph, age 11; 'Paulina, age 3; all b. NJ

--1870 Census, p.113, Caldwell: Jonathan Provost, age 71, farmer; Pauline, age 69; Phebe H. Burnet, age 63; Pauline Williams, age 13, at school; 1 servant; 2 laborers

Children of Jotham M. Williams and Pernella Provost:
Laura Provost, b. abt 1847; d. 1864
Joseph M., b. 1849; d. 1868
Pauline, b. abt. 1857; ?m. 1880, Alfred Whitehead
?m.Rev. J. D. Davis
Jonathan Provost, b. 1862; d. 1883 (bur. Prospect Hill Cem.)
George W., m. Jessie Walsh

- - - - -

Williams, Zadoc   b. (abt. 1740)
(NJ Will 11235G. 1819)   d. (abt. 1819)

wife, **RACHEL** (Kent)   b. (abt. 1741)
(gmnj) (njhs) (lgl) (photo)   d. March 2, 1824

In memory of
Rachel Williams
who died
March 2, 1824
aged 83 years

Notes:

There is conflicting research for this family.

--Zadok Williams, son of Gershom Williams and Hannah Lampson

--Zadok m. Rachel Kent, dau. of Simeon Kent and Mary Speer

--His will, signed 1816, proved 1819: ...wife, Rachel; lands to my son Simeon; to my son, Joseph; as agreeable to the divison made between sons Joseph and Zadock; daughters: Betsey Pierson, Mary Corby, Abigail Corby, Ruth Kent and Rachel King.

Executors: Simeon, Joseph and Zadock Williams.

Children of Zadok Williams and Rachel Kent:

Elizabeth b. abt. 1769; m. abt. 1789, Stephen Pierson

Mary, b. abt. 1771; d. 1831; m. December 1799, Caldwell,
> Peter Corby, b. abt 1776; d. 1851, son of Gideon
> Corby (Desc. of John Corby of Essex County. NY Gen. and
Biog. Record. Vol. 131.   p.30)
> "Peter Corby, son of Gideon Corby to <u>Rachel</u> (??)
> Williams, daughter of Zadoc Williams" (Sentinel
> of Freedom. Newark. February 1800)
> Peter Corby (#2?) m. July 1833, Caldwell, widow
> Catherine 'Stevens'

Abigail Kent, b. abt. 1773; d. bef. 1850; m. July 1801,
> Caldwell, Encrease Corby, b. abt. 1781; d. 1857; son
> of Gideon Corby
> 1850 Census, Caldwell: Yehoncris Corby, age 69,
> res. of dau. Abigail Dickerson, adj.to Ezekiel Corby

Ruth, b. abt. 1775; m. Elias Kent, son of Jacob Kent, q.v.

Rachel, b. abt. 1777; m. Feb. 1795, Caldwell, Gideon King

Zadoc, Jr., m. Mary Corby (Gen. and Memorial Hist. of the State of
> NJ. Francis B. Lee. Vol. 4)

Joseph, q.v.; b. May 1780; d. Apr. 1853; m. Mary
Simeon,(? m. Mary Smith; had daughter Dorcas who m.
    Daniel Corby, (1783-1855) son of Gideon Corby.

- - - - -

Williams, Zenas   b. (1834)
                                 d. (August 6, 1891)
                                 (bur.Fairmount Cem., Newark)

wife, Martha Jane (Keene)   b. (1842)
                                 d. (November 13, 1893)
                                 (bur. Fairmount Cem., Newark)

daughter, **MARY ELIZABETH**
(gmnj)   b. (abt. October 24, 1866)
                                 d. December 16, 1866

Mary Elizabeth
daughter of Zenas Williams
died December 16, 1866
aged 0.1.22

Notes:
--Zenas, son of John A. Williams (grandson of Azel
Williams(1766-1831) and Phebe ..... 1771-1859)
--Zenas m. October 1858, Caldwell, Martha J. Keene
--1840 Census: (Verona) Caldwell Twp: John Williams, near
Geo. P. Martin, Calvin Martin, George Personett
--1850 Census, p.88, Caldwell Twp: John A. Williams, age
55, farmer; Phebe, age 80; Phebe, age 18 (?m. Verona, 1851,
Jacob Sigler); Zenas, age 15, farmer; Henry, age 13; Richard,

age 11; Marcus, age 6; adj. to Abner Williams, age 27, shoemaker

--1850 Census, p.29, North Ward, Newark: Elizabeth Keen, age 48; Mary Keen, age 14; Martha Keen, age 8; Harriet Westervelt, age 17; Luke J. Westervelt, age 21, works at patent leather

--1860 Census, Caldwell Twp: Henry Riggs, age 66 laborer; Elizabeth (Keene?) age 61; Zenas Williams, age 26, shoemaker; Martha Williams, age 18; George H. Williams, Age 1.

--1880 Census, p.260C, Kearney, Hudson Co., NJ: Zenas Williams, age 48, shoemaker; Martha, wife, age 47; Mary, dau., age 19; corset maker; Harriet, age 17, corset maker; Richard, age 15, works at roller factory; Annie, dau. age 7; Daisy, age 4; Zenas, age 2

--1900 Census, p.3A, 4Wd, Harrison, Hudson Co., NJ: Richard Williams, b. Oct. 1864, machinist; Alice, wife, b. May 1876, England; Lulu, sister b. Nov. 1872, housekeeper; Daisy, sister, b. Aug. 1876, clamper at Edison Lamp Works; Charles, brother, b. Mar 1881, grocer clerk; Florence, sister, b. Jan. 1885, glass cutter at Edison Lamp Works

Children of Zenas Williams and Martha J. Keene:
George Henry, b. abt. 1859;d. July 1915; m. Mary Ann
        Dorman (George, bur. Holy Sepulchre Cemetery, Newark)
        (Mary Ann, bur. Holy Cross Cemetery, North Arlington)
Mary, b. abt March 1861
Harriet, b. abt. 1863
Richard Eugene, b. September 1864, m. Alice .....
Mary Elizabeth, b. Sept. 1866; d. 1869.Age 2. (bur. Fairmount
        Cemetery, Newark)
Annie "Lulu", b. November 1872

Daisy, b. August 1876
Zenas, b. abt. 1878; d. 1880
Son, b. Sept. 1880,Kearny, Hudson Co.

Charles, b. March 1881
Florence Belle, b. January 1885; d. Oct. 1947; m. (?Edward)
Littig; (Mrs., bur. Hollywood Memorial Park, Union, N.J.)

- - - - -

WILLIS

Willis, Elias B.   b. (January 29, 1811)
                                    d. (July 27, 1856)

wife, **ELIZA** (Kent)   b. (abt. 1816)
(gmnj)   d. August 21, 1853

Eliza
wife of Elias B. Willis
daughter of Jacob and
Polly Kent
died August 21, 1832 (Aug. 21,1852)
aged 56.10.23 (36.10.23)

Notes:
--gmnj: 'stone difficult to read'
--Elias Baldwin Willis, son of Joseph W. Willis and Mary
Baldwin
--Elias m. February 23, 1833, Eliza Kent, dau. of Jacob Kent

--1850 Census, p. 82&83, Caldwell Twp: Elias B. Willis, age 39, stage driver; Eliza, age 34; Georgianna, age 11; John Henry, age 4; Charlotte L., age 2; all b. NJ
--1870 Census, p.205, East Orange: Wm. C. Freeman, age 30, builder; <u>Georgianna</u>, age 30; Minnie, age 9; Martha, age 6; Lottie B., age 4; Edward age 1; <u>Charlotte Willis</u>, age 21, domestic

Children of Elias Baldwin Willis and Eliza Kent:
Mary E., b. abt. 1835; d. bef. 1850?
Georgeanna, b. abt. 1839; m. July1860, William C. Freeman
John Henry, b. abt. 1846
Charlotte L., b. June 4, 1848

- - - - -

WRIGHT

Wright, **SUSANNA A.**   b. (abt. 1764)
(gmnj)   d. August 9, 1844
(?NJ Will.13590G. Inv.1846)

Susanna A. Wright
died
Augt. 9th, 1844
in her 80th year

Notes:
--prob. Susanna, mother of Moses Wright
--Moses Wright b. Feb. 1795; d. Jan 1859 (bur. Teedtown Cemetery/Federated Baptist Cemetery, Livingston, NJ)

--1850 Census, p.99, Livingston, Essex Co., NJ: Moses Wright, age 54, shoemaker; Hannah 50; Edwin age 18, farmer; Sarah J., age 16; Susanna age 14; Annette age 9; Ann, age 26; Moses Jr. age 6; Joseph,age 26, shoemaker; Joseph, age 4; all b. NJ

--1860 Census: Livingston: Widow Hannah Wright, age 62, real estate $8,000; Susana, age 24; Moses age 14; Aneta (Annette) age 19; Joseph, age 12

--1863, September: Susie F. Wright m. Sept. 1863, Livingston, John B. Kehl

--1870 Census: Livingston: Hannah Wright, age 70, real estate $10,000; Annette, age 38

- - - - -

CHRONOLOGICAL

The below three inscription reports have been compared and studied:

(NJHS):<u>Monumental Inscriptions of Essex County, N.J. Collected in 1904</u>. NJ Historical Society (The latest stone recorded was for Elenor Voorhees Miller, August 1858) Stones marked only(njhs) had 'no trace of remains in 1925'.

(GMNJ): <u>Gravestone Records From The Caldwell Presbyterian Church Yard, Essex County</u>. The Genealogical Magazine of New York. Vol. 2. July 1926. 'Copied Aug. and Sept., 1925, by Sylvester H. M. Agens and Russell B. Rankin' (This report, aided by a copy of the above, seems to be the most reliable.)

(LGL) Lewis G. Lockward. <u>A Puritan Heritage</u>. 1955 (Lockward refers to the 1904 Collection; but not to the 1925 Collection by Agens and Rankin.)

- - - - -

1788, March (gmnj)	Susanna Gould, wife of Timothy
"oldest stone standing in 1955" (lgl)(njhs)(gmnj)	
1789, August (gmnj)	Stephen Grover Gould, s/o Capt.Wm.
1789, Nov. (gmnj)	William Dodd, son of Abel
1790, April (gmnj)	Simeon Ogden
1790, June (gmnj)	Keturah Bond, dau. of William
1790, August (gmnj)	David Ogden
1790, Nov. (gmnj)	Betsy Gould, dau. of Timothy
1791, May (gmnj)	Dennis Bacorn
1791, July (gmnj)	Rhoda Harrison, wife of Joseph Esq.
1793, Jan. (gmnj)	Cornelius Gould, son of Stephen

1793, June (gmnj)	John Osborn, son of Aaron
1793, August (gmnj)	Charlot Bond, dau. of Abner
1794, July (gmnj)	Zebedee Gould, son of Joseph
1794, Sept. (gmnj)	Elizabeth Bond, dau. of Abner
1795, Sept, (gmnj)	John Dodd, son of Abel
1795, Oct. (gmnj)	Daniel Baldwin, son of Ezekiel
1797 (gmnj)	Effie Edwards Kent, wife of Jacob
1797, April (gmnj)	John Ogden (husb. of Elizabeth?)
1797, Nov. (gmnj)	Richard Jacobus, son of Peter D.
1798, April (gmnj)	Mary Personett Gould, w/o Encrease
1798, July (gmnj)	James Wheelock Grover, s/o Stephen
1799, June (gmnj)	John Grover, son of Stephen
1800, April (gmnj)	Eunice Ward, dau. of Capt. Zebediah
1801, March (gmnj)	Moses Personett, son of George Esq.
1801, March (gmnj)	Phebe Personett, dau. of Moses
1801, March (gmnj)	Caleb Pierson
1801, Nov.(gmnj)	Capt. Zenas Crane
1802, August (gmnj)	Elizabeth Ogden, widow (of John?)
1802, Dec. (gmnj)	Thomas Gould, son of Joseph
1803, August (gmnj)	Abigail Harrison, wife of Jabez
1804, August (gmnj)	Jane Simonson, wife of Barney
1804 Sept. (gmnj)	Davis Bayles Baldwin, son of Elias
1804, Sept. (gmnj)	John DeCamp, son of Aaron
1805, Jan. (gmnj)	Dorcas Crane, wife of Timothy
1806, August (gmnj)	Peter I. Riker, husb. of Martha
1806, Sept. (gmnj)	Keturah Bond, wife of Noah
1806, Oct. (gmnj)	Jonas Crane
1806, Nov. (gmnj)	Elias Allen Baldwin, son of Elias
1807, August (gmnj)	John Gould
1808, March (gmnj)	Elizabeth Beach, widow of Zophar
1808, April (gmnj)	Nancy Catharine Bates,d/o Philemon
1808, Oct. (gmnj)	Elizabeth Gould, wife of Thomas
1809, February(gmnj)	Electa Dickerson Bates,d/o Philemon
1810, January (gmnj)	Amanda Nesbit, dau. of Hugh
1810, March (gmnj)	Ambrose Crane, son of Capt. Simeon
1810, June (gmnj)	Mary Condit Personett, w/o Geo. Esq.
1810, Sept. (gmnj)	Enos Martin, Esq.
1810, Dec. (gmnj)	Joseph Gould, husb. of Rebekah P.

1811, Jan. (gmnj)	Capt. Caleb Dodd
1811, Feb. (gmnj)	Samuel Crane, Esq.,husb. of Mary
1811, March (gmnj)	Enos Williams
1811, Nov. (gmnj)	Capt. William Sandford
1812, Jan. (gmnj)	Dr. Abner Reeves, husb. of Elizabeth
1812, March (gmnj)	Ellen Husk, dau. of John
1812, April (gmnj)	Elizabeth Kent, dau. of Jacob
1813, Feb. (gmnj)	Lucius F. Douglass
1813, April (gmnj)	Harriet Henrieta Gould,d/o of William
1813, Oct. (gmnj)	Hannah Grover Riker, dau. of Peter I.
1813, Dec. (gmnj)	Mehitable Gould, wife of Thomas
1814, March (gmnj)	Azariah Crane
1814, April (gmnj)	Phebe Dodd
1814, April (gmnj)	Eliz Gould Reeves, wid. of Dr. Abner
1814, April (gmnj)	Dr. Ezra K. Squire
1814, June (gmnj)	Charlotte Gould Harrison,w/o Joseph
1814, August (gmnj)	Joannah Wardell, wife of Peter
1814, Sept. (gmnj)	John Parliamen Cole, son of John
1815, Feb. (gmnj)	Thomas Gould, husb. of Mahetable
1815, Feb. (gmnj)	Nancy Tucker
1815, April (gmnj)	Henry VanHouten
1815, June (njhs)	Hetty Eliza Baldwin, dau. of Robert
1815, June (gmnj)	Samuel Price
1815, June (gmnj)	Betsey Bond, dau. of Samuel
1815, July (gmnj)	Mary Jane Jacobus, dau. of John R.
1815, July (gmnj)	Ralph Jacobus, son of John R.
1815, Nov. (gmnj)	Ann Plunket, wife of William
1816, Jan. (gmnj)	Sarah Douglass, wife of Nathaniel
1816, Feb. (other)	Sarah Gould, wife of Stephen, Esq.
1816, March (gmnj)	Rebekah Paxton Gould, w/o Joseph
1816, May (gmnj)	Jane Martin, wife of Enos, Esq.
1816, June (gmnj)	George Personett, Esq.
1817, Jan. (gmnj)	Mary Crane, wife of Samuel, Esq.
1817, Feb. (gmnj)	William Cole, son of John
1817, March (gmnj)	Rebeckah Day, wife of Moses
1817, July (gmnj)	Mary Kent, wife of David
1817, August (gmnj)	Jacob Bown, son of John (Kent stone)
1817, August (gmnj)	Deacon Oliver Crane

1817, Oct. (gmnj)	John Lindsley Bates, son of John
1817, Dec. (gmnj)	Henry Gould
1818, Jan. (gmnj)	Mehetable Gould Riker,dau. of Peter I.
1818, June (gmnj)	Annah Burnet, wife of William
1818, June (gmnj)	Martha Gould Hudson, w/o John L.
1818, July (gmnj)	Rachel Maria Openshaw, d/o Richard
1818, July (gmnj)	William Wheelock Gould, s/o Robert
1818, Sept. (gmnj)	Abby Harrison, dau. of Zenas
1819, Feb. (gmnj)	Barney Simonson, husb. of Jane
1819, April (gmnj)	Caroline O. Simonson, d/o Anthony
1819, Nov. (gmnj)	Hannah Maria Baldwin, dau. of Noah
1819, Nov. (gmnj)	John Louis Gould, son of Thomas D.
1820, Jan. (gmnj)	Jane Lee Duryea Crane,w/o Nathaniel
1820, Feb. (njhs)	D. Elizabeth Harrison
1820, June (gmnj)	Mary Gould, wife of Robert
1820, July	Dorcas Eliz. Harrison, of Samuel
1820, July (gmnj)	Stephen Brundage, husb. of Mary
1820, Nov. (gmnj)	Matthew Bowden
1821, June (gmnj)	Widow of Jonas Crane
1821, July (gmnj)	Elizabeth Gould, wife of Josiah
1821, August (gmnj)	Samuel Gibson Crane, husb. of Lydia
1821, August (gmnj)	Hannah Dobbins, wife of David
1821, August (gmnj)	Samuel Gould
1821, Sept. (gmnj)	Nehemiah Crane
1821, Sept, (gmnj)	Jos Freeman Crowell,h/o Ros.Grover
1822, March (gmnj)	Charles Thos Cochran, son of Thomas
1822, Nov. (gmnj)	Esther Cochran, wife of Thomas
1823, Oct. (gmnj)	William Burnet Stiles, son of Moses
1824, Jan. (gmnj)	Peter Westerfield, native of New York
1824, Feb. (gmnj)	Mary Williams Dobbins,d/o David L.
1824, March (gmnj)	Rachel Kent Williams, w/o Zadoc
1824, May (gmnj)	Nathaniel Douglass, husb. of Sarah
1824, July (gmnj)	Elizabeth Gould, wife of Timothy,Esq.
1824, August (gmnj)	William B. Personett, son of Abram
1824, Dec. (gmnj)	Daniel Beach, husband of Joannah
1825, Jan. (gmnj)	Joannah Beach, wife of Daniel
1825, Feb. (gmnj)	Delphine Edgar Crane, son of Nath'l.
1825, March (gmnj)	Susan Colyer

1825, July (gmnj)	Robert Gould, husb. of Mary
1825, August (gmnj)	Sarah Fordham, wife of Stephen
1825, Nov. (gmnj)	Mary Lee Duryea, wife of Rev. John
1825, Dec. (njhs)	Sardius Stuart
1826, Jan. (gmnj)	Elias Northrup, son of John
1826. April (gmnj)	No surname. Martha Ann,d/o Hester
1826, July (gmnj)	Esther Grover, dau. of Stephen R.
1826, Dec. (gmnj)	Francis Moore
1827, Jan. (gmnj)	Nancy Crane, wife of Calvin S.
1827, Jan. (gmnj)	Infant Crane, son of Calvin S.
1827, April (gmnj)	John Cole
1827, June (gmnj)	Pierson Bond
1827, August (gmnj)	Charles Grover, son of Stephen R.
1827, August (gmnj)	Grace Slover, widow of Isaac
1827, Sept, (gmnj)	Peter Morison Arbuthnot, son of Wm.
1827, Oct. (gmnj)	David Harrison Dobbins,son of David
1827, Nov. (gmnj)	Noah Bond
1827, Nov. (gmnj)	Col. Cyrus Crane, husband of Hannah
1828, Jan. (gmnj)	Mary Conselyea
1828, Jan. (gmnj)	Ellen Moore, dau. of Daniel
1828, March (gmnj)	Phebe Baldwin,w/o Ephraim & Hiram
1828, April (njhs)	William Henry Miller, s/o Benjamin
1828, April (gmnj)	John Simonson, husb. of Fanny Lines
1828, August (gmnj)	Marth Riker, wid. of Peter I.
1828, Sept. (gmnj)	Philip Crane, on stone of Nehemiah
1828, Dec. (gmnj)	Cyrus Crane
1829, Jan. (gmnj)	Ann Eliza Cochran
1829, Jan. (gmnj)	Amzi Edward VanGieson, s/o Rynier
1829, Feb. (gmnj)	Francis A. Moore, son of Stephen
1829, March (gmnj)	William S. Burnet
1829, March (gmnj)	Joseph Byram
1829, Oct. (gmnj)	Eliza Reeves Gould, dau. of Thomas
1829, Oct. (gmnj)	George Provost, son of Jonathan
1829, Nov. (gmnj)	Stephen Fordham, husb. of Sarah
1829, Nov. (gmnj)	Elizabeth Gould, dau. of Stephen
1830, April (gmnj)	Sandford Gould, son of Anthony
1830, May (gmnj)	David L. Dobbins, husb. of Hannah
1830, August (gmnj)	Adeline Conover, dau. of Stephen

1830, August (gmnj)	Ezra Jacobus, son of Archibald
1830, Oct. (gmnj)	Maria Crane, dau. of Caleb
1830, Oct. (gmnj)	Peter Jacobus, husb. of Sarah
1830, Oct. (gmnj)	Samuel Gibson Steele, son of George
1830, Nov. (gmnj)	Ann Maria Conover Heath, w/o Aaron
1831, Feb. (gmnj)	Rosina Gould, dau. of Ezekiel
1831, Feb. (gmnj)	Eleanor P. C. Miller, dau. of Isaac S.
1831, June (gmnj)	Abby Faitoute Gould, d/o Nathaniel
1831, July (gmnj)	Zenas Harrison, husb. of Phebe
1831, Sept. (gmnj)	Jeniah Williams,(h/o Charlotte Pierce)
1831, Oct. (gmnj)	Edward J. Crane
1831, Oct. (gmnj)	Elenor Wardell
1831, Dec. (gmnj)	Miranda Harrison, dau. of Jabez
1831, Dec. (gmnj)	Moses Van Ness
1832, Jan. (gmnj)	Rachel Jacobus, wife of Peter D.
1832, Feb. (gmnj)	Elizabeth Sandford, w/o Gamaliel
1832, March (gmnj)	Noah Baldwin, husband of Naomi
1832, March (njhs)	Joseph R. Crane, son of Col. Cyrus
1832, May (gmnj)	Sally VanDuyne, wife of Cornelius
1832, May (gmnj)	Ellen Jacobus Gould, wife of Samuel
1832, May (gmnj)	Marcus Johnson Gould,s/o Nathaniel
1832, June (gmnj)	Maria L. VanDuyne, d/o Cornelius
1832, July (gmnj)	David B. Harrison, son of Jabez
1832, July (gmnj)	Isaac Slover Miller,husb. of Elenor V.
1832, August (gmnj)	Eliza Kent Willis, wife of Elias D.
1833, May (gmnj)	Elijah Pierson Crane, son of Cyrus
1833, May (gmnj)	Mary Jane Low, dau. of Cornelius
1833, June (gmnj)	Hannah Roome Hammell,w/o Dr.John
1833, June (gmnj)	Rhoda Martin, 1st wife of George P.
1833, July (gmnj)	John Low, son of Cornelius
1833, July (gmnj)	James M. VanNess, son of Jacob F.
1833, August (gmnj)	Israel Corby, son of Ezekiel
1833, Nov. (gmnj)	Mary Jane Low, dau. of Cornelius
1834, May (gmnj)	Lydia Crane, dau. of George
1834, Oct. (gmnj)	Phebe Jones Crane, wife of Nehemiah
1834, Oct. (gmnj)	Phebe Gould, wife of Timothy
1834, Oct. (gmnj)	Edward Hoage
1834, Dec. (gmnj)	Sarah Urania Crane, dau. of Stephen

1835, Jan. (gmnj)	Hannah Crane
1835, Jan. (gmnj)	Julia Douglass Crane,w/o Calvin G.
1835, Feb. (gmnj)	Samuel Moore
1835, Feb. (gmnj)	Eliza C. Simonson, dau. of John
1835, Feb. (gmnj)	No name. 'My father'
1835, May (gmnj)	Tamar H. Dodd, wife of Aaron
1835, June (gmnj)	Calvin A. Francisco, son of Thomas
1835, Sept. (lgl)	Pierson Cole
1835, Sept. (gmnj)	Richard Cole
1835, Sept. (gmnj)	John R. Jacobus, husb. of Sally
1835, Nov. (gmnj)	Stephen C. Moore
1836, March (gmnj)	Henrietta Crane, dau. of William G.
1836, March (gmnj)	Jane Chitterling Morris, w/o Stephen
1836, June (gmnj)	Rev. Stephen Grover, husb. of Mary
1836, August (gmnj)	Ezra Jacobus, son of Archibald
1836, Sept. (gmnj)	Mary Gould, dau. of Joseph
1836, Sept. (gmnj)	Priscilla Bush, dau. of Jacob
1836, Oct. (gmnj)	Rev. John Duryea, husb. of Mary
1836, Oct. (gmnj)	Abigail Gould Jacobus, w/o Cornelius
1836, Oct. (gmnj)	Mary Jane Personett, dau. of Abram
1836, Oct. (gmnj)	Josiah Steele, husb. of Phebe
1836, Dec. (gmnj)	Aaron I. Jacobus, son of Aaron
1837, Jan. (gmnj)	Aaron S. Conselyea
1837, March (gmnj)	Calvin S. Crane, husband of Nancy
1837, March (gmnj)	Joseph Harrison Esq, husband of Mary
1837, April (gmnj)	Nancy C. Gould, wife of Thomas D.
1837, May (gmnj)	Sarah H. Francisco, wife of Henry
1837, April (gmnj)	William Wallace Crane, son of Moses
1837, June (gmnj)	Abigail Alling Dobbins, wife of John
1837, April (gmnj)	Nancy Gould, wife of Thomas D.
1837, July (gmnj)	Aaron S. Conselyea
1837, Sept. (gmnj)	Euphemia Martin, 2nd wife of Geo. P.
1837, Oct. (gmnj)	Ephraim S.VanNess, husb. of Sarah
1837, Nov (gmnj)	Cath. Provost Schuyler,w/o John D.
1837, Dec. (gmnj)	Elizabeth Douglass, dau. of Marcus
1837, Dec. (gmnj)	Obadiah Wade, husb. of Nancy
1838 (gmnj)	David Harrison
1838 (gmnj)	Lois Williams Dodd, wife of David

1838, March (gmnj)	William W. Gould, son of Stephen J.
1838, May (gmnj)	Henry A. Jacobus, husb. of Maria
1838, May (gmnj)	Infant dau. of Henry A. Jacobus
1838, June (gmnj)	Gabriel Lewis Baldwin
1838, June (gmnj)	Aaron I. Jacobus, husb. of Abby
1838, August (gmnj)	Benjamin DeCamp
1838, August (gmnj)	Harley W. Crane, son of George
1838, Sept. (gmnj)	George Wheelock Gould,s/o Nath'l. M
1838, Sept. (gmnj)	Byron S. Reuck, son of Aaron
1838, Sept. (njhs)	George VanRiper, son of John
1839, May (gmnj)	Stephen Gould
1839, Nov. (gmnj)	Josephine Bowden, dau. of William
1838, Nov. (gmnj)	Susanna Crane, wife of Oliver
1839, January(gmnj)	Aaron Dodd, husb. of Tamar
1839, January(gmnj)	John Gould
1839, March (gmnj)	Joseph Pryme, son of David D.
1839, May (gmnj)	Ann Maria G. Crane,dau.of Saml G.
1839, May (gmnj)	Stephen Gould
1839, May (gmnj)	Calvin Kent
1839, June (gmnj)	Eliza Mahon, wife of John
1839, Sept. (gmnj)	Jane Bond, wife of Smith Bond
1839, Sept. (gmnj)	David Banks Crane, son of Uzal A.
1839, Sept. (gmnj)	Richard S. Harrison
1839, Sept. (gmnj)	Sarah Jane Riker, dau. of Asa P.
1839, Nov. (gmnj)	Josephine Bowden, dau. of William
1839, Dec. (gmnj)	William Bowden, son of John
1840, Jan. (gmnj)	Joseph Crane, son of Nathaniel G.
1840, Jan. (gmnj)	Edward Nelson Crane, son of Moses P
1840, April (gmnj)	Betsy Bond, dau. of Samuel
1840, April (gmnj)	William G. Jacobus, husb. of Margaret
1840, August (gmnj)	Mary Harrison, wid. of Joseph, Esq.
1840, Sept. (gmnj)	Margaret Gould, wife of Nathaniel M.
1841, Feb. (gmnj)	Zadoc Crane, husband of Joanna
1841, Feb. (gmnj)	Timothy Gould, husb. of Susanna
1841, May (gmnj)	Geo. Moore Reuck,s/o Aaron
1841, June (gmnj)	Jacob Kent, husb. of Effie Edwards
1842, Jan. (gmnj)	Catherine Decamp, wife of Moses
1842, Jan. (njhs)	John M. Dexheimer, son of Jacob

1842, Jan. (gmnj)	Stephen S. Gould
1842, Feb. (gmnj)	George Duryea
1842, Feb. (gmnj)	Fanny Personett, wife of John, Jr.
1842, March (gmnj)	Ellen Husk, dau. of John
1842, April (gmnj)	Jonathan Beach, husband of Sarah
1842, May (gmnj)	Sarah M. Beach, dau. of Jonathan
1842, May (gmnj)	Keziah Dodd Kent, wife of Jacob
1843, Jan. (gmnj)	John G. Jacobus, son of William G.
1843, Jan. (gmnj)	Dr.John T. Lockward, h/o Charlotte P.
1843, March (gmnj)	Abby E. Baldwin, dau. of Ira
1843, March (gmnj)	Elizabeth Baldwin, dau. of Ira
1843, April (gmnj)	Hannah Jane VanEmberg
1843, July (gmnj)	Suwarrow S. Bedford, dau. of Moses
1843, Dec. (gmnj)	Mehetable Gould, wife of Gen. Wm.
1844, Jan. (gmnj)	Sarah VanNess, wife of Ephram S.
1844, Feb. (gmnj)	Mary Sandford Gould, w/o Anthony
1844, Feb. (gmnj)	Joshua Moore
1844, March (gmnj)	Mary Banks Crane, dau. of Uzal A.
1844, March (gmnj)	Lucetta Banks Crane, dau. of Alexdr.
1844, April (njhs)	Francis Alexr. Harrison, s/o Jared F.
1844, May (gmnj)	Hannah Moore, wid. of Samuel
1844, May (gmnj)	George Moore Reuck, son of Aaron
1844, June (gmnj)	Judson Irvin Beach, son of Jared
1844, June (gmnj)	Caleb Crane
1844, June (gmnj)	Rev. Joseph Moore
1844, June (gmnj)	Judson Irvin Beach, son of Jared
1844, August (gmnj)	Susanna Wright
1844, Sept. (gmnj)	George H. Grover, son of Stephen R.
1844, Nov. (gmnj)	Elizabeth Baldwin
1845, Dec. (gmnj)	John Henry Francisco, son of Andrew
1844, Dec. (gmnj)	Harriet Maseker, dau. of Peter
1845, Feb. (gmnj)	Joanna Frances Riker, dau of Asa P.
1845, May (gmnj)	Josiah Gould, husb. of Elizabeth
1845, June (gmnj)	Zophar W. Ward, son of John
1845, July (njhs)	George Jacobus, son of Cornelius
1845, August (gmnj)	James Backus, son of Calvin G.
1845, Dec. (gmnj)	John Henry Francisco, son of Andrew
1846, Feb. (gmnj)	Harriet P. Beach, dau. of Jonathan

1846, March (gmnj)	Martha Bowden, wife of Matthew
1846, March (gmnj)	Rachel Dobbins, wife of Isaac
1846, March (gmnj)	Thomas Francisco, husb. of Nancy F.
1846, March (gmnj)	Sarah Jacobus, wife of Peter
1846, May (gmnj)	Electa Bond, wife of Samuel
1846, May (gmnj)	Eliza Crane, dau. of George
1846, May (gmnj)	John Husk, husb. of Abigail
1846, June (gmnj)	Ann Harrison, wife of Henry W.
1846, August (gmnj)	Frances R. Ward, wife of Job D.
1846, Sept. (gmnj)	Ichabod B. Ward
1846, Nov. (gmnj)	Richard Cadmus, son of William
1846, Dec. (gmnj)	Sarah E. Condit, dau. of Wm. S.
1846, Dec. (gmnj)	Hannah M. Gould, dau. of Thomas D.
1847, Jan. (gmnj)	Sarah Beach, wife of Jonathan
1847, Feb. (gmnj)	Gen.William Gould, h/o Mehitable
1847, Feb. (gmnj)	Joannah Miller, wife of Philetas
1847, March (gmnj)	Elizabeth Backus, wife of Calvin G.
1847, March (gmnj)	Cornelius Gould, husb.of Eliza Beach
1847, April (gmnj)	Matthias Canfield
1847, May (gmnj)	Suwarrow A. Bedford, dau. of Moses
1847, May (gmnj)	Sarah Pierson, wife of Jeptha
1847, June (gmnj)	Phebe Harrison, wife of Rufus
1847, June (gmnj)	Sophia Stager, dau. of Thomas
1847, July (gmnj)	Mary Grover, wife of Rev. Stephen
1847, July (gmnj)	Frances R. Ward, dau. of Job D.
1847, August (gmnj)	Rev. William Bull
1847, August (gmnj)	Harriet Matilda Stiles, dau. of John
1847, Dec. (gmnj)	Phebe Steele, wife of Josiah
1848, Feb.(gmnj)	Cathalina Jacobus, wife of Ephraim
1848, March (gmnj)	Rhoda Maria Crane, wife of Caleb S.
1848, March (gmnj)	Sarah E. Stager, dau. of John
1848, May (gmnj)	Malvina M. Potter Baldwin, w/o Caleb
1848, May (gmnj)	Samuel Dodd
1848, June (gmnj)	Marcus E. Jacobus, son of Henry A.
1848, July (gmnj)	Eliza Beach Gould, wife of Cornelius
1848, July (gmnj)	Rufus Harrison, husband of Phebe
1848, July (gmnj	James Provost, son of Jonathan
1848, August (gmnj)	Walter Dodd, son of Elijah

1848, August (gmnj)	Elizabeth Grover, wife of Stephen
1848, August (gmnj)	Nancy Haywood
1848, Sept. (gmnj)	Florence Baldwin, dau. of Alfred D.
1848, Sept. (gmnj)	Leah Bush, dau. of Absalom
1848, Oct. (gmnj)	Elizabeth, wife of Stephen R. Grover
1848, Dec. (gmnj)	Mary Supenor, wife of Christopher
1849, Jan. (gmnj)	Catharine DeCamp, wife of Moses
1849, Feb.(gmnj)	Betsy Condit, wife of Stephen
1849, Feb.(gmnj)	Susan Gould
1849, Feb. (gmnj)	Sarah J. Stager, dau. of Thomas
1849, March (gmnj)	Elizabeth Baldwin, dau. of Ira
1849, March (gmnj)	Mary Dobbins, wife of David
1849, March (njhs)	Samuel Harrison
1849, April (gmnj)	Eunice Crane, wife of Asher
1849, April (gmnj)	Caroline O Simonson, d/o Anthony
1849, May (gmnj)	Jabez Harrison, husb. of Abigail
1849, Sept. (gmnj)	Hyacinth Maria Hopkins
1849, Sept. (gmnj)	William Harris Hopkins
1849, Sept. (gmnj)	Joseph B. Stager, son of Thomas
1849, Sept. (gmnj)	Sarah J. Stager, dau. of Thomas
1849, Oct. (gmnj)	Joanna Crane, wife of Zadoc
1850 (gmnj)	Patick Hoage, husb. of Matilda Lane
1850, Jan. (gmnj)	Thomas Cochran
1850, Jan. (gmnj)	Stephen Condit. husb. of Betsy
1850, Jan. (gmnj)	Sarah Jacobus Vanderhoof, w/o Henry
1850, Feb. (gmnj)	Ellen Low, dau. of Cornelius
1850, March (gmnj)	William S. Burnett
1850, March (gmnj)	Sarah Eliz. Harrison, wife of Saml O.
1850, April (gmnj)	Charles C. Condit, son of William S.
1850, May (njhs)	Silas Baldwin, son of Amos
1850, May (gmnj)	Willie M. Crane, son of James H.
1850, May (gmnj)	Hannah Crane, wife of Col. Cyrus
1850, May (gmnj)	Willie M. Crane, son of James H.
1850, June (gmnj)	Henry VanNess, son of Jacob F.
1850, July (gmnj)	Caleb D. Burnet
1850, August (gmnj)	Charity Wade Davidson,w/o of Henry
1850, Oct. (gmnj)	Joseph Wade
1850, Nov. (gmnj)	Amelia Naomi Harrison, d/o Saml O.

1850, Nov. (gmnj)	Rebecca Demarest Sindle, w/o Jacob
1850, Dec. (gmnj)	Eliz. Baldwin Harrison,dau. of Saml O
1851, March (gmnj)	Betsey E. Condit, wife of Stephen J.
1851, March (gmnj)	Sarah Jacobus Crane, w/o William G.
1851, March (gmnj)	Aaron B. Heath, h/o Ann M Conover
1851, May (gmnj)	Parnella Moore, wife of Joshua
1851, July (gmnj)	Caroline Provost, dau. of Jonathan Sr.
1851, July (gmnj)	Caroline Stager,dau. of John VanRiper
1851, August (gmnj)	Caleb S. Crane, husb. of Rhoda Dodd
1851, August (gmnj)	Charlotte Martin Hartley, wife of John
1851, August (gmnj)	John Ossian Hulbert, son of O. W.
1851, August (gmnj)	Jeptha Pierson, husb. of Sarah
1851, August (gmnj)	Joseph H. Sindle
1851, Sept. (gmnj)	Thomas J. Sindle
1851, Sept. (gmnj)	Catherine Supenor, wife of Abraham
1851, Sept. (gmnj)	Christopher Supenor, husb. of Mary
1851, Nov. (gmnj)	Martha Pierson, 1st wife of Elijah
1852, Feb. (gmnj)	Moses DeCamp, husb. of Catherine
1852, Feb. (gmnj)	Charles P. Kirker
1852, March (gmnj)	Mary Cecelia Beach, dau. of James
1852, April (gmnj)	Mary Allen, wife of Alpheus
1852, April (gmnj)	Henrietta O. Beach, w/o James H.
1852, May (gmnj)	Ann Eliza Dobbins, dau. of Joseph
1852, Oct. (gmnj)	Sophia Cole, wife of John
1852, Oct. (gmnj)	William P. Riker
1852, Nov. (gmnj)	Joanna Harrison
1852, Dec. (gmnj))	Julia F. Hedges Crane, w/o Nathl. S.
1853, Feb. (gmnj)	William Fairchild
1853, June (gmnj)	John L. Hudson, husb. of Martha G.
1853, August (gmnj)	Eliza Kent Willis, wife of Elias B.
1853, Sept. (gmnj)	Mary Elizabeth Bedford,dau. of Moses
1853, Sept. (gmnj)	Frank Gould Carman(?), son of Joseph
1853, Sept. (gmnj)	Justus Soverill Dobbins, son of Isaac
1853, Sept. (gmnj)	Emeline Beach, dau. of Jared
1853, Oct. (gmnj)	Stephen R. Grover, husb. of Elizabeth
1853, Oct. (gmnj)	Ann Mott, widow
1854, Feb. (gmnj)	O. W. Hulbert, husb. of Mary S.
1854, Feb. (gmnj)	William H. Supenor

1854, March (gmnj)	Thomas D. Gould, husb. of Nancy C.
1854, July (gmnj)	Jonathan Provost, Sr., husb.of Paulina
1854, Sept. (gmnj)	William Fairchild, husb. of Mary B.
1854, Oct. (gmnj)	Peter V. Miller, husb. of Electa C.
1855, Feb.(gmnj)	Joseph Dobbins, husb. of Abigail
1855, March (gmnj)	William Bush, son of Absalom
1855, March (gmnj)	Samuel Edgar Harrison,son of Saml O
1855, March (gmnj)	Caroline Nichols, mother of Holmes P
1855, April (gmnj)	Mary Baldwin Dodd, wife of Linus
1855, May (gmnj)	William W. Gooding
1855, May (gmnj)	Sarah M. Williams, dau. of Daniel Z.
1855, July (gmnj)	James M. Van Ness, son of Jacob F.
1855, Sept. (gmnj)	Daniel Corby
1855, Oct. (gmnj)	Lydia Steele Crane, wife of Samuel G.
1855, Nov. (gmnj)	Jacob Courter, husband of Ellen
1856, Feb. (gmnj)	Mary B. Fairchild, wife of William
1856, Feb. (gmnj)	Joseph W. Harrison, son of Cyrus F.
1856, March (gmnj)	Anthony Gould, husb. of Mary S.
1856, April (gmnj)	Harriet S. O'Neal, dau. of Hiram D.
1856, June (gmnj)	Nancy F. Francisco, wife of Thomas
1856, Sept. (gmnj)	Lucy Provost, wife of John
1856, Oct. (gmnj)	Willis Pierson Bond, son of Wm. H.
1856, Oct. (gmnj)	Sally Jacobus, wife of John R.
1856, Nov. (gmnj)	Ellen Courter, wife of Jacob
1856, Dec. (gmnj)	Walter S. Mann, son of John J.
1857, Jan. (gmnj)	Georgianna Cadmus, dau. of William
1857, April (gmnj)	Lucy Provost, dau. of John
1857, May (gmnj)	Adelia Ann Bush, wife of Absalom
1857, May (gmnj)	George S. Condit, son of William S.
1857, May (gmnj)	Fred G. Gooding
1857, May (gmnj)	Edward Clark Harrison, s/o Saml O.
1857, May (gmnj)	Phebe C. Stiles Whitney, w/o Rev. E.
1857, June (gmnj)	Holmes P. Nichols, son of Caroline
1857, Dec. (gmnj)	Phebe Mowerson, wife of Aaron
1858, July (gmnj)	William J. Mead, son of John
1858, August (gmnj)	Eleanor Voorhees Miller,w/o Isaac S.
1859, March (gmnj)	Elizabeth Martin,(dau. of Enos)
1859, May (gmnj)	Calvin Kent

bef. 1860, March	John H. Stager, husb. of Sophia
1860, Jan. (gmnj)	Dorcas Corby, wife of Daniel
1860, Jan. (gmnj)	Ezekiel Corby, husband of Rebecca
1860, May (gmnj)	Cornelius Low, husb. of Ellen
1860, May (gmnj)	Sarah Williams Mesler, w/o Abraham
1860, June (gmnj)	Ann C. Dobbins
1860, July (gmnj)	John Bowden, son of Anthony
1860, Nov. (gmnj)	John M. Courter
1861, Jan. (gmnj)	Marcus I. Jacobus, son of James O.
1861, Feb. (lgl)	Hattie Randolph Gould, d/o Stephen R
1861, Feb. (gmnj)	Arminda C. Mead, dau. of John
1861, Feb. (gmnj)	Laura Provost Williams, d/o Jotham
1861, March (gmnj)	Phebe Harrison, wife of Zenas
1861, April (gmnj)	Mary Bowden Hulbert, d/o John B.
1861, June (gmnj)	Phebe Burnet
1861, August (gmnj)	Halsey Martin, s/o George P. Martin
1861, Sept. (gmnj)	Sarah Ann Kent, wife of Ira M.
1861, Dec. (gmnj)	Ellen Low, wife of Cornelius
1862 (gmnj)	Hannah Eliza Hoage, dau. of Patrick
1862, Jan. (gmnj)	Willie M. Mann, son of John J.
1862, Feb. (gmnj)	Eliza Duryea Harrison,dau. of Philip H
1862, Feb. (photo)	Hattie Randolph Gould,d/o Steph. R.
1862, March (lgl)	Pernella Provost Williams, w/o J.M.
1862, May (gmnj)	Sarah F Crane McChesney,w/o John
1862, May (gmnj)	Nancy D. Gould, wife of Nathaniel M
1862, May (gmnj)	Sarah F.Crane McChesney, w/o John
1862, June (gmnj)	Stephen Bond
1862, July (lgl)	Elijah Anderson
1862, July (gmnj)	Elijah Pierson, husb. of Martha
1862, August (gmnj)	Lucetta G. Mann, wife of John J.
1862, Sept. (gmnj)	Caroline Gould, 2nd w/o Thomas D.
1862, Oct. (gmnj)	Clarence E. Colyer, son of Ezra
1863 (gmnj)	Peter Cadmus
1863, Jan. (gmnj)	Harvey Baldwin, son of Ira
1863, March (gmnj)	Ira Baldwin, husband of Emeline
1863, April (gmnj)	Joanna Personett, wife of Abram
1863, May (gmnj)	Jesse Jacobus
1863, June (gmnj)	Lydia Personett Crane, wife of Caleb

1863, Sept. (gmnj)	Peter A. Francisco, son of Josiah
1863, Oct. (gmnj)	Henry Francisco
1863, Oct. (gmnj)	Stephen Randolph Gould, h/o Harriet
1863, Nov. (gmnj)	John H. Colyer, son of Ezra
1863, Nov. (gmnj)	Clarence E. Colyer, son of Ezra
1863, Nov. (gmnj)	Esther E. Hopping, wife of Joseph T.
1863, Dec. (gmnj)	Alice B. Courter,d/o John Bowden
1863, Dec. (gmnj)	Lizzie Baldwin Harrison, d/o Saml O.
1863, Dec. (gmnj)	Electa C. Miller, wife of Peter V.
1864 (lgl)	Nicholas Williams
1864, Jan. (gmnj)	Mary Brundage, wife of Stephen
1864, Feb. (gmnj)	Rachel Brown Albert, wife of Charles
1864, Feb. (gmnj)	Caleb C. Pierson, husb. of Hannah M.
1864, Feb. (gmnj)	Laura Provost Williams,dau of Jotham
1864, April (gmnj)	John Provost, husb. of Lucy
1864, August (gmnj)	Calvin G. Backus
1864, August (gmnj)	Jacob Sindle, husb. of Rebecca D.
1864, August (gmnj)	Nancy Wade, wife of Obadiah
1864, Sept. (gmnj)	Electa C Dobbin Baldwin w/o Marcus
1864, Dec. (gmnj)	Mary Bond Harrison, wife of Harvey
1865, January (lgl)	Samuel Bond
1865, February (lgl)	Jane M. Jackson, wife of William
1865, August (gmnj)	Phebe Harrison Cook, wife of Joseph
1865, Sept. (gmnj)	Sarah M. Pierson Schuyler,w/o John D
1865, Oct. (gmnj)	Joseph A. Pierson, son of Caleb C.
1865, Dec. (photo)	George W. Barnett
1865, Dec. (gmnj)	Louis August Frenson,husb. of Martha
1865, Dec. (gmnj)	Louis August Frenson, son of Louis
1865, Dec. (gmnj)	Harriet E. Westervelt, wife of Luke J.
1866, August (gmnj)	Maria C. M. Harrison, wid. of Richard
1866, March (gmnj)	Joanna Anderson, wife of Elijah
1866, May (gmnj)	Rhoda M. Adams, dau. of Ezekiel
1866, Sept. (gmnj)	Ezekiel Adams, husband of Martha
1866, Dec. (gmnj)	Dorcas Williams DeCamp,w/o Benj.
1866, Dec. (gmnj)	Elizabeth Williams, dau. of Zenas
1867, April (gmnj)	Mary Jones Conover, w/o Stephen
1868 (gmnj)	Eliz. Jones Cadmus, wife of Peter
1868, Jan.(gmnj)	Stephen A. Grover

1868, June (gmnj)	Sarah Dobbins, 2nd wife of John
1868, April (gmnj)	Isaac Dobbins, husb. of Rachel
1868, June (gmnj)	John Dobbins, husb. of Abigail
1868, July (gmnj)	Joseph M. Williams, son of Jotham M
1868, Oct. (gmnj)	Elizabeth Crane Canfield, w/o Matthias
1868, Oct. (gmnj)	Mary Pierson, 2nd wife of Elijah
1869, Sept. (gmnj)	Harvey Harrison, husb. of Mary Bond
1869, Dec. (gmnj)	Fanny Lines Simonson, w/o John
1870, July (gmnj)	Nathaniel S. Crane
1870, Dec. (gmnj)	Sophia Stager, widow of John H.
1871, March (gmnj)	Mary Davenport, wife of Ezra
1872, Sept. (gmnj)	Joseph T. Hopping, husb. of Esther E.
1873, Nov. (gmnj)	Rosalinda Grover Crowell,w/o Joseph
1876, Dec. (gmnj)	Stephen Conover, husband of Mary
1878 (gmnj)	Martha Lane Hoage, wife of Patrick
1879, March (gmnj)	Abigail Williams Dobbins,w/o Joseph
1881, May (gmnj)	Abram Personett, husband of Joanna
(the last burial allowed)	

- - - - -

PRIMARY SOURCES

(Many sources are shown online.)

Agens, Sylvester and Russell B. Rankin (gmnj)	*Gravestone Records from the Caldwell Presbyterian Church Yard, Essex County* Genealogical Magazine of New Jersey. Vol.2
Baldwin, Charles C.	*The Baldwin Genealogy* Cleveland, OH, 1881
Condit, Jotham H. and Eben	*Genelogical Record of the Condit Family.*Newark, 1885
Derrie, Daniel Steele	*Steele Family Genealogical History.* Albany, NY, 1862
Dodd, Bethuel L. and John R. Burnet	*Genealogies of the Male Descendants of Daniel Dod, of Branford, Conn.* (Newark, NJ; 1864)
Eberhart, Edith Whitcraft	*The Doremus Family in America* Gateway Press Baltimore 1990
Lewis Publishing	*Biographical and Genealogical History of Newark* (Lewis Publ. Co., NY, 1898)
Lockward, Lynn G. (lgl)	*A Puritan Heritage. The First Presbyterian Church in*

	Horse-Neck (Caldwell, N.J.) 1955
New Jersey Historical Soc. (njhs)	*Monumental Inscriptions of Essex County, N.J. Vol. II Collected in 1904*
Nicholas, George King	*The Corby Family* New York Genealogical and Biographical Record Vol. 131. No. 1-4. Jan. 2000
Sanford, Carlton E.	*Thomas Sanford The Emigrant to New England.* Carlton E. Sanford. Tuttle Co.,Rutland VT. 1911. Volume I
Shaw, William H.	*History of Essex and Hudson Counties.* Wm. H. Shaw, Everts and Pack Phildadelphia 1884
Ullman, Judith Courter	*Database of Judith Courter Ullman* Rootsweb.com
Underhill Society	*12th Annual Report of the Underhill Society. 1904*
Williams, Lyle Keith	*The Williams Families of New Jersey* Anundsen Publ Co. Iowa 1998

www.ingramcontent.com/pod-product-compliance
Lightning Source LLC
Chambersburg PA
CBHW060129290226
41932CB00012B/1464